The Historic Gardens of England Series
Historic Gardens of Somerset

The Historic Gardens of England Series

Historic Gardens of Somerset

Timothy Mowl

Marion Mako

redcliffe

For Mark Horton

The publication of this volume has been made possible by a grant from
THE LEVERHULME TRUST
to cover all the necessary research work

The Walk by Harry Brockway, 2008. By kind permission of Harry Brockway

First published in 2010 by Redcliffe Press Ltd.
81g Pembroke Road, Bristol BS8 3EA
T: 0117 973 7207
E: info@redcliffepress.co.uk
   www.redcliffepress.co.uk

© Text and photographs: Timothy Mowl and Marion Mako
© map: Stephen Morris

ISBN 978-1-906593-56-8

British Library Cataloguing-in-Publication Data
A catalogue record for this book is available from the British Library
All rights reserved. Except for the purpose of review, no part of this book may be reproduced, stored in a retrieval system, or transmitted, in any form or by any means, electronic, mechanical, photocopying, recording or otherwise, without the prior permission of the publishers.

Designed by Stephen Morris, smc@freeuk.com www.stephen-morris.co.uk

Printed by HSW Print, Tonypandy, Rhondda

Contents

ACKNOWLEDGEMENTS   7

INTRODUCTION: ALFRED, ARTHUR AND THE HOLY THORN –   9
A COUNTY OF DARK AGE LEGENDS

1   WATER CLOSETS, BANQUETING HOUSES AND   17
A LOST BOTANICAL GARDEN
Kelston Manor · Low Ham · Montacute · Cothelstone Manor
Lytes Cary · Mells Manor · Clevedon Court

2   EARTHWORKS, AN EPISCOPAL CANAL AND WILDERNESSES –   36
FORMALITY EVENTUALLY SUBVERTED
Nether Stowey Manor · Low Ham · Witham Charterhouse
Hinton House · Brympton d'Evercy · Orchard Portman · Fairfield
Nunney Castle House · Wells Bishop's Palace · Ven House
Sandhill Park · Orchard Wyndham · Marston Bigot

3   RIVALS IN ARCADY   59
Marston Bigot · Halswell · Hatch Court · Hestercombe
Dunster Castle · Crowcombe Court · Terhill

4   POETRY, POLITICS AND MOSES' HOLY TABERNACLE   93
IN THE BATH HINTERLAND
Prior Park · Widcombe Manor · Lilliput Castle · Batheaston Villa · Burton Pynsent

5   SOMERSET GENTRY SPURN LADY NATURE'S SECOND HUSBAND   112
Earnshill · Redlynch Park · Mells Park · Barwick Park · Orchardleigh Ammerdown
Enmore Castle · Midford Castle · Kelston Park · Nettlecombe Court
Harptree Court · Ashton Court · Ston Easton Park · Newton Park · Leigh Court

6   SCIENCE, TECHNOLOGY, BIBLICAL EXEGESIS AND THE   147
TRUE SOURCE OF *FRANKENSTEIN*
Fyne Court · St. Audries · Jordans · Ashwick Grove · Ironstone Cottage
The Chantry · Hapsford House · Pondsmead · Beckford's Ride · Oakwood
Ashley Combe · Banwell Caves

7   GARISH BEDDING, TERRACES AND A CONFUSION OF STYLE –   173
THE VICTORIANS
Cricket House · Nynehead Court · Parish's House · Camerton Court
Brockley Hall · Claverton Manor · Tyntesfield · Maperton House
Cranmore Hall · Clevedon Court · Hestercombe · Brympton d'Evercy
Orchardleigh · Lydeard House · Crowe Hall · Inwood House

8   WHERE STONE FLOWERS AT LEAST AS VIGOROUSLY   188
AS THE PLANTS – THE EDWARDIAN GARDENS
Barrow Court · Montacute · Tyntesfield · Milton Lodge · Wootton House
Lytes Cary Manor · Hinton House · Nailsea Court · Ammerdown House
Redlynch Park · Mells Manor · Hestercombe Gardens · Barrington Court
Mells Park · Glencot · Wayford Manor · Burton Pynsent · The Old Court
Widcombe Manor · Barley Wood · North Cadbury Court
St Catherine's Court

9   TWENTIETH-CENTURY PLANTSWOMEN TAKE CENTRE STAGE   229
East Lambrook Manor · Brympton d'Evercy · Tintinhull House · Montacute
Greencombe · Barford Park · Hadspen House · Cothay Manor · Lady Farm

10   MODERNIST AND TRADITIONAL – A VERY PATRICIAN COUNTY   247
Caveman Restaurant · Pen Pits · Clapton Court · Kilver Court
Yarlington House · Barcroft Hall · Aislaby · Babington House
Camerton Court · Dillington House · Stoberry Park · Wells Bishop's Palace
Honeywick House · Hatch Court

NOTES   273

GAZETTEER   291

MAP   293

INDEX   294

Acknowledgements

As with the last six books in this series, my first thanks go to Professor Sir Richard Brook and his Trustees at the Leverhulme Trust, whose generous funding of the research has made the Somerset travelling and garden visiting a pleasure rather than a financial worry. Their generosity has made it possible for Marion Mako, who worked on the *Cheshire* volume, to be appointed again as consultant for *Somerset*, and she has undertaken all the research and co-ordinated the site visits in a calmly professional manner. I should also like to thank Dr Clare Hickman, Research Fellow of the project, who has overseen the progress of the writing and research with her usual efficiency.

Owners, archivists, friends, colleagues and Bristol University MA Garden History students and postgraduate researchers who have been particularly helpful include Primrose Mallet Harris and Patricia Davies-Gilbert of Somerset Gardens Trust, who brought several gardens to our notice, the staff at Somerset Record Office, particularly Jenny Christoforou and Brian Cahill, the staff at Somerset Studies Library, particularly Anne Nix and Wilf Deckner, Richard Higgs of the National Trust, Lord Oxford, Viscount & Viscountess Asquith, the Hon Andrew Joliffe, Professor Ronald Hutton, Professor Mick Aston, Susan Palmer, Anne Buchanan, Chris Holloway, Jonathan Naylor, Edwyn Martin, Yvonne & Ron Sargent, John Haynes, John Chapman, Denise & Brian Herrick, Mike Lane, Michael Stancomb, Iann Barron, David Selwyn, Sarah Fitzgerald, Jo Collins, John Horsey, Dr Stuart Prior, Robert Turner, Helen & Ivan Knight, Jane Dunn, Nicholas Ostler, Bryan Smith, Sarah & George Glossop, Tim Schroder, Nick Owen, Dipti & Ravi Sarathy, Ivy & Ken Biggs, Suzi & Mark Bullough, Dr. Cathryn Spence, Daniel Brown, Tessa & William Theed, Mary Anne & Alastair Robb, Jane & Hugh Warmington, Nicki Faircloth, Harry Godden, Hazel Malcolm, Dr Pat & Richard Smith, Anthony Trollope-Bellew, the estate of John Barrett, Lorna Howarth, David Carrington, Wayne Bennett, Nick Rigden, Judith Patrick, Bridget and Richard Combe, Gail & Mike Werkmeister, Anne & Simon Stoye, Lady Elizabeth Gass, Maureen Lehane Wishart, Joan Loraine, Penelope Hobhouse, Niall Hobhouse, Michael Coles, Mark Cranfield, Graeme Bond, Raj Russell, Mary Hill, Linda & Charles Hill, John Townson, Melanie & Philip Gibbs, Yvonne Davis, Philip White, Robert & Fiona Alfred, Rupert Lewin, Camilla Carter, Isabel & Richard de Pelet, Joan & Peter Speke, Judy & Malcolm Pearce, Vaun & Colin

Wilkins, Simon Larkins, Michelle & Kevin Adeson, Graham Adeson, Michael McGarvie, Michael Samuel, Jonathan Liebert, Simon Tudway Quilter, Shona Grant, Tom Wolsey, Jacqueline McKenna, the late Tony Dewberry, David Timms, Professor Frank Morgan, Jane & Robin Canon, George Smith, Elizabeth Montgomery, Diana Hathaway, Alec Reed, Justin Cole, Jack Broom, David Critchell, Judith Williams, Merrial Laverack, Pep Hill, Chris Silverwood, Aisha & Andrew Baker, Tara Kahan, Paul Thomas, Konstantia & Charles Woodruff, Ian Strong, Mike Jackson, Rebecca Goulden, Alison Jenkins, Hein van Vorstenbosch, Francis & Tim Young, Kathleen Hippisley, Dorian Poole, Ian Jupp, John Powell, Peter Facey, Pam & Roger Entwistle, Paul Evans, Jasper Conran, Karin Grainger, Garry Abbot, Sir Mervyn Medleycott, Tim MacCaw, Wendy & Robin Goffe, Robin Whalley, Andrew Davisson, Andy Smith, Sylvia Wray, Michael Eavis, Carolyn & Charles de Salis, Peggy Stembridge, Susan Palmer, Dr Jane Bradney, Dr Kate Felus, Dr Kate Harris, Noni & Sam Bemrose, Simon Bonvoisin, Jim Bartos, Nick Dixon, Sue Shephard, Max Taylor, Frederica Coker, Gillian Sladen, Amy Frost, Magdalene Cordel, Wendy Smayle, Vivienne Lewis, Celia Downie, Kate Hughes, Helene Gammack and Charles Hind.

I must thank Michael Richardson of the University of Bristol's Special Collections for bringing many important texts to my notice. John Sansom has been an encouraging and enthusiastic editor, and Stephen Morris has achieved another elegantly designed volume. Alexandra Denman has proofed the typescript most conscientiously, and Douglas Matthews has produced yet another definitive index.

Somerset has been researched alongside my teaching of Bristol University's MA in Garden History, so I must thank my fellow university colleagues for their lively encouragement. My agent, Sara Menguc, has continued to support the project with her affectionate enthusiasm. My wife, Sarah, and daughter, Olivia, went with me to check out Dragonfly Barn, North Newton, which provided Marion and me with the ideal base for forays into the county and archival trips to the Somerset Record Office; thanks are due to Alison & Chris Pendry for their hospitality at the Barn. I should also like to thank Pete Barnes for his unstinting support of Marion and for his technical excellence in handling our photographs. My son Adam, having just completed an MA at the University of London, has been equally supportive. Finally, I should like to thank Professor Mark Horton, to whom this book is dedicated, for his archaeological advice and valued friendship. I now leave the Arthurian Moors and head back up the M5 to tackle Warwickshire, Shakespeare's county.

TIMOTHY MOWL, Bristol,
May 2010

Introduction

Alfred, Arthur and the Holy Thorn – a county of Dark Age legends

▼

THE WIDE EXTENT AND SINGULAR BEAUTY OF SOMERSET WAS REVEALED TO me early in the travelling for this survey, as I was driving one day in late March from my base at West Newton, due east to Castle Cary in the south-eastern corner of the county. Shafts of bright spring sunshine cut through a numinous morning mist rising from Curry Moor, the road lined with pollarded willows and snaking in serpentine fashion as it followed the route of an old track. Withies edged the ditches and rhynes, strengthening the banks of the watercourses and marking field boundaries and ancient droves. In the distance stood Athelney Hill, where King Alfred is thought to have hidden before going on to defeat the Danes at the Battle of Ethandun in 878,[1] while all around the landscape stretched out in a level vastness like an East Anglian watercolour by Cotman or Crome.

Suddenly a knoll, crowned by a ruined tower, rose up on the horizon. It could easily be mistaken at this distance for Glastonbury Tor. But this was Barrow Mump, a natural hill in the marshy midst of Zoyland, or Sealand, where Alfred may have sited his fort in 879. It is an outcrop of Keuper Marl, at the strategic point in the royal Isle of Athelney where the river Tone and Cary join the Parrett at Burrowbridge. The Mump was garrisoned by Royalist forces in 1642 and 1645, and occupied by a detachment of the King's army in 1685 during Monmouth's Rebellion. Today the abandoned church, dedicated as one would expect to St Michael, cuts a jagged profile, its tower tricked up in 1724 to serve as an early Gothick eyecatcher; a later, 1793, attempt at rebuilding ran out of funds. This landscape of intense historic associations unfolded as the road wound towards Othery, where I turned off to skirt the escarpment on which the outworks of a great seventeenth-century formal garden survive at Low Ham. Then on to Huish Episcopi and eventually to Castle Cary, an eighteenth-century town of Palladian merchants' houses inspired by Henry Hoare, the Lord of the Manor, who had set that architectural fashion in the 1720s at nearby Stourhead.

My destination that day was Hadspen at Pitcombe, another Palladian-style house owned by Niall Hobhouse, where his mother, the influential garden designer Penelope Hobhouse, has returned to live in the Clock House. Here there were unexpected surprises. The flower-filled garden created after 1987 by Nori and Sandra Pope, with its emphasis on colour, has been mercilessly bulldozed. Penelope's walled garden is in decay, and she is planting a completely new garden outside her apartment, while Niall holds court in a portable library housed within a metal container which he has shunted around the estate to different locations as the whim takes him. Hadspen will be given its due in later chapters of this survey, particularly in a consideration of a group of Somerset-based women designers at the cutting-edge of twentieth-century garden design, and also in an analysis of exactly what Niall Hobhouse intends for the scarred site of the Popes' former garden.

So I had travelled from the seventh century to the twenty-first in a matter of an hour and a half, crossing the county from west to east. That was just one day of many memorable excursions up and down and across a county which Nikolaus Pevsner felt the need to divide into north and south for his *Buildings of England* volumes. However, it separates more readily between east and west, with the Moors and the M5 motorway defining the central area. The industrial areas to the east, clustered around Frome, Midsomer Norton and Shepton Mallet, are characterised by new money and populated now by recent settlers from London, while the patrician belt to the west, around the Brendons, the Blackdowns and the Quantocks, is where old-established families still cling on to their estates. To drive the deep-delved lanes of the Quantocks, their hedgerows bristling in spring with wild flowers, directed by cast-iron road signs to villages nestling in the lee of hills, where local pubs like the White Horse at Stogumber serve wholesome ploughman's lunches with hunks of bread and ripe Cheddar, is to be transported to England in the 1950s. Or, on the other flank of the Quantocks, to the Romantic 1790s at Nether Stowey, where Coleridge wrote the *Ancient Mariner* and *Kubla Khan* and Wordsworth lived just three miles away at Alfoxton House, its approach road guarded by an ancient Dog Pound of the St Aubyns, and its escarpment carriage drive giving spectacular views out to Bridgwater Bay. Here, on the northern slopes of the hills, in appropriate poetic isolation, they wrote experimental poems of rural simplicity aiming to catch the 'language of conversation in the middle classes of society....adapted to the purposes of poetic pleasure'.[2] The result was *Lyrical Ballads*, first published in 1798, which became the manifesto of the English Romantic movement. In the plain below Alfoxton is Fairfield, with the remnants of its formal gardens obliquely aligned now on Hinkley Point power station, and Stogursey, famous for the local saying: 'Out of the world and into Stogursey, and out of Stogursey and into the sea'.

In garden history terms, however, one Somerset visit will serve to encapsulate the wide chronology of historic intervention on a site and will help to define the essential character of a county that is often passed by, as holidaymakers from Bristol and Birmingham hare down the M5 to Devon and Cornwall. This is Poundisford Park, about three miles south of Taunton near Pitminster, which has the best surviving medieval deer park in the county, even though the pale of its northern reach has been severed by the M5. Once the Taunton suburbs are left behind, the B3170 passes the race course at Orchard Portman, the forlorn site of a once important late-seventeenth-century garden, and just before Corfe, a right turn, Green Lane, leads in a dizzying zig-zag of bends towards Poundisford. At a sharp corner in the lane, a conical-roofed Regency Gothic lodge with green bargeboards, like a Staffordshire china ornament set loose from the mantelpiece, comes into view. This turns out to be an estate boundary marker for a vanished sixteenth-century mansion at Barton Grange. As the lane turns left it is lined with a substantial rubble-stone wall. This forms the eastern boundary of the horseshoe-shaped deer park, now entirely divided into hedged fields, which was originally enclosed by the medieval bishops of Winchester.[3] It is known to have been in existence in 1210-11 when King John sent deer from Hereford to Bishop Peter des Roches to replenish the herd at Poundisford.[4] The presence of

Poundisford Lodge on the pale edge to the north of Poundisford Park is another indicator of the hunting landscape, for Sir Hugh Luttrell of Dunster Castle is recorded as being the Park Keeper there in 1487.[5]

Turning off the lane and into the park, the drive crosses a small stream that cascades down into a hollowed-out basin, its walls constructed as if to provide a bathing pool, and heads towards tall gatepiers and the entrance forecourt of the house. Here there is a lead water tank dated 1671, set up when the Hill family were in ownership.[6] Its leadwork is modelled with mermaids, a dramatic sporting scene of dogs pursuing a stag, moustachioed rustics tending fruit trees, and botanically accurate flowers sprouting from vases. The date may well be significant, as soon afterwards Sir Roger Hill inherited the Park, and was probably responsible for remodelling the grounds and building the Garden House on the south lawn. Today, Poundisford Park is owned by Charles and Konstantia Woodruff, who have recently begun to restore the great rooms with their beautiful plasterwork ceilings, of the mid-sixteenth century in the Hall and of the 1680s in the Library, the latter decorated with arabesques, fruit and flowers.

Outside, the gabled vernacular ranges of William Hill's house, begun in 1546, are studded with honey-coloured ironstone mullioned windows, and its rendered walls are patterned with burgundy lichen. The lawns are bisected by randomly paved paths which lead to an Ionic-columned Loggia set against a doorway in a side wall, dating from a post-1928 restoration by Mr A Vivian-Neal, and to a line of columnar yews flanking the west lawn. However, the most important garden structure is the Garden House (1) commanding the south lawn, the site of a formal parterre or perhaps a bowling green. This is clearly of mixed dates, but the English bond of its brickwork walls and the floating pediment on brackets above the main door, broken at the apex to accommodate a bust, could easily be pre-Commonwealth. It was refenestrated and given internal plasterwork after Roger Hill took over in 1673; the roof looks to be of early twentieth-century date. There is a similar summerhouse at Poundisford Lodge, which was owned by the Hills until the late seventeenth century when it passed out of the family by marriage. This is early-eighteenth-century in date, constructed of roughcast render over

1 The seventeenth-century Garden House at Poundisford Park must once have overlooked a formal garden or a bowling green

brick, but with an identical conical roof to the Garden House at the Park.[7] It was not possible to visit the grounds around the Lodge, but these had been considerably developed in the Regency period by the Helyars of Coker Court when the Revd Edmund Butcher saw the house:

> the taste that has been displayed in the small pleasure-grounds of the lodge is very considerable – many of the trees, particularly the firs and acacias, were planted, several of them from seed, by the present occupier of the domain – and to see them rearing their tall heads, and spreading their beautiful leafy branches in the manner they now do, must give him great satisfaction.[8]

In Somerset the garden historian can move effortlessly from a medieval deer park of King John's reign to a twentieth-century garden which celebrates the legend of Joseph of Arimathea and actively promotes New Age spiritualism. Not surprisingly it is to be found in Glastonbury, its approach on Chilkwell Road signalled by a Banksy stencil, which wittily fuses the American Hip Hop artist Jay-Z with Michael Eavis, impresario of the annual rock festival held at nearby Worthy Farm.[9]

The chalybeate waters of the Chalice Well, which leave an iron-red stain on the stones over which it flows, are said to represent the blood of Christ issuing from the spot where Joseph of Arimathea buried or washed the cup used at the Last Supper.[10] As such it has been a place of pilgrimage for centuries, sought for baptism and healing; even the mathematician and astrologer Dr John Dee visited in 1582 to drink the water and 'declared himself possessed of the *Elixir Vitae*'.[11] Its survival into the twenty-first century, surrounded now by beautiful gardens, is due to Wellesley Tudor Pole, who came to see the Well in the spring of 1904 after having a vision of himself as a monk at Glastonbury Abbey. This followed early experiences of seeing the colours of prayers when meditating in church. In more prosaic moments he was a managing director of flour, grain and cereal merchants engaged in government work. After World War One, during which he conceived the idea of a one minute's silence each evening, an act of observance that continues to this day on Remembrance Sunday, he established his own firm with business interests in New York, Paris, Amsterdam, Constantinople, Alexandria and Haifa.

In 1959 Tudor Pole bought the Chalice Well, together with the two orchards on Chalice Hill and the playing fields on the slopes of the Tor, and vested it in a trust with the words: 'I hope you will feel that we are doing our best to cherish and safeguard this holy place, filled as it is with the atmosphere of history, legend and tradition; filled also with a sense of hope and expectation for the future'.[12] Since then the Well and Gardens have developed and are now promoted as 'the ancient red spring of Avalon, a natural sanctuary of peace and healing'. On the hillside slope the separate garden areas connect via a winding path which leads to the Well itself at the head of the Gardens, its oak cover decorated with writhing wrought-ironwork of Art Nouveau sinuosity (2), dating from 1919 and representing 'the Bleeding Lance and the Visible and Invisible Worlds interlocked with one another'.[13]

2 The eponymous Chalice Well in Glastonbury. The Art Nouveau-style well cover dates from 1919 and represents the visible and invisible worlds interlocked

Easily the most striking element in the Gardens is the 'Flowform', a cascading stone watercourse of decidedly labial shapes issuing via a helmeted erection into double pools (*colour 1*) 'where the waters dance and swirl'. Next to it in a grass clearing is the Holy Thorn Tree (*Crateagus monogyna praecox*), a living symbol of the story of Joseph's staff, which is said to have taken root, blossoming each year at Christmas. Further up the garden, Tudor Pole's 'Silent Minute' is recalled in a wooden lattice summerhouse; there is a Lion's Head where visitors may drink the water, the path above lined with white *Rosa rugosa*; King Arthur's Court has a healing pool and mini waterfall; and for contemplation there is the Meadow, which flanks the garden. Each garden room and pathway is bordered by a profusion of flowers, and linking all is the sound of running water emanating from the Well. The planting, predominantly herbaceous perennials, is abundant and reassuringly relaxed. Foxgloves, Japanese anemones and Welsh poppies are allowed to fill the spaces they seed, and the gravel paths are overhung with lush fragrance. It is a delightfully homespun place with an intensely soothing atmosphere that, it has to be admitted, comes close to spiritual calm. There may well be something in the legends: Joseph and the Grail, Arthur and Guinevere sleeping in the Abbey grounds nearby, the Levels around the Tor being the Isle of Avalon. As the short history of the Well concludes, 'Tradition, for all the distortions and additions made by centuries of oral repetition, yet persists in retaining its grain of Truth. So many of these ridiculed tales have in modern times been proved true by research or excavation, that it is quite within the bounds of possibility that discoveries may one day be made round the Well which will confound the doubting Thomases of this materialistic age'.[14] Wellesley Tudor Pole certainly thought so before he 'returned once again to his own plane of spiritual consciousness on 13th September 1968'.[15]

The most evocative demonstration of the complex historical and spiritual associations of the county can be found at Worthy Farm. Bleary-eyed festival goers could be forgiven for thinking that they had been miraculously transported to Stonehenge, as they emerge from their tents on the sloping fields towards the perimeter of the Festival enclosure, surrounded by a stone circle centred by a dolmen. The Swan Circle, which reflects the star pattern of Cygnus, is sited within view of the great Tor, next to a single veteran oak. It is not, however, of prehistoric vintage, but was commissioned in February 1991 and built in time for the Midsummer solstice of June 1992. The Swan Circle (*colour 2*) has many resonances, but in essence it 'celebrates the Stone Beings, the guardians and memory holders of the earth'.[16] As its maker Ivan explains in a booklet written to inform the uninitiated, the Stone Beings 'are very much alive and ready to make contact with us again in a new contemporary way. They will guide us in our journey to understand how to work with and heal this wonderful Being, the Earth, who supports, cares for us, and gives us our very life'. After such a blissful spring and early summer criss-crossing this extraordinary county, a sceptical academic might be persuaded to believe that those stones could actually talk.

1

Water closets, banqueting houses and a lost botanical garden

▽

Kelston Manor · Low Ham · Montacute · Cothelstone Manor
Lytes Cary · Mells Manor · Clevedon Court

IN WARWICKSHIRE, WHICH HAS BEEN SURVEYED FOR THIS SERIES, BUT NOT yet published, the presence of Queen Elizabeth I in the county sent aesthetic shockwaves throughout the nobility, which was anxious to curry favour with the monarch on her annual summer Progresses. The most audacious and brilliantly orchestrated entertainment for her pleasure was staged in 1575 by Robert Dudley at Kenilworth Castle. This lasted several days, during which time the Queen was entertained with poetry readings, masques and dumb shows, and showered with gifts. She went on hunting expeditions, was served lavish banquets and enjoyed endless dancing. In addition to decorating special apartments for the Queen and her retinue, Dudley also constructed a spectacular formal garden for her private enjoyment, centred by a marble fountain set within an octagonal basin, from which rose two back-to-back figures of Atlas holding a sphere of the world. This spurted water through metal pipes into the basin below, which was carved with further classical figures: Neptune, Thetis, Triton, Prometheus and Doris. Robert Laneham's sensual description evokes the abundant beauty of the enclosure:

> A Garden then so appoynted, az wherein aloft upon sweet shadoed walk of terres, in heat of soomer, too feel the plaezaunt whysking winde aboove, or delectabl coolnes of the fountain sprin beneath: to taste of delicious strawberiez, cherryes, and oother frutez, eeven from their stalks: too smell such fragrancy of sweet odooruz, breathing from the plants, earbs, and floourz: too heer such naturall meloodioous musik and tunez of burds.[1]

Tall obelisks punctuated the garden parterres, and on one side there was a huge cage for birds. It was the epitome of an Elizabethan garden, and where intellectual artifice combined with the scents of flowers and fruit, where visitors might take exercise or relax in quiet contemplation listening to birdsong.

Dudley was the Queen's royal favourite, but even he felt the need to impress. A lesser courtier without the backdrop of a medieval castle set above a lake to work with would have to try even harder to create a setting worthy of a royal visit. It is just possible that one such Somerset-based courtier – Sir John Harington of Kelston – went to great lengths to provide a setting for his queen's enjoyment at **Kelston Manor**, sited above the banks of the Avon to the west of Bath. If so, it would be completely in character, for Harington spent most of his life at court pursuing the patronage first of Elizabeth, then, after her death in 1603, of King James and subsequently his son and heir, the fated Prince Henry. Harington did this by writing punning epigrams and translating the Psalms and classical texts: Ludovico Ariosto's *Orlando Furioso* in 1591 and, whilst he was incarcerated in prison for an uncle's debt, the sixth book of Virgil's *Aeneid*. The mixture of ribald wit and classical learning in Harington's writings suggests that Shakespeare may have used him as a model for both Orlando and Jacques in *As You Like It*. His intellectual assiduity was not, however, rewarded by royal favour, and by 1603 he was writing:

> Thus muche I have livede to see, and (in good soothe) feel too, that honeste prose will never better a man's purse at cowrte; and, had not my fortune been in terra firma, I might, even for my verses, have daunced bare foot with Clio and her school-fellowes untill I did sweat, and then have gotten nothing to slake my thirste, but a pitcher of Helicon's well.[2]

Starting out in court life as Queen Elizabeth's godson, whom she affectionately called 'Boye Jacke', he had some natural advantages, and on inheriting the manor house at Kelston when his father died in 1582, he determined to make the most of them.[3] The Somerset historian John Collinson reports that the house, which stood next to the church, 'was erected in 1587 by Sir John Harington, after a plan of that celebrated architect James Barozzi, of Vignola'.[4] This must refer to Harington's use of Vignola's 1563 *La Regola delli Cinque Ordini d'Architettura*, which gave guidance for setting out the five orders on a modular system, rather than a specific design prepared by the great Mannerist architect. The house is likely to have been begun in the 1560s, after which it was completed by Sir John 'as a proper reception for queen Elizabeth during a summer's excursion, who here visited her godson in her way to Oxford 1591'.[5] It is not easy to determine exactly what had been achieved on the Kelston site before he took over, but a letter appended to Harington's most bizarre publication – *The Metamorphosis of Ajax*, published in 1596 – offers some insights into the grounds around the house.

The letter, written by *Philostilpnos* to his cousin Misacmos ('hater of filthiness') prefaces Harington's scatalogical comedy, with its reflections on current morality. This social satire grew out of a convivial gathering at Wardour Castle, home of Harington's school friend, Thomas Arundell.[6] *Philostilpnos* is Edward Sheldon, who married Harington's cousin Elizabeth Markham; *Misacmos* is, of course, Harington himself. Philostilpnos writes: 'Sir, I have heard speech of your house, of your picturs, of your walks, of your ponds, and of your two boats....all which God willing (if I live another summer) I will come of purpose to see; as also a swimming place, where if one may beleeve your brother Fraunces, Diana did bath her, & Acteon, see her without hornes'.[7] This must be a tongue-in-cheek reference to the Queen's visit to Kelston, with a risqué aside about Harington spying on her like Actaeon, but managing to suppress arousal on seeing her bathe. *Philostilpnos* continues to list the three elements of the garden that he is most keen to see:

> The one a fountaine standing on pillers, like that in Ariosto, under which you may dyne & suppe; the second a shooting close...in which I heare you have hit a marke that many shoot at, viz: to make a barren stony land fruitfull with a little cost; the third is a thing that I cannot name well without save-reverence, & yet it sounds not unlike the shooting place, but it is in plaine English a shyting place.[8]

Of the three, the 'shyting place' or 'jakes', hence the title of his book, is the most significant, in that it appears to be the very first attempt at contriving a flushing water closet, and it was certainly invented by Sir John. However, it is the ornamental, as opposed to the earthily practical, water feature which suggests that Sir John's father had already laid out an ambitious garden at Kelston long before his son inherited, and even before Dudley's 1575 pleasance at Kenilworth. Collinson illustrates the 'Fountain of the Haringtons at Kelweston Court' on a plate (3) of the baths at Bath as they stood in 1676.[9] The finial on top of the column has the rebus of a hare and barrel (hare and tun – Harington) and the date 1567, proving that it was the centrepiece of John Harington's garden, rather than that of his son. This would be the garden that Elizabeth visited in 1591 on her way to Oxford. Sir John 'had received the promise of a royal visit at his country mansion, at Kelweston near Bath; and that he might afford the queen a proper reception there, had fitted up his house in a stile of elegance and magnificence suitable to the taste of the age'.[10] Harington gives the best contemporary description of this romanticising of the Queen during her Progresses: 'Her mind was oftime like the gentle air that cometh from the westerly point in a summer's morn; 'twas sweet and refreshing to all around her. Her speech did win all affections, and her subjects did try to show all love to her commands; for what she would say, "her state did require her to command what she knew her people would willingly do from their own love to her"'.[11] That willingness often resulted in bankruptcy; but there is no suggestion that, as well as preparing his house for her reception, Harington also laid out a garden expressly to amuse and entertain her. He may have had no need, as one terrace was already in place with the dramatic focal point of the Fountain, its classical columns reflecting those of the Manor whose east façade it faced. Elizabeth was as good as her word, stopped at Kelston and, significantly, if somewhat strangely, 'dined right royally under the fountain which played in the court'.[12] So, even if she did not take a bath in it, she dined beneath the canopy to the sound of splashing water above.

Not surprisingly, given that the action takes place in Italy, a magnificent fountain features prominently in Ariosto's *Orlando Furioso*, which Harington

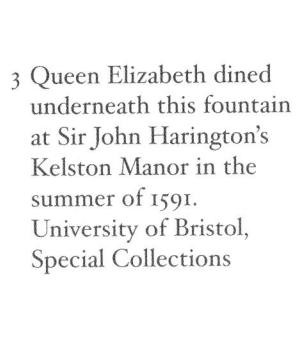

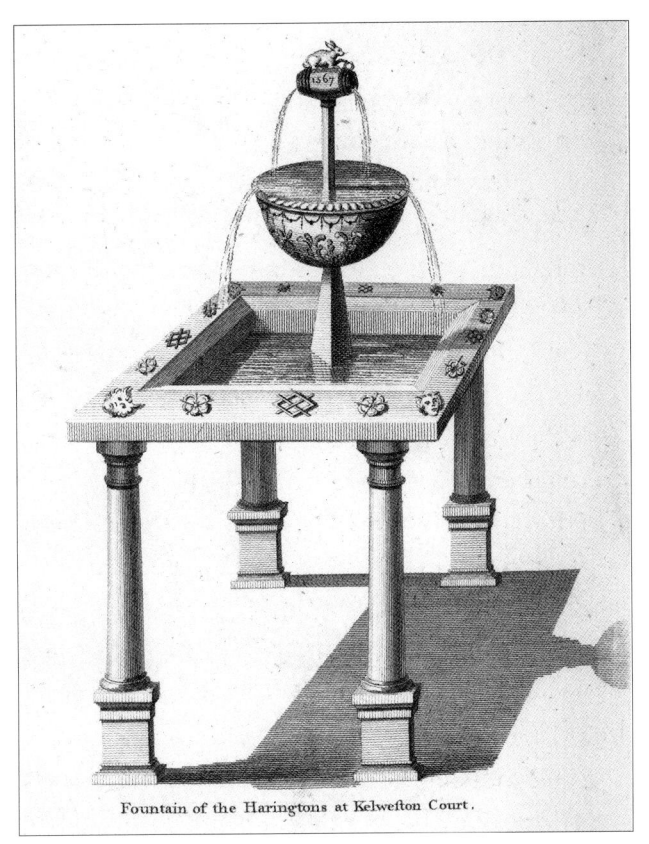

3 Queen Elizabeth dined underneath this fountain at Sir John Harington's Kelston Manor in the summer of 1591. University of Bristol, Special Collections

Fountain of the Haringtons at Kelweston Court.

was to publish in translation during the year of the Queen's visit:

> The fountain had been fashioned with endless subtlety and care by a diligent craftsman. It was shaped like a pavilion or loggia consisting of eight distinct arches. It was roofed with a gilt enamelled sky. Eight white marble statues supported the sky left-handed. The ingenious sculptor had carved cornucopias which each one held in her right hand; from these water fell with a pleasant murmur into the alabaster basin. With greatest craft he had reduced the eight pillars to the shape of women, more than life-sized, each one different in dress and face, though all equally fair and beautiful.[13]

This Italian example also functioned like an outdoor room for dining, while its water source was connected to the wider landscape, suggesting a formal water garden: 'The statues delimited a circular basin floored with dry coral, blissfully cool with the crystal-clear water collected there before being channelled into a canal which irrigated the green meadow, dotted with blues, whites and yellows; it branched into several streams – balm to the soft grasses and tender shrubs'.[14] This may be significant, for on the site of the vanished manor house at Kelston there are earthworks that indicate a lost formal layout of pools and terraces. Given Sir John's fascination with water and mechanics, it is not unreasonable to suggest that he might have extended his father's garden from the Fountain Court into the landscape beyond.

Today, the site of the old Manor lies in fields between St Nicholas' parish church alongside Church Road, and the Tower House on the main road between Bath and Bitton. A field survey undertaken in 1981 for the Bristol Archaeological Research Group by James Edgar and Rob Iles identified the remaining earthworks in this area, and subsequent reports have succeeded in interpreting the banks and ditches as garden features.[15] The most useful visual source for the several areas and the Manor itself is a plan taken from the 1744 tithe map illustrated by the Revd Francis Poynton in his *Memoranda* of the parish.[16] This marks the Manor, adjacent to the eastern churchyard wall, as a quadrangular house with an inner courtyard and a south-east corner tower. To the south is a 'Bowling Green' next to an area of raised terracing, and further out the Lay Mead with a direction given to the 'Summer House'. Fronting the east façade of the Manor is the 'Italian Garden', laid out in rectangular beds with the Fountain at one end. To the east of all these enclosures is the 'Gaston', centred by a tree-lined pool and crossed by tree avenues to the south. There are further enclosed sectors to the north, which included a fruit garden and the Green Court on the approach to the main entrance front. A later map of about 1814[17] names the outer fields of the estate, one of which, to the west of the manorial site, is called the 'Shooting Close'; no doubt where Sir John practised archery. This map shows the path from the riverbank cutting up the slope between Tennant's Wood and Summerhouse Wood to cross the 'Conygeare' and head for the Manor. Sheldon's remark about Harington's boats suggests that one way to approach the Manor was up the river from Bath, alighting at the break in the woods where the

Summerhouse on the ridge above may have acted as a postern.

The position of the Fountain is indicated on the 1744 plan, but its specific dimensions were not determined until 1921, when the Revd Poynton's son investigated the foundations of the Manor and found that, on the plan, it was equal in size to the south-east tower, which measured approximately 50 feet by 25 feet.[18] Scales in plans of this type are rarely accurate, so this must remain a tentative speculation, but it suggests that the Fountain would easily have accommodated the Queen and her retinue for dinner.[19] Joy Brown has discovered the footings of two of the four columns, under which there is a culvert with running water, supplied from a well in the 'Sandpits' to the east of the main road. Her conjectural siting of the Fountain places it centrally across a path, so that visitors could walk beneath and then up steps to the raised lawn next to the Bowling Green. Quite where Harington's 'swimming place' was located is uncertain, but it may have been the rectangular pool in the Gaston, its sides lined with trees for privacy.

The Privy is now located in the garden of Moores Cottage, built on the enclosure of quadrant beds adjacent to Church Road marked on the 1744 plan.[20] It is a semicircular castellated screen wall of stone, punctuated with round-arched openings and with an arched tunnel giving on to a circular basin paved with flagstones (4). This may well be only a fragment of the original structure, as a manuscript drawing by Harington suggests that it would have been entirely circular, in imitation of one of the wonders of the Ancient World. A note accompanies this drawing: 'My privy shall be a round built like the Tower of Babel and upon vaults too well tarassed after the finest fashion: now for the tunnel: I mean to raise it in the midst provided that divers doors and windows shall be made on every side'.[21] The mechanics of the Privy are illustrated in Harington's *An Anatomie of the Metamorphosed Ajax* where 'unsaverie places may be made sweet, noysome places made wholesome, filthie places made cleanly'.[22] The device is a simple cistern of water that is flushed by a screw, covered by a scallop shell when it is not in use. Beneath the seat the 'stoole pot' connects with a vault below; Harington advises: 'always remember that at noone and at night, emptie it and leave it halfe a foote deepe in fayre water. And this being done, and orderly kept, your worst privie may be as

4 The remains of Harington's Privy, the mechanics of which are described in his 1596 *Metamorphosis of Ajax*

sweet as your best chamber'.[23] As well as the Privy at Kelston, Harington presented one to the Queen at Richmond Palace and another to William Cecil at Theobalds. In the prefatory letter to the *Metamorphosis*, *Philostilpnos* remarks on the prospect of mass-producing this aid to personal cleanliness in an age of slovenly hygiene:

> If you have so easie, so cheap, & so infallible a way for avoyding such annoyances in great houses; you may not only pleasure many great persons, but do her Majestie good service in her pallace of Greenwich & other stately houses, that are oft annoyed with such savours....Also you might be a great benefactor to the Citie of London, and all other populous townes, who stand in great neede of such convayances.[24]

Chronologically, the next important Elizabethan garden is that laid out by Sir Edward Hext after he bought the manor of **Low Ham** in 1588.[25] He had built his Elizabethan house on the site by 1593 and laid out gardens on an

5 A parish church as mausoleum – the Gothic Survival church of Low Ham, built by Sir Edward Hext in 1620 as his final resting place

elevated site above the rare Gothic Survival church (5) that he was to build later in 1620, more as a mausoleum to receive his mortal remains than as a place of worship. Hext died in 1623 and his wife followed him ten years later; the church was not consecrated until 1669. This strange, angular building sits at the foot of Hext Hill in green isolation without a churchyard, surrounded instead by farm machinery. There is an expansive view down to it from the top of the terraced hill, with Glastonbury Tor prominent on the skyline. It is a place of rare beauty, the gardens stripped now of all their architectural support save some scraps of stone walling. Unlike Kelston, the site of whose gardens has been preserved along with several of the manorial buildings – the dovecote and tithe barn at the Manor Farm, the stables and, most importantly, the screen wall of Harington's Privy – the Elizabethan and Jacobean garden earthworks at Low Ham have been overlain by formal gardens of the late seventeenth century, so we have no record of what they comprised. It is even unclear where the Elizabethan mansion stood,[26] so an analysis of the formalities at Low Ham will need to wait until the gardens of the late seventeenth century are discussed in the next chapter.

Fortunately, that is not the case at **Montacute**, where not only do twin Jacobean banqueting houses survive, but there is also a short description of the gardens as they were in 1633: 'large and spacious Courtes, gardens, orchards, a parke',[27] and a more detailed survey of 1667. This, coupled with a late-eighteenth-century estate map of Montacute by Samuel Donne, taken before the park was naturalised into a Brownian vapidity, give a clear impression of how the Jacobean gardens functioned and what they comprised.[28]

The beautiful honey Ham stone house, its roofline bristling with ogee-shaped gables and tall columnar chimneystacks, its Nine Worthies surveying all they guard from niches set between a battery of mullioned windows, was built for Sir Edward Phelips in the 1590s.[29] Phelips was a wealthy lawyer, a powerful man who entered Parliament in 1584 and was knighted in 1603. He rose to the high offices of Speaker of the House and Master of the Rolls. There was an Old Park at Montacute, essentially a deer larder to the south-west of the present park, but Phelips decided to create a new park and site his house close to the village centre dominated by its cone-shaped hill – *mons acutus* in Latin – that was to become visually appropriated into the estate landscape in the mid-eighteenth century. Entry into the estate today is directly off the village square via a nineteenth-century lodge in the ogee-domed style of the Banqueting Pavilions on the East Court. The National Trust car-park is sited in what until 1971 was the walled Kitchen Garden, and a gate in the wall leads to the Cedar Lawn, marked 'Pigs Wheatle Orchard' on the Donne survey, which was converted into a bowling green in the nineteenth century. The line of trees marked on the Donne survey is gone, replaced now by a tall yew hedge, while an avenue of columnar yews on a raised walk leads to the south-east Banqueting Pavilion in the corner, overshadowed by a veteran sweet chestnut; its twin is directly opposite to the south-west (6). In 1667 this area was 'a large Woodyard and necessary buildings for Dayres Washing Brewing and Bakeing, a Pigeon house, and on the South side thereof, and of the Court before the house, are severall Orchards of Cherryes, Pares, Plumbs, others of Apples, and also good Kitchen gardens with 2 fish pounds all incompassed within a wall'.[30] The most intriguing

6 One of the two Banqueting Pavilions at Montacute, built by Sir Edward Phelips in the 1590s to command both the entrance forecourt and the deer park beyond

building in this sector of the grounds is the arcaded Garden House at the south-western corner. At first sight this seems to be of Elizabethan date and coeval with the house and gardens, with its cabochon decoration around the arches, shaped gable and balustrading. However, it was probably brought from Barrington Court – the arms of the Strode family are set in the gable – by Lord Curzon, who leased the estate after 1915.[31] Behind the yew hedge is the Column Garden, again of Curzon vintage, its row of Doric columns reflecting the columned terrace on the east front of the house. This is a contemplative space bordered by curving yew hedges and studded with beds of spiky yucca.

The East Court is the best preserved of the Jacobean enclosures, but even this has undergone some changes. It was originally stone-paved rather than laid to grass as befits an entrance court,[32] and its approach from the park across the Bowling Green was guarded by a gatehouse.[33] Each wall had a stone porter's lodge shown in a naïve eighteenth-century drawing preserved at Mells Manor;[34] both gatehouse and lodges were demolished in the late eighteenth century. Nevertheless, the space is one of the most exhilaratingly architectural enclosures in late Elizabethan and Jacobean garden design, perfectly in harmony with the house that commands it. The ogee gables, balustrades, pyramidal obelisks, free-standing columns, mullioned and lead-latticed windows and oriels of the main house are all reflected in the screen wall and Banqueting Pavilions. The 1667 survey is so precise in its description of the Court that it is worth quoting at length:

> There is a descent of 6 Stepps into a faire Court with a Freestone walke in the midst leading to a Gatehouse which Court is walled about with Freestone Ashler Wall topped with Rayles and Ballesters and Piramids and Turrets of Ornament, in the middle of the East Wall part of the said Court is a faire Gatehouse with lodging Chambers of Freestone and at each corner of the said Court are 2 faire Turretts with lodging Chambers.[35]

The 'Turretts of Ornament' are the circular gazebos from which no view could ever be enjoyed, as they are above head height on the boundary walls. Their sturdy Doric columns support openwork canopies, which are decorated inside with Gothic-style rib vaults ending in pendants. There is a minor mystery to the Banqueting Pavilions in that they are two storeys high, yet there is no staircase in either. The survey reports that these 'Turretts' had 'lodging Chambers', which would imply that there were two rooms for habitation, so they must originally have had internal stairs. However, their architectural detail is of such sophistication that it is more likely that they functioned as elegant private spaces for family retreat from the hustle and bustle of the main house with all its servants. The ground plans of each are particularly interesting in that they are formed by quatrefoils overlaid on squares echoing the sixteenth-century delight in conceits and 'devices'.[36] Their close proximity to the main house suggests that the upper rooms were used for the banquet course of sweet-meats, crystallised fruit and dessert wines served after dinner.[37]

The North Garden was extensively remodelled in the 1890s by R S Balfour and Reginald Blomfield and will feature in a later chapter on Edwardian gardens. For its contemporary Jacobean appearance we have another detailed description from the 1667 survey:

> On the North side of the house is a very faire Spacious Garden walled about and furnished with all sorts of Flowers and fruits and divers mounted walkes without which Garden there is a descent of about 10 stepps into Private walkes walled about and furnished with store of fruit, and at the end of the East walke there is a faire Banqueting house built and Arched with Freestone wainscoted within and leaded on the Toppe thereof, and without the West Walke of the garden there is a faire Orchard furnished with good fruit and divers pleasant Walkes.[38]

The bones of this layout are present today, particularly the raised walks to the east and west sides, but the Banqueting House has gone. The survey fails to mention the pond and the Mount, which are both shown in this enclosure on the Donne map. Mounts are a typical Elizabethan and Jacobean garden feature, and it is highly likely that the North Garden had such a viewing platform early on to give elevated views down to the flowerbeds.

This series of enclosures, which originally included an extension to the East Court 'walled about and coped with Freestone sett with Severall walkes and Rowes of Trees'[39] contiguous with the Bowling Green on the edge of the park, is typical of a period in which gardens had a leisure purpose distinctly different from that pursued in the wider landscape. This insistence upon tightly defined spaces, either walled or hedged, is apparent at another Jacobean house, **Cothelstone Manor**, which shelters under the southern slope of the Quantocks to the west of the county.[40] On approaching the estate from the west the road bends sharply and a volumetric Regency Lodge, set back behind screen walls with chunky ironwork railings, marks the early-nineteenth-century drive to a house that has vanished. This was Cothelstone House, built in 1818 for Edward Jeffries Esdaile by the Bath architect, Charles Harcourt Masters, who must also have designed the Lodge.[41] But it is the old Manor that appears next, guarded at the roadside by a triumphal-arched entrance of rural proportions,[42] and further on down the drive by a diminutive Gatehouse behind which the courtyard and garden areas extend.

The medieval manor house at Cothelstone, which was remodelled by Sir John Stawell, who held the manor from 1541 to his death in 1603, was originally approached by a series of courts and gateways. During its restoration in the 1850s, Edward Jeffries Esdaile kept diaries that record his conservation work and provide a useful description of the environs of the Manor: 'Passing through an archway [the extant gatehouse] we find ourselves in a wide open space, all walled, and another porter's lodge before us'.[43] This layout of enclosures is confirmed by an estate map of 1733,[44] and there was a further 'white-stoned, semi-circular arch' leading out of the immediate surroundings of the Manor.[45] Arched niches on the Gatehouse entrance front and further niches under the archway suggest that visitors and owners were encouraged to sit and view the enclosures, much as the seating niches on the east front of Montacute offered vantage points for relaxation on the terrace.

Moving from the Gatehouse, the surviving terraced gardens are set high up to the east, right above the courtyard, while there are remains of further walled enclosures below the house to the west. On the upper terrace there are two distinct areas, probably originally defined by walls, which comprise a formal parterre or perhaps a bowling green and another formal garden towards the parish church of St Thomas of Canterbury. The first is dominated at the north-east corner by the arcaded Summerhouse (7), its round arches studded with cabochon decoration, its parapet, like that of the Gatehouse, castellated. This has been reconstructed in fine ashlar stone on a rubble stone plinth course, so it may be on the site of an earlier building associated with the old medieval manor house. Inside it has a beautiful king post timber roof that looks sixteenth- or early seventeenth-century, and the cabochon decoration is identical to that on Sir John Stawell's 1603 alabaster monument in the church. Conversely, it may date from the mid-nineteenth century when Esdaile was restoring the house and grounds.[46] If this grassed area was originally a bowling green, it may be that the two stone seats at either end offered views of the game. These again are difficult to date, but their angularity and crispness of detail are suggestive of mid-Victorian work. The further sector is commanded by a two-storey Banqueting House, now cut off from its garden enclosure by a later rubble stone wall. This has been extensively altered and extended, but the central baluster mullion to its southern canted bay is identical to others on both the Manor and the Gatehouse; it is a most singular motif that has, apparently, neither precedent nor rival in the area.

A similar set of walled enclosures survives around **Lytes Cary**, at first sight a perfect small manor house of the sixteenth century. Unlike the garden compartments at Cothelstone, however, which remain relatively

7 Sir John Stawell's arcaded Elizabethan Summerhouse at Cothelstone Manor was built on an elevated site above the house to overlook a formal garden area and offer views out across the landscape

intact and have early features, what was left of the original house at Lytes Cary was extensively remodelled after 1907 by Sir Walter and Lady Jenner. Most of the walls date from that period, so its grounds have a distinctive Arts and Crafts feel.[47] However, in the very year of Elizabeth's accession to the throne in 1558, John Lyte made over his property to his son Henry, who in 1578 published the *Niewe Herball, or Historie of Plants*, an English version of a French translation by Carolus Clusius of the Flemish herbal, the *Cruydeboek*, by Rembert Dodoens. Not surprisingly, Lyte dedicated his book to the Queen, 'from my poore house at Lytscarie', and it is said to have directed Shakespeare in the references to plants in his plays,[48] and most probably informed Edmund Spenser:

> Bring hither the Pincke and purple Cullumbine,
> With Gellifloures;
> Bring Coronations, and Sops-in-wine
> Worne of Paramourse;
> Strowe me the ground with Daffodowndillies,
> And Cowslips, and Kingcups, and loved Lillies,
> The prettie Pawnse
> And the Chevisaunce,
> Shall match with the floure Delice.[49]

Lytes' own copy of the *Herball* is still at the house and contains copious marginal notes revealing his deep knowledge of plants, particularly local Somerset flora.[50] Sadly, the family fortunes dipped in the eighteenth century, and in 1755 Thomas Lyte and his son John surrendered all rights to the estate. Thereafter, the house was let to tenants and much of the fabric was either left to rot or demolished. So, although John Aubrey reported that Henry Lyte had 'a pretty good collection of plants', and his son Thomas had extensive orchards, the Elizabethan gardens have not survived.[51]

Another predominantly Edwardian garden, but one which was also developed within the structural walls of a much earlier layout, is at **Mells Manor** near Frome, the home of the Horners. Any mention of that family immediately brings to mind the nursery rhyme of Little Jack Horner who pulled the rich plum of the manor out of the Dissolution pie. However, as the deed bearing the king's seal that survives at the Manor proves, Thomas Horner bought Mells from the crown for a considerable sum in 1543. His nephew Sir John was succeeded in 1587 by his son Thomas, by which time the Manor had been enlarged and gardens laid out. These must have been contained within the high walled enclosure to the rear of the house, which is very likely a survival of the monastic manorial complex built by Abbot Selwood of Glastonbury before his death in 1493. John Leland visited the site in about 1543 and wrote:

> There is a praty maner place of stone harde at the west ende of the churche. This be likelihood was partley builded by Abbate Selwodde of Glasteinbyri. Sins it served the farmer of thye lordship. Now Mr Horner hath boute the lordship of the King.[52]

Whilst the whole area at the back of the Manor was remodelled during Frances Horner's ownership in the late nineteenth century, there are definite signs that this enclosure is of fifteenth-century origin. The west wall has a series of attached, semicircular buttresses with shaped caps (8), and there is a Tudor-arched doorway that gives access now to the Kitchen Garden. John Harvey believes the garden walls to be the work of Richard Beere, who succeeded Selwood at Glastonbury and died in 1524.[53] Whether they are by Selwood or Beere, they are certainly early in date and a reflection of the medieval hortus conclusus, which was to be sustained and developed well into the Jacobean period. Harvey is also convinced that the garden 'formerly had internal mounds at its northern angles, looking over raised parapets into the countryside'.[54] This speculation is intriguing, for there are definite changes in the stonework on the northern wall, particularly at the eastern corner, which has two bands of long-and-short quoins, suggesting a corner pavilion rather than a mount. A crudely drawn estate map of 1680 shows the enclosure as 'The Garden', but there is no record on it of corner pavilions.[55] There can be no definitive answer to these speculations, but the grey-walled enclosure to the north of the Manor may well be the earliest domestic, as opposed to ecclesiastical, garden enclosure to survive in Somerset.

There is a similar arrangement at **Clevedon Court**, south of Bristol, without doubt the most beautiful small manor house in the country, let alone in Somerset. At Clevedon the Elton family were to reshape and remodel the house and grounds in both the early eighteenth century and the nineteenth century, but they kept the existing layout of terraced and walled enclosures below the steep, wooded hillside to the rear of the house.[56] The grounds were first described in 1629 as 'two gardens, an orchard, a fayre court, a strong and large barne, and other out houses, besides 60 acres of woods and coppice'.[57] Many of these features are shown on a large oil painting by Peter Tillemans (*colour 3*), which still hangs in the house. The Manor is surrounded by walled compartments on three sides: a yard before the forecourt, three enclosures to the south, the last crenellated, and a narrow transverse garden room along the top of the ridge – now the Pretty Terrace – with a buttressed perimeter wall. This last was possibly rebuilt by the Eltons after they bought the estate in

8 The buttressed walls around the North Garden at Mells Manor are survivors of the monastic complex owned by the abbots of Glastonbury. They were built by either Abbot Selwood, who died in 1493, or Abbot Beere before his death in 1524

1709, but presumably replaced an earlier boundary wall. The walled area immediately behind the house is commanded on the north wall by a circular bastion tower, which survives today. The Round Tower is likely to have acted as a gazebo for views down to a formal parterre or knot. Further out on the hillside above is a gatehouse defining the formal entrance drive, and beyond that the silhouette of Walton Castle overlooking the Bristol Channel.

The presence of three long canals in the foreground of the Tillemans painting is indicative of a later seventeenth- or early-eighteenth-century remodelling of the grounds, as is the planned wilderness to the north with its winding walk and axial path commanded by a summerhouse. However, the Octagon at the south end of the Pretty Terrace and the Summerhouse at the other were added by Sir Abraham Elton IV in the mid-eighteenth century.[58] These features are salutary reminders that, especially on sites where later gardens were laid out, the walls of the enclosures are likely to be much older than their fashionable planting would suggest. With this in mind it is a short step back to the great earthworks at Low Ham, where extensive late seventeenth-century gardens were formed around the compartmented core of Sir Edward Hext's earlier Elizabethan layout.

2

Earthworks, an episcopal canal and wildernesses – formality eventually subverted

Nether Stowey Manor · Low Ham · Witham Charterhouse · Hinton House
Brympton d'Evercy · Orchard Portman · Fairfield · Nunney Castle House
Wells Bishop's Palace · Ven House · Sandhill Park · Orchard Wyndham
Marston Bigot

THE FORMAL CANAL AT CLEVEDON SHOWN ON PETER TILLEMANS' PAINTING must date from the early eighteenth century, after 1709 when Sir Abraham Elton I, a self-made entrepreneur, bought the Court as a country retreat from his business base in Bristol. His status as Master of the Merchant Venturers is reflected in the grounds, not only by the fashionable canal, but also in the formal beds divided by gravel paths and the Pretty Terrace with its wall of espaliered plants. This, however, is the last gasp of a formalism that had begun in the 1630s and was soon to be eclipsed by the coming informality in garden design of the next two decades of the century. But changes in garden fashions take time, especially in the provinces away from the capital. A 1750 estate map of **Nether Stowey Manor House** shows the house still surrounded by walled enclosures, with a formal layout in the front garden commanded by an ogee-domed gazebo.[1] While the walled compartments must date from the seventeenth century, if not earlier as at Clevedon, the Gazebo is mid-eighteenth-century in date, built of brick on an earlier stone substructure, with a Venetian window to the garden.[2] There was a similar walled garden with formal beds and a gazebo, but one that overlooked the river, at Ladymead House, Walcot in Bath.[3] There the Gazebo appears to be late seventeenth-century in style, with cross-mullioned windows and decorative urns. So caution must be exercised when examining formal sites, particularly where there has been a succession of owners interested in garden improvements.

It will be instructive, therefore, to track back to the great earthworks at **Low Ham**, where Sir Edward Hext, the Elizabethan gardener, lies in his church-mausoleum next to his wife Dionysia, to review the second phase of garden intervention on Hext Hill. Fortunately this has been interpreted by two sensitive and thoughtful archaeologists: Michael Aston first identified the site as of importance in 1978 and, more recently,

9 Low Ham has the most extensive series of earthworks in the county. They represent lost formal gardens laid out by Lord Stawell after 1690, with advice from Jacob Bobart, Superintendent of the Oxford Physic Garden

Robert Wilson-North surveyed it for the Royal Commission on the Historical Monuments of England between September 1995 and March 1996.[4] Neither of them has the definitive answer to what was actually achieved at Low Ham, nor are there helpful visual records of the great layouts there, but the RCHM report is as close as we will get to determining the ornamental and practical functions of the site. After Sir Edward's death in 1625 the estate passed to his daughter Elizabeth, wife of John Stawell. Thereafter the family did little to the Elizabethan house and gardens, though there was rebuilding work on the church in 1688. Ralph, 1st Lord Stawell, died in 1689 and his son John, 2nd Lord Stawell, inherited and began a major rebuilding campaign to create what Collinson was later to describe as 'a most sumptuous and expensive edifice'.[5] However, John died tragically three years later at the age of twenty-four, so it is not clear just how much he had achieved before his death.

The surviving earthworks (9) are roughly rectangular in shape, defined by a limestone wall of dressed and squared blocks on the east and the village road to the west. They rise steeply up the hill from the south front of the church and then expand across the au at the top. As we have seen, this elevated site offers spectacular views across the Moors to Glastonbury Tor in the far distance. A 1779 map of the estate shows this area as completely walled, with a further wall in the centre defining two rectangles of equal size.[6] It is marked 'Hare and Rabbit Warren', to which the gardens must have reverted by the late eighteenth century. The map shows the west elevation of the Stawell mansion at the foot of the hill to the east of the church; its site is now covered with modern farm buildings, but to their rear are the remains of the former Kitchen Garden wall, also shown on the map. This siting of the house would accord with Collinson's description of it as having been built in a 'very low and bad situation'.[7] By his time the mansion was ruined and a farmer was living in its kitchen. The approach was through gates from the village road to the west, and the formal gardens were laid out above the house to the south.

It is presumed that Sir John, newly married to a daughter of James Cecil, 3rd Earl of Salisbury, determined to remodel the existing terraced gardens south of the church. The evidence for this is contained in a letter that Jacob Bobart, Superintendent of the Oxford Physic Garden, wrote to Stawell in 1690. It begins with a general overview of how the gardens were to be reorganised: 'First we suppose the Tarras walke to be the basis of the whole thence a perpendicular to arise to take the middle of the passage out of the house and from this line all the side walls to run parallel'.[8] Robert Wilson-North has extrapolated measurements and height changes from the letter which correspond exactly with the earthwork evidence, so there can be no doubt that Stawell was remodelling the existing Elizabethan gardens in the central section of his newly walled area. The pronounced depression at the heart of the enclosure, which runs down to the former site of the house, must be the 'perpendicular' alignment mentioned by Bobart.

Bobart's letter gives tantalising glimpses of what Stawell hoped to lay out before the work was abruptly halted at his death. It is worth quoting in some detail, as a conjectural reconstruction of the gardens can be formed from his directions. Indeed, the meticulous measurements given in the letter suggest that Bobart was himself the designer of the fated scheme:

> The Tarras to be about 90f broad which may imperceptibly rise 6 or 8 inches from thence a pair of stairs of 10 steps riseing 70 inches which carries up to the first plot 262 f square assending 168 inches. Then arising 5 steps or 35 inches which carries up to the plot where the canall is to be the plot 74 f with the canall in the middle of the same 40 f broad and 80 f long (if it be concluded to be a parallelogram or whither an Octagonall figure would not keep cleaner considering there is no great flux of water). From this plot arises another pair of staires of 10 steps 70 inches which deliver you up to a plot of 260 f square ascending 192 inches. Then 10 steps more 70 inches high carryng up to the Wilderness 260 f square ascending allsoe 192 inches. The length of the whole with what the steps take up is about 980 f ascending 848 inches.[9]

As Wilson-North has argued convincingly, these compartments or 'plots' can be seen on the hillside, rising up from the church in a sequence of terraces and staircases connecting large planting areas, the first with a central water feature and the last a Wilderness of shrubs, trees and winding walks. Quite whether the water feature was ever constructed is uncertain, as there would need to be a 'great flux of water' to support a canal at that height, but the siting of the Wilderness sector at the end of the layout, where it connects with the wider landscape, is typical seventeenth-century practice. Given his Cecil connections it is to be assumed that Sir John would have filled his plots with all manner of flowers and shrubs and lined his terrace staircases with urns and statuary, but that inveterate traveller Celia Fiennes seems not to have visited this part of

Somerset to record its gardens in her travel diaries, and by 1722, when a survey was taken after the death of the 2nd Baron, the Phelips family were preparing the estate for sale.[10]

At **Witham Charterhouse**, Wilson-North has surveyed another Somerset site where earlier layouts have been overlain with later formal gardens, but there the dating is inexact and the earthworks are less revealing.[11] Witham is a tantalising site close to Frome with the Great Western Railway slicing through its rectangular enclosure (*colour 4*). It has had a chequered history since the Dissolution, when it was bought by Ralph Hopton, one of Thomas Cromwell's advisors, who converted parts of the monastic buildings into a residence. Thereafter the Wyndhams owned it, and in 1717 William Wyndham commissioned the architect James Gibbs to make improvements to the house. In 1754, when Dr Richard Pococke visited the site, he found it in 'a low situation; the old chapel and some other parts of the Nunnery remain'.[12] Sir Charles Wyndham, by that time Earl of Egremont, had 'lately removed all his furniture from it, not purposing to live there any more'.[13] Finally, in 1762, he sold the estate to Alderman William Beckford, who immediately commissioned Robert Adam to design a new mansion on another site to the south. The foundations at least of this Neo-classical house were built, but the Alderman died in 1770, the house was abandoned, and the younger William Beckford of Fonthill Abbey finally sold it in 1810. So the earthwork remains on the site are of at least three periods and difficult to interpret, but it is possible that a seventeenth-century layout was, like that at Low Ham, constructed within the environs of earlier gardens associated with the Charterhouse.

The significance and complex layering of the site were first discovered in the 1960s by Mick Aston when, in conjunction with the Royal Commission and English Heritage, he was carrying out a survey of all the Carthusian monasteries in the UK and Ireland. Ian Burrow wrote up the 1960s excavations in the late 1980s, and the findings published in 1991 have informed Wilson-North's own researches. He believes that the bulk of the earthworks are formal gardens for the Hopton house, commandeered after 1717 for the Wyndham remodelling by Gibbs. To the west of the house was an octagonal area, still visible today but partly obliterated by the railway, and to the south, terraced walks with a pavilion overlooking the formal gardens. The pavilion also gave views across to a series of lakes developed from the river Frome in a large cutting. The principal rooms of the house gave on to the private garden, which was built over the Great Cloister of the monastery containing the monks' cells. The original cloister walk may well have survived as a covered garden feature. All this is, of course, informed speculation, and it is still not certain who laid out the gardens at Witham. Wilson-North opts for Ralph Hopton, who was created Knight of the Order of the Bath at Charles I's coronation; 'His status is in keeping with gardening on this scale and as such provides a date in the 1620s-1640s'.[14] However, that octagonal area is more likely to date from the Wyndham-Gibbs phase of the improvements, and it is by no means clear on what 'typological grounds' the earthwork evidence supports a pre-Civil War date.[15]

Lacking contemporary visitor accounts, the precise dating of the earthworks at Witham will remain unproven.[16] Fiennes mentions some parks in the north of the county and saw the Bishop's Palace at Wells, to which we shall return, but she sheds little light on formal garden improvements. While Witham survives only in earthworks and lacks descriptive elucidation, the formal gardens created by the Pouletts at **Hinton House**, Hinton St George, have completely disappeared, but there is a seventeenth-century description of the layout which gives a detailed account of the grounds. Cosimo III, Grand Duke of Tuscany, visited Hinton on 9 April 1669 and was impressed by both house and gardens:

> The dwelling rooms are noble, fine and spacious, and there are also gardens both for utility and pleasure. On the one hand they contain all those sorts of plants and fruits which the climate will allow, and on the other a parterre, very different from the common usage of the gardens in England. For, where these have sanded walks perfectly levelled by rolling them with a stone roller.....and between the walks several flat spaces covered with very green turf and without other adornment, this garden of mylord Pawlett is a meadow with different beds having borders of bricks on end...filled with flowers.[17]

The concentration on utility and productivity is typical of the Commonwealth period with its emphasis on husbandry, but the flowerbeds set within brick borders sound like a *parterre de broderie*, fashionable after the Restoration. It is likely that this flowery meadow was directly in view of the house; Cosimo mentions the wider park 'of three miles in circumference, shut in by a thick plantation of trees', but not the location of the flower garden.[18]

As well as the paucity of visitor accounts, there are also few informative country house views for Somerset gardens until the 1730s and 1740s, when several paintings were made of the layouts at Fairfield and Orchard Wyndham. Somerset rates only two of the 'Principal Seats of the Nobility and Gentry' in Leonard Knyff and John Kip's 1707 *Britannia Illustrata*.[19] These are Orchard Portman, south of Taunton, and **Brympton D'Evercy**, just south of Yeovil. Both estates were remodelled after the Civil War, Brympton in the 1660s and Orchard Portman slightly later. Brympton's is shown encircled by a series of walled enclosures, echoing medieval and mid-seventeenth-century practice, but Orchard Portman has embraced the new post-Restoration fashion, derived from France, of axial alignment through the centre of the house.

Both sites had existing Tudor manor houses, which were reconstructed and expanded, but while Brympton d'Evercy (*10*) was given a striking new south front by Sir John Posthumous Sydenham, clearly inspired by the Jonesian classicism of his wife's family home at Hinton St George, its gardens were developed piecemeal within surviving compartments.[20] A detailed engraving taken closer to the house,[21] which was published in 1699 by James Fish of Warwick (*11*), gives a clear picture of the formal areas. A transverse raised terrace gave on to a walled Bowling Green, its wall lined with espaliered bushes and its green flanked by rectangular grass strips defined at the corners by conifers. Then, after a narrow alley of fruit trees, came a shrubbery grove leading to an orchard. Returning to the Kip and Knyff engraving, to the west below the churchyard was a rectangular pool, possibly an arm of the original moat, set alongside more vegetable plots, with another orchard beyond this. The water extended in a narrow canal between the fruit tree alley and the grove, across open grassland to perimeter planting on the east. Further wooded enclosures

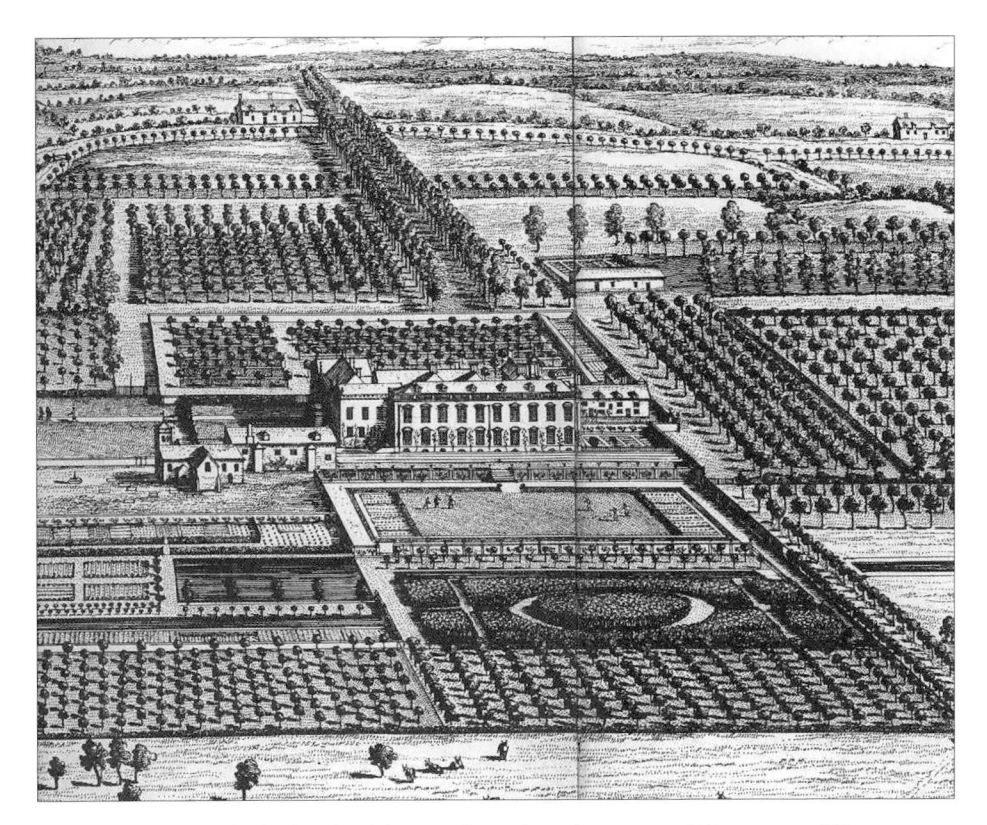

10 John Posthumous Sydenham's elaborate formal gardens around Brympton d'Evercy, as illustrated in Jan Kip and Leonard Knyff's 1707 *Britannia Illustrata*. University of Bristol, Special Collections

hemmed in the house on the north and east, while an axial avenue of trees ran north-south on the east side of the house rather than on an alignment with its centre. The emphasis was on trees rather than flowers and must have owed much to John Evelyn's *Sylva, or a Discourse of Forest-Trees*, published in 1670. Evelyn's book introduced seventeenth-century owners to the exotics recently imported from the Mediterranean like the cypress, holm oak and phillyrea, and cedar of Lebanon. Brympton's sister house, Hinton St George, had a celebrated cedar lawn, planted in 1684 and wrecked in the great storm of May 1897.[22] Today, the gardens below the house at Brympton are laid to lawn and the central section of the canal has been broadened out into a small lake,[23] but the rectangular pool survives and also the run of stone and brick walling that separated the vegetable plots from the Bowling Green in front of the house.

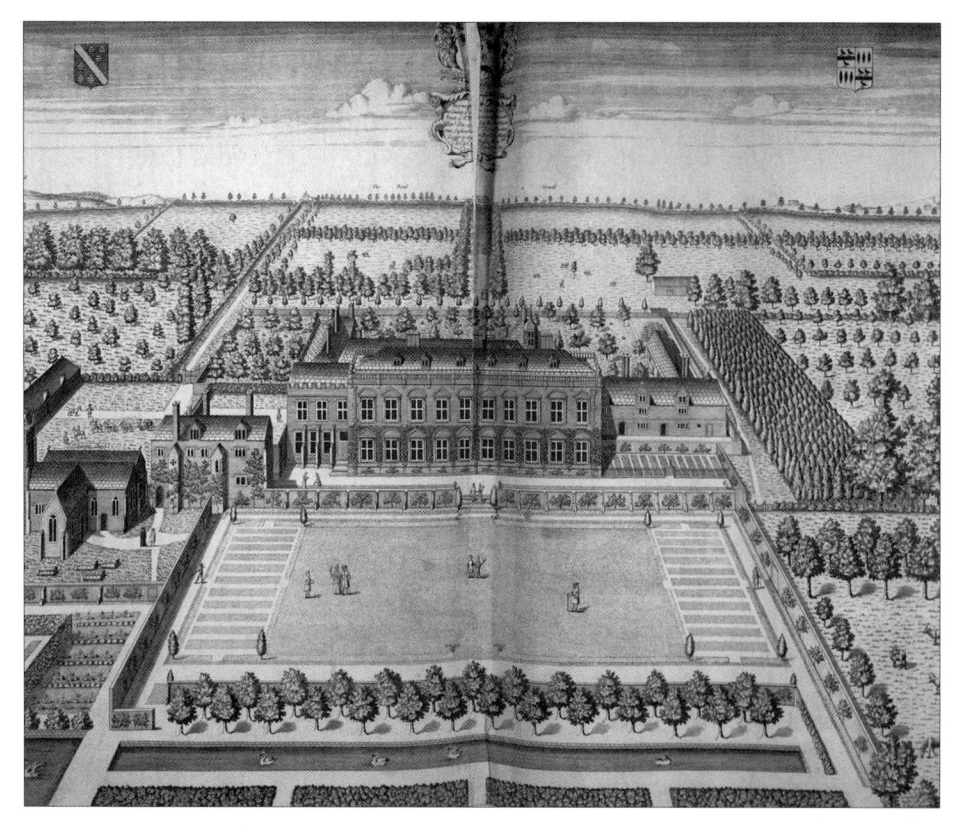

11 A detail of the walled compartments around Brympton d'Evercy from a 1699 engraving; vestiges of the walls and canal system survive today. The Bodleian Library, University of Oxford, Gough Maps 29, f.20B

While there are substantial remnants of the formal layout at Brympton, only vestiges of the gardens at **Orchard Portman** remain around the parish church, and nothing survives of the house itself, which was demolished in the latter half of the nineteenth century. The site is now occupied by a later, nondescript building, which serves as a nursing home, and much of the original estate has been taken over by Taunton Racecourse. This is a tragedy, as Orchard Portman represents a major stylistic leap in garden design from medieval enclosures to a more expansive layout with an axial focus (*12*). The Tudor house was recovered by Sir William Portman after the Civil War and underwent remodelling between 1683 and 1684 when William Taylor was working in the southwest for several clients, including Sir Halswell Tynte of Halswell Park and Lord Weymouth at Longleat.[24] Taylor's work must have included a certain

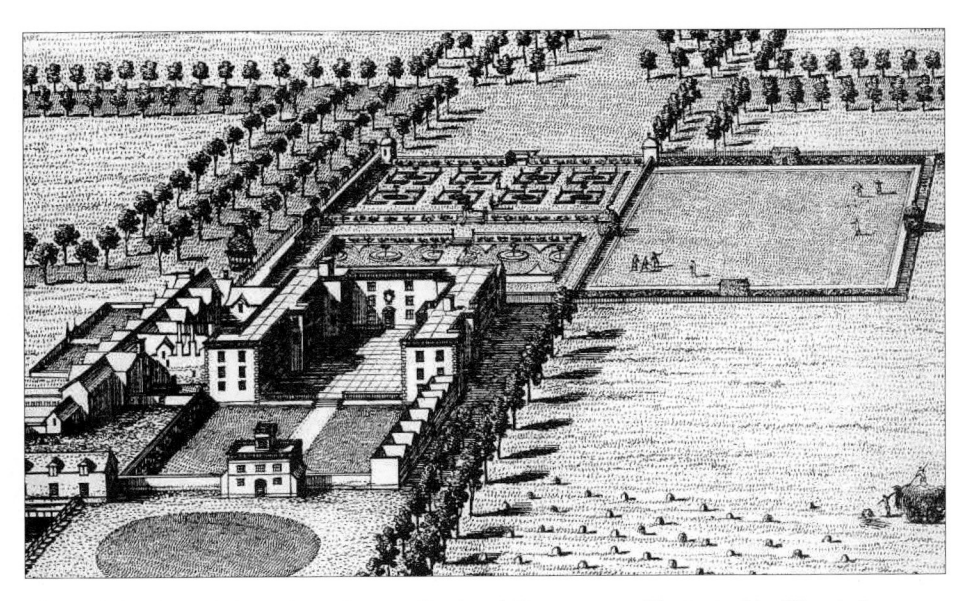

12 The axially aligned formal gardens at Orchard Portman, as illustrated in Kip and Knyff's 1707 *Britannia Illustrata*. University of Bristol, Special Collections

classicising of the main façades and the provision of leads on the flat roofs of the house, as well as a banqueting pavilion at the north-west angle to take in views of the new formal gardens below. These comprised two areas of parterres, the first of cut-work grass plats, the latter of eight square compartments, each centred by a tree, with arbours at the mid point between them and corner banqueting pavilions where the wall gave on to parkland. The Bowling Green alongside was paled and hedged with two green pavilions developed from the hedging. Radiating out from the main northern tree avenue were further avenues to the east and west. To the south of the house were productive areas with vegetable plots, orchards, and a vast walled kitchen garden with what look like double dovecotes at its northern end.

This grand axial layout lacks canals, fountains or other water features usually associated with seventeenth-century formal design, and these do not appear in Somerset gardens until the new century. The earliest canal seems to have been developed from a medieval moat surrounding the manor house at **Fairfield** near Stogursey. Fairfield is a richly textured place with outbuildings and rustic courtyards more suggestive of a village in Provence than a windswept park close to the sea and in sight of the power station at Hinkley Point. The approach is via a yard with a weatherboarded granary and majestic stone barn, through a gabled archway clad in warm pink render and thence to the back door of the house. The entrance front, which faces east, is in complete contrast: a colourwashed, E-shaped formal range, looking more Scottish baronial than Somerset vernacular. At its core is a fifteenth-century house, originally encircled by a crenellated wall with seven towers and a moat. This was rebuilt by Elizabeth Verney and her husband William Palmer in 1589, as recorded on a coat of arms above the porch.

There are great family treasures at Fairfield, including three paintings of the house and grounds which show a formal garden to the east centred by a canal.[25] This is not artistic licence, as the canal, its angular corners now softened, is recorded on an estate map of about 1770.[26] Judging by the paintings the garden was a simple affair, laid out after the orientation of the house was changed, as the earliest painting shows this area as a walled forecourt. The new garden was laid out on the lawn in front of the house as a grid of gravel paths, their angles defined by sentinel conifers, with the canal extending out from the centre of the house eastwards. The remains of three of the bastion towers and the crenellated wall projected on each side of the house (*colour 5*). The foreground of one painting has what looks like a set of steps leading down into the garden, though there is no fall in the land on the site. Another shows the house at a slightly later date with the canal isolated in a sea of lawn, the gravel paths having disappeared. Whatever the true nature of the garden, these paintings are a rare and important record of a lost formal layout. It is likely that the garden was laid out by Thomas Palmer before his death in 1735. His retention of the medieval walling and towers accords perfectly with Palmer's antiquarian and scientific interests. He was a fellow of the Royal Society and wrote a history of Fairfield and other parishes in the county. More significantly, he presented the Saxon Alfred Jewel, found on his family's land at North Petherton, to the Ashmolean Museum in Oxford.

Another simple layout of paths and conifers is shown on a 1733 engraving of **Nunney Castle** by Samuel and Nathaniel Buck. While there are unlikely to have been any formal gardens around the Castle itself, the

Castle House, as it was originally called, was built in the precincts in the latter half of the seventeenth century and given a high-walled rectangular garden with gravel paths studded with conifers and flower borders. While the Castle is a welcoming ruin, managed by English Heritage, the Manor Farmhouse alongside is intensely private, with a special hand-made sign of a Doberman with blood dripping from its mouth warning visitors to beware of the dogs. Unsurprisingly, the garden was not visited for this survey, but the walled enclosure survives with much later planting.

Whilst most ecclesiastical sites in the county have lost their early garden layouts, the Cathedral at Wells has retained its moated **Bishop's Palace**, and there is sound cartographic and archaeological evidence that a complex formal garden was laid out in its walled enclosure.[27] This is, of course, to be expected, as the grounds must always have been a favourite retreat for clerics, their high bastioned walls offering walks for contemplation and internal views down to the gardens, with more expansive prospects out to Bishop Jocelin's thirteenth-century deer park beyond the moat and the Glastonbury Tor in the far distance. They are now open to the public, so preserve little of their original privileged seclusion, but the whole enclosure, now replanted with Victorian specimen trees and studded with modern sculpture on our visit, instils an air of tranquillity in the visitor. And within the sight and sound of this *hortus conclusus* are the bubbling wells which give the town its name, their pools reflecting the great central tower of the Cathedral. In 1698 Celia Fiennes stopped off at Wells expressly to visit the Cathedral and the Palace. She noted how St Andrew's Well 'bubbles up so quick a spring and becomes the head of two little rivers which encreases a little way off into good rivers' and 'saw the Bishops Pallace and Garden; there is a long walke as well as broad shady and very pleasant, which went along by the ditch and banck on which the town wall stands'.[28]

There are several maps and plans which record the formal gardens that were laid out by 1733, the most important being Samuel and Nathaniel Buck's precinct view of that year, Simes' 1735 map of Wells and the antiquary John Carter's later sketches[29] of the ecclesiastical buildings (*colour 6*). These all indicate an ornamental canal system, which took advantage of the wet nature of the Palace grounds, set within a complex of compartments defined by grass plats and clipped shrubs. Buck's engraving shows a culvert and part of a canal at the south-west corner of the site, while Carter's plan of the Palace grounds marks the L-shaped canal clearly to the south of the Great Hall. Mark Horton has suggested that this Dutch-style layout might have been inspired by one of two bishops who had contact with the Netherlands – Thomas Ken, bishop from 1685 to 1690, and George Hooper, bishop from 1704 to 1727 – through their appointment as chaplain to Queen Mary when she was living in The Hague between 1678 and 1690. Significantly, Bishop Ken, who was known to have a keen interest in gardening, was resident at Longleat while the great formal gardens were being laid out between 1682 and 1694 for the 1st Viscount Weymouth by George London and Henry Wise.[30] At the heart of the Longleat layout, to the side of the house in the marshy valley of the Leat, there was a long canal, widening at its centre to accommodate a spectacular fountain. Also resident at Longleat was a fellow non-juring bishop, George Harbin, who wrote his 'Memoirs of Gardening' of the years 1716 to 1723, though his unpublished manuscript was almost entirely confined to descriptions of plants.[31] Horton believes that Bishop Hooper is the more likely candidate for this scheme, citing his longer episcopate and the contemporary currency of this style in the early eighteenth century, though one of the promenades is still called 'Bishop Ken's Walk'. The canals were probably filled in when Bishop George Henry Law landscaped the gardens in the current Gardenesque style after 1824.[32] Whatever its date, the canal garden set an important precedent for other formal layouts in the county, most notably that at **Ven House**, near Milborne Port, in the far south-east corner of the county.

Some idea of how the Bishop's Palace gardens might have looked can be experienced at Ven, where one sector of the elaborate layout, commissioned in about 1725 by James Medlycott, has been brilliantly recreated by Tommy Kyle. Ven's gardens continue to undergo further enlightened and creative restoration and expansion under the present owner, Jasper Conran. Unlike the Bobart-inspired scheme at Low Ham, drafts and a plan of the completed layout by Richard Grange (*13*) survive to show how he intended to wrap a series of canals, parterres and shrubberies threaded with winding walks around the skirts of the house at Ven which Medlycott

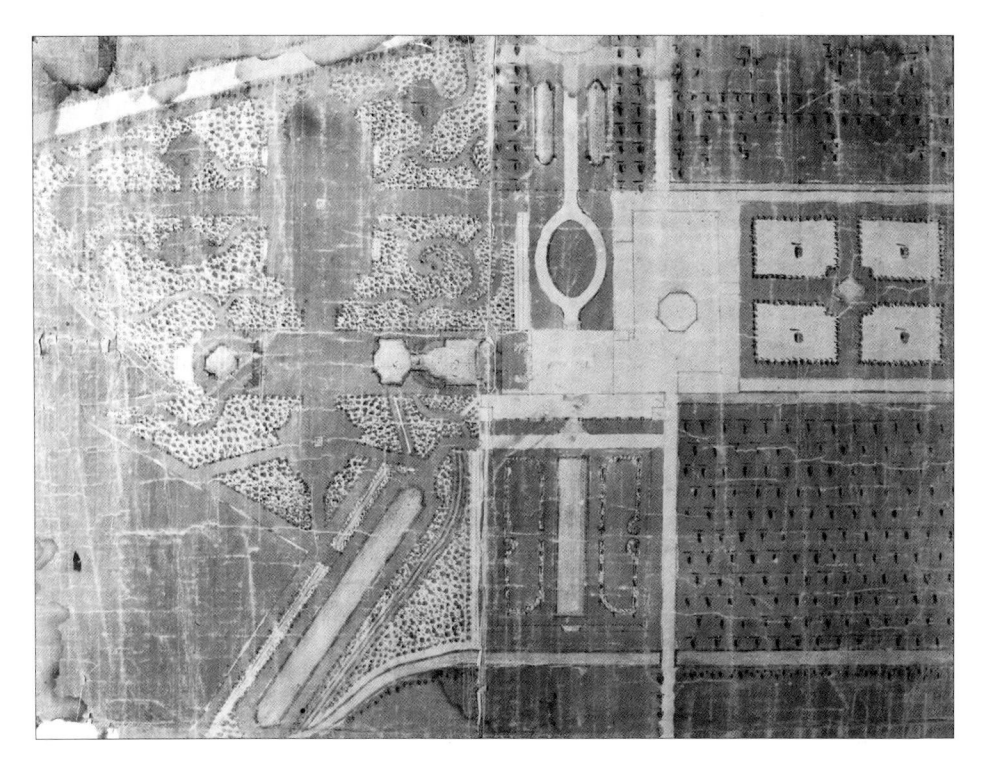

13 Richard Grange's plan for the grounds at Ven House shows garden design in flux, with formal areas around the house on three sides, while the fourth is dramatised by a Wilderness with serpentine walks and garden buildings. Reproduced by permission of English Heritage. NMR

had bought from Sir Charles Carteret before his marriage to Anne Howard, a City heiress. Medlycott drew up his account of 'the cost of my house at Ven and gardens in the year 1700 which was begun in 1698',[33] so presumably that refers to a precursor of the grand Baroque brick house that Nathaniel Ireson of Wincanton built for Medlycott in the early 1720s.[34] But there is a complication here. Although there are extensive accounts of the building works at Ven, it appears that the new house had not been completed at James Medlycott's death in 1731. Furthermore, Grange's drafts of the gardens are entitled: 'Prospects of Ven House, the seat of James Medlycott, Esq. in Milborn Poort, Somersett', proving that they were, indeed, prepared for Medlycott, but the plan of the gardens is dated 19 September 1739'.[35] This seems an inordinately long time to lay out a garden, and there can be no definitive answer to this conundrum, but the layout has elements of late seventeenth-century practice and also of the emerging fashion in the first two decades of the eighteenth century for wildernesses.

Grange's plan for Ven is best analysed as if the house were being approached today from the road to the north. In this way it can be seen that many of the original walled enclosures survive, though the area of the eastern Wilderness has now been informalised around the stream. An exedra of gates and railings guards the entrance forecourts from the road, the first laid out with rectangular beds flanked by double avenues of trees, the latter a turning circle in front of the house. To the west there is an orchard with a tree avenue at its centre and beyond that to the south a walled garden with four compartments and a central lobed pool. Between this and the west front of the house is a plain area with an octagonal pool. To the south of the house there is a balustraded terrace with a banqueting pavilion at either end and steps leading down to a sunken garden with a central canal bordered by serpentine flowerbeds. This is flanked on the east by an orchard of regimentally lined trees, and on the east by a huge Wilderness comprising geometric pools, a long rectangular canal at a forty-five degree angle to the house, straight and serpentine grass walks, open glades and dense shrubbery in between.

The Wilderness is accessed from the house via a double-flight staircase at the head of the first geometrically shaped pool. Plinths for statues and urns are dotted around the glades and there is a pyramidal-roofed pavilion at the centre of the pentagonal-shaped clearing, mirrored by another further down the axis, and a large rectangular building on the edge of the shrubbery below the linked geometric pools. The style of this particular area is more advanced than that of the more prosaically formal areas on the other sides of the house, which suggests that the Wilderness at least may be coeval with the rebuilding of Ven in the mid-1720s. It has certain affinities with late-1720s layouts by Charles Bridgeman, such as Spring Wood at Hackwood in Hampshire.[36] If the Wilderness was ever laid out it would have conformed to the description given in a contemporary publication by Philip Miller:

> The usual method of contriving Wildernesses is, to divide the whole Compass of Ground either into Squares, Angles, Circles, or other

Figures, making the Walks correspondent to them; planting the Sides of the Walks with the Hedges of Lime, Elm, Hornbeam, &c. and the Quarters within are planted with various kinds of trees promiscuously without Order.[37]

Walking the grounds at Ven today it is apparent that much has survived of the bones of the formal garden. Although the Wilderness is unlikely to have been achieved in its original elaborate form, the present serpentine lake is a remnant of the obliquely axial canal, and the orchard to the east is now informal woodland with specimen trees threaded by a winding stream. The Kitchen Garden walls still define the extent of the former quadrant garden, its central pool now circular, while its east wall is enlivened by a later classical Loggia. The sunken garden to the south retains its original brick walls, but has been replanted with sentinel yews, which echo the giant Corinthian pilasters of the house. This is shown as laid mainly to lawn in a photograph of 1898, the canal and formal parterres having been swept away in the nineteenth century.[38] The change probably coincided with Decimus Burton's 1835 proposals for altering the house and the addition of the great Conservatory and linking glazed colonnade on the west terrace (*14*). Burton intended to provide a pendant building to this on the other end of the terrace with a Palladian-style Summerhouse, which was never realised.[39] It may be that this would have been developed from the easterly of the two banqueting pavilions shown on the Grange plan.

Hill House, now **Sandhill Park**, near Bishop's Lydeard, is another house of similar date and style that also had elaborate formal gardens. John Periam had it built between 1728-34 in a vernacular Baroque style, close to that deployed by Ireson, with giant pilasters and an attic storey.[40] A contemporary painting, now in private ownership, shows it to have been surrounded by brick-walled compartments entered by gateways, one of which appears to be almost Rococo in style with side scrolls and a pedimented overthrow.[41] Periam's Account Book includes a specific entry relating to Aaron Palfreman's work on forming the gardens. Palfreman was paid in May 1730 'for leveling of ye bowling green garden and parterre'. At least two tree avenues radiate from the walled complex by

14 Tommy Kyle's reconstruction of the early-eighteenth-century sunken garden at Ven House is commanded by Decimus Burton's 1835 Conservatory

the house, but the outer parkland is used for grazing only and there are no other designed features present. Hill House was renamed Sandhill Park in the 1780s when the formal gardens were swept away and the landscape remodelled with a chain of lakes. It is shown in its new state in Collinson's *History*, a small summerhouse dominating the ridge to the north of the house. The grounds and house were further developed in the Regency period when a long Doric pilastered conservatory was added to the house. Today Sandhill Park is derelict, having been used first as an American military hospital from 1940 and then an NHS hospital of self-care flats until its closure in 1991.

Wildernesses are key features associated with the coming informality in garden design in the 1720s and 1730s. At this period they are usually set apart from the formal areas around the house as places of retirement in which to escape and enjoy a leisurely solitude. In his 1718 *Ichnographia Rustica*, the landscape architect and writer Stephen Switzer advises that they should be set at a distance from the house to provide diversion further out in the landscape, and he gives elaborate planting suggestions

15 The early-eighteenth-century Garden House at Orchard Wyndham is shown on a contemporary painting of the house and grounds by Robert Griffier

to produce the ideal combination of shady areas and open glades, all connected by axial and meandering walks. This is exactly what Sir William Wyndham achieved in his Wilderness in Blackdown Wood, on the rise opposite his house at **Orchard Wyndham**.[42] The woodland was laid out sometime between 1715 and 1740,[43] when Wyndham was also constructing a walled garden and garden house, both of which survive on site, and a series of tree avenues radiating from the house: a poplar avenue leading to the Walled Garden, oriental planes on the Stream Drive and a majestic Long Walk of native oaks, horse chestnuts and holm oaks leading up to the Wood; the drive from Williton still has veteran sweet chestnuts. John Gay wrote to Pope in 1732 that 'Sir William Wyndham is at present amusing himself with some real improvements and a great many visionary castles',[44] so that gives us a more precise dating of the works. The Wood was originally known as the 'Blackdown coverts', as in John Beadford's estimate of his annual charge of £43.14.6d for looking after the estate,[45] which suggests that the copse was used for hunting, as well as for gentler pursuits. The 1891 Ordnance Survey records the original layout: there is a circular clearing – 'The Roundabout' – accessed via a serpentine path from the Long Walk. Close to this path is 'Mother Shipton's Stone', which survives today, a menhir-like shard with a decayed inscription. From the central point six axial walks cut through dense planting, one heading out to the 'Giant's Cave' near the perimeter.

All of this and more is shown on a mid-eighteenth-century painting at the house (*colour 7*), which has been attributed to Robert Griffier, son of Jan Griffier I, one of the early Netherlandish country-house artists.[46] It is very close in style to the more expansive landscape view of nearby Fairfield, so may have been painted at the same time. The house sits in front of a small deer park, but surrounded by hedged fields, and with the patchwork quilt of the Quantocks in the distance to the rear. To the right is the Wilderness with the Roundabout and the axial walks in the sector closest to the house, while a patte d'oie of rides radiates out from a summerhouse to the north-east, with winding walks cut in between them, much as at Clevedon Court. While the summerhouse has gone, the ruins of the Giant's Cave, its walls constructed with huge blocks of stone, are still visible in the undergrowth. This was contrived for his son, the 3rd Earl of Egremont, born in 1751, by Sir Charles Wyndham, who inherited in 1750. The deer park is shown enlivened by a circular pool and fountain, the remains of which survive today. To the west, though out of shot in this detail of the painting,[47] is the Walled Garden with its Garden House, faced with brick and lit by sash windows and oculii (*15*).

A very similar garden, of uncertain date but also dominated by a planned wilderness, was laid out at **Marston Bigot** for Charles Boyle, 4th Earl of Orrery.[48] However, instead of employing a local man who has left no biographical record, as James Medlycott did at Ven, Lord Orrery commissioned Switzer, the author of *Ichnographia Rustica* and his later *Hydrostaticks and Hydraulicks* of 1729. In the Preface to the latter book Switzer talks of his difficulty in consulting original texts when in the country and cites Lord Orrery's collection as the most helpful in his researches: 'The greatest Help that I had being out of the Library ('tho as yet unfinished) of my very worthy learned and noble Friend and Master, the right honourable the Earl of Orrery, at his seat at Marston in Somersetshire'.[49] This proves that Switzer was Lord Orrery's guest at Marston,

16 Lord Orrery's grounds at Marston Bigot were laid out with advice from Stephen Switzer. This illustration of their joint collaboration is taken from the 1739 volume of *Vitruvius Britannicus*. University of Bristol, Special Collections

but it is not proof that Switzer laid out the formal gardens there. However, it is clear from the surviving evidence, both on the ground and in the archival record, that Switzer had at least a hand in designing the layout within an existing garden. This had retained two viewing mounts, first referred to in 1683, at the extremity of the gardens to the north of the house, overlooking the road from Bruton to Frome. These circular stone bastions are clearly marked on Rene Parr's 1739 bird's eye image of Marston, which was included in the fourth volume of *Vitruvius Britannicus* (*16*). They would have provided views over Sharpshaw towards Whatley, as an alternative to the southern prospects of the wooded Wiltshire ridge commanded by the house.50 At this period, when the house was lived in by a succession of dowager countesses, the grounds to the north of the house were mainly orchards, while on the south there were walks.

The last dowager countess died in 1714 and the 4th Earl inherited. He had taken the title of Baron Boyle of Marston when he was given an English title in 1711, which suggests his affection for the place. It may also have been a matter of expediency, as Charleville, the Irish family seat, had burnt down in 1690. Lord Orrery was a diplomat and soldier, a cultured man with wide interests in literature and science. Even though family papers for the period 1714 to 1732 are missing, it is known that Lord Orrery employed Switzer in 1723, paying him £20, and Switzer dedicated his 1724 *Practical Fruit Gardener* to his employer. The publication of *Hydrostaticks* in 1729 suggests that the waterworks at Marston were completed by that time. However, they are not mentioned by visitors and do not feature in later Orrery correspondence. If they were indeed realised, they would be the two circular basins of water, presumably with water spouts, shown to the south of the house on the Parr print.

The main gardens were to the north of the house, clinging to the wooded slope and offering spectacular views across the Vale of Witham below. A contemporary poem of 1733 by Samuel Bowden describes:

> Deep, mossy banks in artless Hills decline,
> And Sloping verdures beautifully shine.
> Behind, with slow Ascent, the Gardens rise,
> Whose airy top looks downward to the skies.[51]

In addition to these terraced gardens there was a Bowling Green bordered with classical statues:

> Below, an Area of Enamel'd Green
> Displays its Robes, where Statues rise between,
> And shine with features of a Roman mien.[52]

The grass amphitheatre rising up the hillside shown on the print survives at Marston and leads into a densely wooded area in which there is a stone Grotto with an arched opening in the front and entrances at either end. This is most likely to have been added by John Boyle, the 5th Earl, after his succession to the earldom in 1732. It is roughly in the area of walled woodland to the north-west of the house. The 5th Earl was in the process of designing and planting this sector of the gardens in 1733:

> The wood-walk, which I designed a labyrinth, is almost finished.

Three little fountains at three several distances add to the beauty of the place. The goddess of spring, and to follow, the deity of the summer, stand smiling at the beautiful prospect in the distant vale, while Bacchus in another cabinet of wood, presents you with the produce of the autumn, to banish melancholy and dissipate gloomy thoughts, Winter is seen shivering in a corner, to remind us of mortality.[53]

At other points in the wood there were seats and 'little closets...where I may count my beads and say my Mattins'.[54] The layout recalls other planned wildernesses like those at Wray Wood and Castle Howard, or the Classical Grove at Heythrop in Oxfordshire, seen by Switzer in about 1710.[55]

These informal experimental groves led to a loosening of the rigidities of formal design, but here at Marston they co-existed with the formal areas. Switzer advocates the creative use of water in such secluded woods, both for contemplative amusement and for practical purposes. At the heart of the Heythrop Classical Grove there is a Cold Bath, and when Lord Orrery returned to Marston in 1738 his wife brought with her the finance needed for further works, which included the Grotto and a Cold Bath (*colour 8*), originally set in isolation, but now close to the 1775 Kitchen Garden and Gardener's Cottage, subsequently the Home Farm. Switzer was recalled for advice in 1739 and the work entrusted to James Scott, nicknamed by the Orrerys 'the Great Surveyor'.[56] Switzer worked on until at least 1741, when the Countess, writing to her husband from Caledon, her family home in County Tyrone, remarked that she was musing over 'the new beauties of Marston, where I see your Lordship, the Great Surveyor, and the great Switzer, all busy, and at least one happy'.[57] Lady Cork's Bath, as it was called after her death in 1758, her husband having inherited the second earldom in 1753, was built in this period of busy activity and, apart from the Grotto, is the only eighteenth-century garden building to survive.[58] Dr Richard Pococke saw it in 1754: 'Two or three fields below the house is a cold bath, as in an enclosure of an ancient Cemitery, with several old inscriptions made for it, and at the end is a small room very elegantly furnished, this I take to be Lady Orrery's place of retirement'.[59] Pococke's description is apt, as the surviving fragment of

Lady Cork's bath-house looks like the remains of an Italian wayside chapel, its pedimented end wall lit by an elegant Venetian window. The trees that must once have given it privacy, and which are shown on the 1886 Ordnance Survey map, have been felled, yet the bath is still full of clear spring water, the rough stone walls are studded with quartz, and a fragment of an inscribed stone can be traced in the ruins.

With Pococke's detailed description of the grounds at Marston we have reached the mid-Georgian period, when tightly contained formal parterres, angular canals and rigidly planted tree avenues gave way to a softening of the planting lines and a dispersal of the garden buildings across the whole parkscape, to be encountered in shrubberies and plantations as surprise objects of curiosity and fascination. Here at Marston, in the second phase of work which began in 1749, that leap into the wider landscape was taking place. Just before his return to Marston from Ireland in that year, Lord Orrery wrote to his friend Thomas Carew that he hoped to find 'hamadryads there in perfect health, and their shady habitations making great progress towards the arch of Heaven'.[60] These classical groves, their secret corners enlivened with statues, temples, hermitages and druids' cells, will be the focus of the next chapter.

3

Rivals in Arcady

▼

Marston Bigot · Halswell · Hatch Court · Hestercombe ·
Dunster Castle · Crowcombe Court · Terhill

DR POCOCKE'S DESCRIPTION OF LADY CORK'S BATH AT **MARSTON BIGOT**, which concluded the last chapter, was taken from a much more extensive record of his July 1754 journey through Dorset, Wiltshire and Somerset. The wandering bishop was obviously taken with Marston, as the account is one of the longest in his travel journals. The garden laid out by the 5th Earl of Orrery and his Irish Countess encapsulates perfectly what mid-century owners were trying to achieve with their improvements. Pococke continues:

> The Earl is improving the place in a very elegant taste. There is a lawn with a statue of Minerva at the end of it; then to the right another lawn with a plantation of wood adorned with busts, and an open temple with an altar in it, and ancient statues. To the left of the first lawn is a winding walk to the cottage built near the place, where a person lived (in the times of confusion after King Charles the first) in a little house under the park wall …This cottage is built and furnished as it is supposed a person in his situation [a deprived clergyman] might have done it, and there is a window with a wooden shutter to it opening to the road, with this inscription on it: 'Sunt quos pulverem collegisse juvat'. At the other end of the garden in a corner is a little Hermitage near finished for my Lord's youngest son; there is a deep way cut down to it with wood on each side, a seat or two in it – one is made in the hollow of a tree; it leads to a little irregular court, with a fence of horses' heads and bones. It is a cabin, poorly thatch'd, and a bedstead covered with straw at one end, a

chimney at the other, and some beginning made of very poor furniture. In one part of the garden a very fine horse of my Lord's is buryed with a monument – a pedestal, with an urn, I think, on it; on three sides, in English, there is an account of the horse and on the fourth side is this latin inscription 'Hic sepultus est Rex Nobby Equorum Princeps omnium sui generis longe praestantissimus obiit Feb. 12, 1754, Aetat. 35'. Two or three fields below the house is a cold bath.[1]

The key phrase in this passage is 'a very elegant taste', but this taste was not simply an enthusiasm for classical statuary with its coded iconography, and the use of Latin inscriptions to denote erudition. This mid-century fashion also embraced the humble cottage of an indigent clergyman, the thatched retreat of the holy man – or at least the Earl's son masquerading as one for visitors' amusement – horses' skulls and bones as decorative ornaments and a memorial to King Nobby, a faithful steed. It was a combination of the Virgilian pastoral near the house and the native rustic with touches of religiosity further out in the park. Orrery had already built a hermitage and a bizarre bone house at his Irish country seat, Caledon in County Tyrone.[2] The columns of the Bone House there, which was built in 1747, were lined with the knuckle bones of oxen, 'to strike', as Lord Orrery wrote, 'the Caledonians with wonder and amazement by fixing an Ivory Palace before their view. We have already gathered a great number of bones, and our friends the butchers and tanners have promised to increase their number'.[3] This fascination with animal remains is apparent at the Banwell Bone Caves near Weston-super-Mare, but they were constructed almost a century later. Here at Marston and Caledon they are part of the so-called 'Rococo' garden aesthetic, a short-lived but delightfully playful phase of rich eclecticism.[4] Mary Delany visited Caledon in August 1748, and after a tour of the grounds in which she saw the Hermitage stocked with 'everything you might imagine necessary for a recluse', she summed it up perfectly: 'I never saw so pretty a whim so thoroughly well executed'.[5] Significantly, the creation of Caledon was a productive partnership between the Earl and his Countess, but not the usual one where the gentleman took charge of the estate and his wife dabbled in garden making; Delany remarks that 'they are both fond of the country; she delights in farming, and he in building and gardening, and he has very good taste.'[6]

Travelling throughout England and Ireland in the 1750s, before the dull Brownian revolution blighted such eccentricities, Pococke was the inveterate chronicler of these whimsical layouts.[7] Everywhere he went he delighted in the artistic lengths owners and their workmen would go to achieve such exotic fancies. But there was often a more serious purpose to these folly circuits, none more so than at **Halswell**, Goathurst, in the lee of the Mendips. However, this is to pre-empt the friendly aesthetic rivalry that existed in these hills south of Bridgwater, their contours chequered with fields of rich red soil and their deep lanes lined with lush floral hedgerows. Sir Charles Kemeys-Tynte of Halswell, who also raised a monument to a dead horse, was just one owner among several who competed with each other in much the same way as William Shenstone at The Leasowes in Worcestershire tried to upstage Lord Lyttelton at neighbouring Hagley. Shenstone was constantly bemoaning his lack of funds to construct garden buildings of lasting materials but, fortunately for garden history in Somerset, many of the structures raised in these Quantocks estates have survived, even if in ruins. There is also a rare collection of architectural sketches by Richard Phelps in the Somerset Record Office,[8] many of which are designs for temples, Gothic ruins and bridges that were actually built and can be tracked down in hidden valleys and deep woods. Little is known about Phelps, but a later account of the family suggests that they were all competent artists:

> A respectable family of the name of Phelps, has long resided at Porlock; many of the individuals of which seem to possess an hereditary talent for drawing and painting, and several churches in the neighbourhood have been ornamented by them. The oldest member of this family, Mr. H. Phelps, Surgeon, was seen by the writer of this article, engaged in painting a head, in the autumn of 1828; though then he was upward of ninety years of age, nor did he use glasses. A nephew of this gentleman's is now an artist of some celebrity in London.[9]

The presence of one artist in the area providing sketches for gardens and their buildings at this time is extremely valuable, but to have two artists is rare indeed. Neither has left artistic impressions to rival the beautiful gouache studies of Rococo layouts by Thomas Robins, but their drawings throw light on the friendly rivalry that existed in these most welcoming of hills. The other artist is, of course, Copplestone Warre Bampfylde of Hestercombe, who was one of the major players in this spate of competitive garden improvement in the 1750s and 1760s. His drawings, as well as those of Phelps, have recently been used to create evocations of the garden buildings that once existed at Hestercombe, including the Gothick Alcove and the Octagon Summerhouse.[10]

Bampfylde had a close connection with Sir Charles Kemeys-Tynte at Halswell, so much so that he raised a Friendship Urn to Kemeys-Tynte and Henry Hoare of Stourhead in the valley behind his house at Hestercombe. At Halswell, Sir Charles had already begun to lay out an eccentric landscape by the 1740s. Full of strange garden buildings, it seems to reveal a deeper, more arcane iconography than the usual haphazard circuit of stylistically eclectic structures. He had inherited a house fronted by a formal garden, with a bowling green alongside commanded by a small temple and, adjacent to the green, a straight canal.[11] His first two improvements were to return this area to more informal, sweeping lawns and build a rockwork dam at the head of the canal. According to a memorandum written in 1781 by Sir Charles' steward, Richard Escott, this 'Rock Work' screen was in place by 1754,[12] but it has since disappeared. However, another Rockwork Screen was built at the end of the canal where the land drops down to the ha-ha; this is shown cloaked in trees in Thomas Bonnor's engraving in Collinson's *History* (17). This will have provided a numinous counterpoint to Mrs Busby's Temple, named after Lady Tynte's sister, which was built in 1755 on a rise of the shaven lawns to the north. On approaching the house today the lower Rockwork Screen is now visible, its vegetation having been stripped away, but Mrs Busby's Temple is still shrouded in trees and wreathed in scaffolding awaiting restoration.[13]

While the Temple is a typical product of the mid-century, though perhaps not all that appropriate for dedication to a woman with its

17 The Arcadian landscape at Halswell, achieved by Sir Charles Kemeys-Tynte, from John Collinson's 1791 history of the county. University of Bristol, Special Collections

masculine Doric order and frieze of bucrania, the Rockwork Screen (*18*) is something else. This is a cyclopean building of immense presence with a tripartite centrepiece of round-headed arches and niches, flanked by what were once pedimented elements with oculii. Its scale is difficult to appreciate until someone sits in the niche to give it scale. It seems as if water originally flowed from the canal above it through an arch in the centre, which would have produced a curtain of water behind which visitors would sit, and via further outlets at a lower level in the arches of the flanking sections, to a circular pool in front. The central arch has an inscribed plaque, now sadly decayed so that the wording is no longer visible, while the flanking sections must once have been decorated with circular cameos. What makes the Screen so unique is the studied use of different materials – three different types of stone – and the combination of stone treatments: coursed rubble for the flanking piers, fine grey ashlar for the recessed sections and rock-faced rustication with wildly protruding, tapered stones for the arches.

The style and use of materials is so close to that advocated in his twin publications *Arbours* (1755) and *Grottos* (1758) by the landscape designer,

18 The 1750s Rockwork Screen at Halswell in magnificent ruin. It was sited at the foot of a canal whose waters gushed through openings in the stonework

mathematician and cosmologist, Thomas Wright of Durham, that Sir Charles must have either commissioned the building from him, or taken the design directly from one of Wright's drawings (*19*). The closest in style is Design L, which Wright intended to be 'dress'd with Shells, Fossils, and Ores', and 'cloathed with Plantations suited to the Scene'. This makes the dating of the lower screen so important, for Wright did not publish *Grottos* until 1758, and Sir Charles was one of its subscribers. This suggests at least an acquaintance, if not a friendship, between the two before Wright's *Grottos* appeared. They may well have been brought together socially by the 4th Duke of Beaufort, for whom Wright was working at Badminton in Gloucestershire after 1748, and who was an acquaintance of Sir Charles; either by him, or by Norborne Berkeley of Stoke Park, who had provided Wright with an annuity for life.[14] Wright may well have provided the inspiration for some of the garden buildings at Halswell, but a portrait of Kemeys-Tynte, attributed to William Hogarth, suggests that Sir Charles acted as his own landscape architect. He is shown sitting down with his favourite dog, a large volume entitled 'Garden Plans' open

1 This erotically charged watercourse – the Flowform – is at the heart of the Chalice Well Garden in Glastonbury, revived in the mid-twentieth century by Wellesley Tudor Pole

2 The Swan Circle at Michael Eavis' Worthy Farm, site of the annual Glastonbury Festival, was constructed for the 1992 summer solstice as a gesture of pantheistic communion with the 'Stone Beings' of the earth

3 This Peter Tillemans painting of Clevedon Court reveals three layers of intervention in the grounds: an Elizabethan approach through a triumphal Archway, a later formality of enclosures and Canals around the house and a mid-eighteenth-century designed Wilderness commanded by a Summerhouse. *Panoramic View of Clevedon Court* by P. Tillemans, Clevedon Court, The Elton Collection (The National Trust), ©NTPL/John Hammond

4 Earthworks at Witham Charterhouse, cut through by the Great Western Railway, record the lost monastic complex and two separate eighteenth-century garden layouts. By kind permission of Michael Aston

5 An early-eighteenth-century formal layout with axial canal and gravel paths laid out at Fairfield, shortly before his death in 1735, by Thomas Palmer. By kind permission of Lady Gass

6 When the antiquary and Gothic fancier John Carter visited the Bishop's Palace in Wells he found an early-eighteenth-century formal garden centred by an L-shaped canal. Mark Horton; by kind permission of the Society of Antiquaries of London

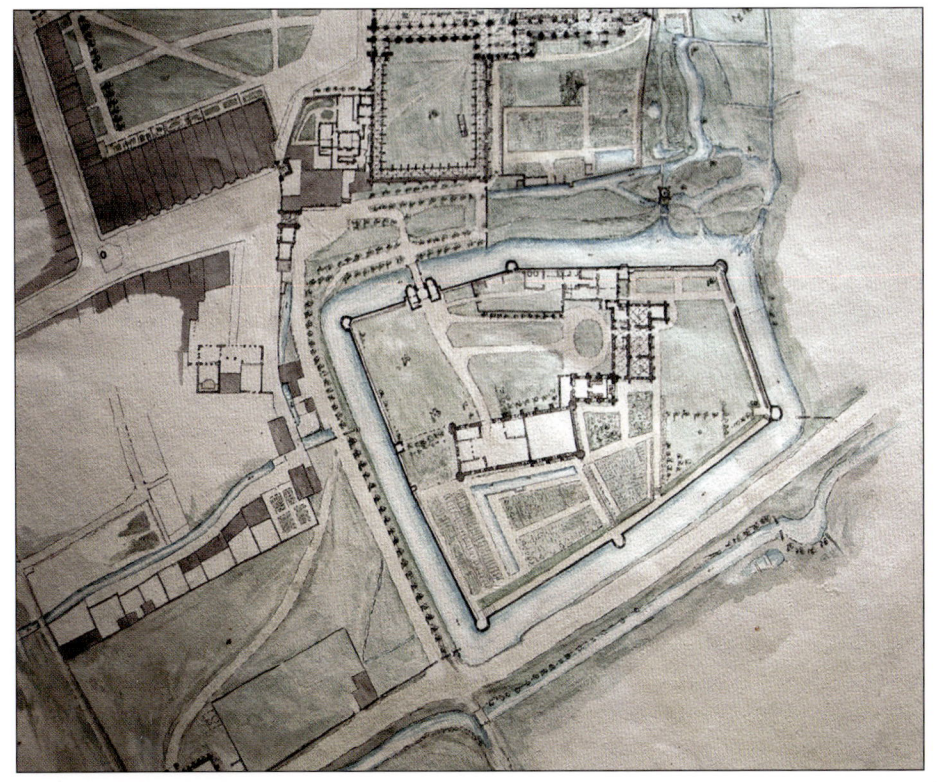

7 A landscape on the cusp between formality and informality in Robert Griffier's painting of the Orchard Wyndham estate. By kind permission of the Trustees of Orchard Wyndham

8 Marston Bigot's archivist, Michael McGarvie, framed in the Palladian façade of Lady Cork and Orrery's Cold Bath at Marston

9 One of the most curious and obscure garden buildings in the country – the 1750s rockwork and shell-encrusted Bridge at Halswell. It formed part of Sir Charles Kemeys-Tynte's freemasonic-inspired circuit of garden buildings in Mill Wood

10 Coplestone Warre Bampfylde's Cascade at Hestercombe was the prototype for a similar waterfall at Henry Hoare's Stourhead

11 The Doric Temple at Hestercombe has a dual function: to be seen as an object in a consciously framed view of the valley, and also to offer views out across the Vale of Taunton

12 Together with an arch and a bridge, this ruined Convent was built in the 1770s in the valley behind the house at Crowcombe to produce a Gothic frisson on a walking tour of the estate

13 Ralph Allen commissioned the Palladian Bridge at Prior Park as a political gesture of Whig solidarity with the Boy Patriots; it was designed in 1755 by Thomas Pitt, 1st Lord Camelford

14 A perfect Rococo conceit – Thomas Robins' 1760 watercolour sketch of Jeremiah Peirce's Hermitage at Lilliput Castle on Lansdown above Bath. Photo © Victoria and Albert Museum, London

15 Mr Nicholas' farm on Charmy Down near Bath is shown in this Thomas Robins sketch to have been a Gothick eye-catcher contrived to be seen in the landscape. Photo © Victoria and Albert Museum, London

16 A detail from James Blackamore's 1774 map of the Earnshill estate records yew-hedged shrubbery walks around the Kitchen Garden. By kind permission of Richard Combe

19 A design by Thomas Wright of Durham from his 1758 *Grottos* is close in style to the Rockwork Screen at Halswell. Wright intended this building to be decorated with shells, fossils and ores. University of Bristol, Special Collections

on the table before him, together with a set of drawing instruments, and in the background there is an open window with a view to a garden building being erected in a wood.[15] Again, dating is crucial here: there is a payment of £42 to the artist in June 1753, recorded in Kemeys-Tynte's account at Hoare's Bank.[16] It would seem, therefore, that by 1753 Kemeys-Tynte had turned his attention to Mill Wood, which runs from south to north, parallel to the house on the western side of the estate, at least two years before Wright's first book on Arbours appeared.

Walking across to the Wood today the visitor passes a striking stepped pyramid, topped with a griffin holding the family coat of arms. This is purported to be a monument 'dedicated to a pure nymph', Sir Charles' young niece who died in 1744, though the inscription has long since weathered and decayed.[17] Its curious shape is perhaps better understood here as symbolic of Freemasonry: the cube surmounted by a pyramid is the form of Moses' Tabernacle in the Wilderness, the first building directed by God and sacred to freemasons.[18] Kemeys-Tynte was a prominent freemason and, not surprisingly, there is further Mosaic and Druidic symbolism deep within Mill Wood.

Mill Wood was originally a slightly sinister place of dark shadowed plantations threaded with a stream breaking into cascades at each change of level. The best contemporary description we have of it is by Arthur Young, who made a tour of England in 1770 and published his account the following year.[19] Walking down from the hill above the house he encountered 'a wood of noble oaks, which shade a wild sequestered spot; where a limpid spring rises at the foot of a rock, over-hung in a fine bold manner by wood which grows from its clefts. The water winds away through the grove in a proper manner'. Here, in a deep thicket, are the ruins of the cavernous Spring Grotto, another tripartite building with round-arched seats fronting a cold bath. An inscribed tablet set in the wall was aimed to encourage in the visitor thoughts of Moses leading the Israelites out of Egypt:

> When Israel's wand'ring sons the desart trod,
> The melting rock obey'd the prophet's rod;
> Forth gush'd the stream, the tribes their thirst allay'd,
> Forgetful of their God they rose and play'd.
> Ye happy swains for whom these waters flow,
> Oh! May your hearts with grateful ardors glow;
> Lo, here a fountain streams at his command,
> Not o'er a barren, but a fruitful land;
> And smiling Plenty gladdens ev'ry hill.

Moses was 'an iconic figure in hermetic tradition, perceived as the first Grand Master providing a link between ancient and modern times; his rod, often transformed into a serpent, was significant in Masonic regalia'.[20]

This biblical allusion is contrasted with the Druid's Temple, in a wooded grove nearby:

> Turning the corner you catch a bridge, under a thick shade, and then come to the Druid's temple, built in a just stile of bark, &c, the view quite gloomy and confined; the water winds silently along, except a little gushing fall, which hurts not the emotions raised by so sequestered a scene.

If Young's description of the placement of the Druid's Temple in relation to the Spring Grotto is accurate, it was perfectly judged to have been another surprise for visitors on a prescribed circuit. Wright's influence is apparent here, as the Temple was taken directly from the frontispiece of Wright's 1755 *Arbours*, its columns of twisted tree trunks resembling Masonic temples. Its siting reflects his views on eclectic layouts: 'Buildings of Different genius aught never to be plac'd in sight of one another nor admitted in ye same scene to avoid a Masquerade of Building ... No Plantation should be so dispos'd as capable of being Discover'd from any point all at once'.[21] On a more intellectual level these buildings might have been contrived to produce an architectural progress fulfilling the Masonic concept of 'God's Wide Open Space as a cult room...associated with the ancient notion of the Garden of Eden...as the freemasons believed in a Utopia on Earth, the landscape garden provided a ritual space for Masonic work and for contemplating Divine Nature'.[22] Escott's memorandum records that the Druid's Temple was built by Jacob de Wilstar, an architect and surveyor who produced an estate map of Halswell in 1756. This contemporary interest in the ancient Britons dates back at least to the founding of the Society of Antiquaries in 1707 and was fostered by William Stukeley's excavations of Avebury and Stonehenge.[23] Wright had designed a Bladud's Temple for Norborne Berkeley at Stoke Park, near Bristol, to commemorate the legendary Celtic founder of pre-Roman Bath.

The next structure, further down the Wood and at a point where the upper lake drops down at least ten foot, is the 'Bridge in the Wood', built slightly earlier in 1755. This is the most bizarre of all the garden buildings in this sector of the landscape and has so far eluded precise interpretation (*colour 9*). It is a screen wall on a dam, with a central round-arched niche for a seat flanked by balustrades terminating in strange female terms shaped like canoptic jars. The arch is studded with blocked rustication of writhing vegetable forms, while the ramped sections either side of the arch are encrusted with stonework coral, rocks and shells. This is the epitome in stone of the twin characteristics of mid-century Rococo: 'rocaille' (rockwork) and 'coquille' (shellwork). The terminal figures, of which only one survives on site (the other is in safe keeping in a local shed),[24] are decidedly female, with one bare breast on display, the torso covered in bullrushes and sashed by a garland of flowers. Kemeys-Tynte's diary for 1756 records the flurry of activity in Mill Wood and a constant stream of visitors, including the Egmonts from Enmore Castle, Bampfylde from Hestercombe and the gentleman architect, Thomas Prowse of Berkeley, who was later to design the Temple of Harmony at the bottom of Mill Wood in 1764. A diary entry for 3 August 1756 has Sir Charles going out early in the morning to the Wood 'with Ly Tynte to fix the Hemogenius'.[25] Might these curious figures be presiding deities representative of Wright's obsession with pansophism or universal nature? *Arbours* and *Grottos* were intended to be 'the two parts of Universal Architecture', and his Durham manuscripts include the following overview of mid-century designed landscapes that comes close to a design philosophy as explored in Halswell's Mill Wood:

> The Business of Building and Planting well understood Depends upon the knowledge of so many of ye Branches of Natural and experimental Philosophy that it is no wonder we find most of ye antient & even many of the Modern productions of Both kinds so very defective…Without great Reading, observation, Science and invention the very Clearest Head, Best Judgement, and most active understanding can never arrive at any tolerable Degrees of rational Tast….Every Naturalist, I mean every genius comprehending architecture & gardening as Sciences aught to be well acquainted with ye natural Dependency the one has upon the other, and ye consequent beauty, grace and utility resulting from the Coordiante harmony of every part of Creation.[26]

Wright's final, withering criticism of many mid-century landscapes was that 'to attempt anything without meaning will always be insipped and only once a surprise'.[27]

Further down the Wood, at yet another fall in the series of lakes, there was a tall rock fronted by a statue of Neptune, water issuing from his feet. Fragments of the rock survive, but the planting has been cleared, making it difficult to imagine the effect of such a dramatic figure emerging out of dark foliage. However, Young's description helps to evoke the atmosphere of Mill Wood, in contrast to the open lawns around the house, even though it is conveyed in the contemporary language of sentiment: 'the awful shade – the solemn stillness of the scene, broken by nothing but the fall of distant waters; have altogether a great effect, and impress upon the mind a melancholy scarcely effaced by the cheerful view of a rich vale with the water winding through it, which is seen on crossing the park towards the house'.[28]

After a break in landscaping, the park was extended to the east in 1761 and the Temple of Harmony was built in 1764, while Robin Hood's Hut was constructed behind the house, offering expansive views down towards Goathurst and out across the Vale of Bridgwater. The approach to this last was carefully contrived for maximum theatrical effect, which was enjoyed by Arthur Young on his 1770 visit. He took the riding 'by the side of a woody precipice, and up through some new plantations; from a dark part of which you enter through a door into a temple dedicated to Robin Hood; upon which a most noble prospect breaks at once on the beholder; which acts not a little by the surprise of the entrance'.[29] The 'Robin Hood house' was built in 1765, but still being fitted up in 1767 when Sir Charles wrote: 'as for the Building on the Hill in the Park, the first room, wch I call the hermits room, must have an *earthen floor*, the kitchen on the left, a brick, and the little room for China, must be board'd'.[30] From the back the Hut looks like a blockish *cottage ornée*, yet from the front towards the view it is a graceful loggia with clustered Gothick columns and ogee arches derived from Batty Langley's 1741-2 Antient Architecture. It was almost certainly designed by Henry Keene, and named after the great defender of ancient liberties because the agent's house on the eastern edge of the park was called Sherwood.

Further garden and park structures followed – a monument to a favourite horse, a riding school and a Temple of Pan – but this second phase of landscaping lacks the tight iconographical programme of Mill Wood. Sir Charles seems to have lost his way somewhat, for a letter written to him from Bampfylde talks of the success of the pool below the Rockwork Screen, which Kemeys-Tynte had recently naturalised, but describes the upper pond on the lawn as an 'eye-sore', because of its artifical nature. He advised his friend to remove the pond and, thereby,

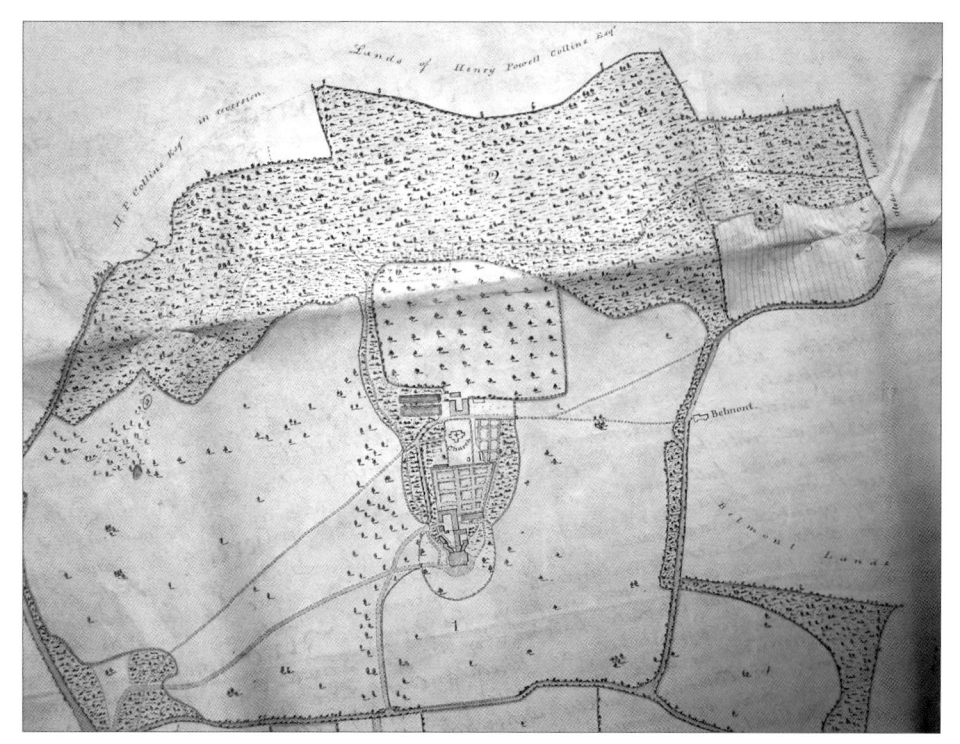

20 An 1820 plan of Hatch Court showing the Line Wood Walk and its attendant garden buildings. Somerset Record Office, DD\TN/9

destroy the Screen at its southern end. Bampfylde continued: 'if you differ in opinion, I shall with pleasure make any design for decorating the Head that my poor fancy can furnish'.[31] Garden historians will forever be grateful that Bampfylde's 'poor fancy', so apparent in the buildings set around his own landscape at Hestercombe, did not prevail at Halswell and that we still have the Rockwork Screen to prove, if not Wright's certain authorship of the early landscape there, but at least the inspiration for it from his *Arbours* and *Grottos*.

Thomas Prowse appears to be the link between the landscape at Halswell and the Line Wood Walk, which was laid out by John Collins after Prowse had built **Hatch Court** at Hatch Beauchamp for him in 1755. The family had made their money from cloth-making at Ilminster, but Collins was determined to break away from family tradition and live the life of a country gentleman. His house is a delightful Palladian villa with corner towers like those at Hagley Hall in Worcestershire, but with the addition of an arcaded loggia on the entrance front.[32] Collins must have begun his woodland walk soon afterwards, for Edward Knight saw it in June 1761. Knight's valuable shorthand entry in his pocketbook mentions a Gothic shell temple, a serpentine river that lacked water, a chapel and bastion with a fine view, a bowling green, a bone house, a hermitage, a square summerhouse, a grotto and a root house.[33] The woodland walk, to the north of the house on a ridge overlooking West Sedge Moor to the east, the Vale of Taunton Deane to the west and the Blackdown and Brendon Hills to the south, is shown as 'Lyne Wood' on a 1787 map,[34] but with no garden buildings, and on an 1820 plan attached to deeds,[35] which marks several structures (20). Collinson visited Hatch Court in 1787 and mentions that 'several temples and seats are erected on the brow of the hill, which is steep, finely indented and adorned with hanging woods'.[36] The only visual proof we have of any of the buildings achieved by Collins is an engraving in Collinson's *History* of the Hermitage (21). This is a night scene of Sublime horror with the natural cave lit by a lantern, revealing the cloaked hermit kneeling at his devotions in front of a crucifix. Beside him is an open book and on a stone shelf above there is a skull and an hourglass. Trees close in on the right framing the cave, while to the left a blasted tree is lit by a crescent moon. Behind this a cascade crashes down to rocks and eventually streams out into a pool in the foreground.

There are no plans, drawings or correspondence relating to the Line Wood Walk, so any analysis of the features and their placement must be speculative, or based on knowledge gained from archaeological investigation.[37] In an act of generosity and pride in his ownership, John Townson, with the support of Taunton Deane Borough Council, opened the woodland walk to the public in 2003. From the car-park off Belmont Road, the visitor follows a linear walk through the Wood, taking in the Bastion, the Bowling Green, which has recently been cleared, the Urn, the Summerhouse, the Icehouse and the Grotto.[38] Unlike most contemporary layouts, which are circuitous, the precipitous edge of the ridge forces visitors to loop back along the same route. It is an exhilarating walk punctuated by the ruined buildings that would once have offered spectacular views south. The footings of the Bastion and its attendant Chapel have been uncovered, an Urn has been re-sited on the Walk, while a new Obelisk provides a vertical accent on the northern edge of the route, and there are

21 As well as a Summerhouse, a Root House and a Grotto, the Line Wood Walk at Hatch Court had a Hermitage, seen here in an idealised view of rocky cliffs and a crashing waterfall. By kind permission of John Townson

painted wooden seats at intervals, lending the Walk an air of Eastern Europe. Close inspection of the Grotto site reveals the use of Ham stone, blue lias and tufa. The archaeological investigation confirmed that there was an artificial cave at the northern end with a passage leading to another room containing Diana's Pool, or cold bath.

Even without documentary proof, there can be little doubt that Collins was attempting to emulate his neighbours' layouts at Halswell and Hestercombe. In fact, it is possible to see Hestercombe from one of the Line Wood Walk garden buildings. If Collins' correspondence had survived it would surely have mentioned his rival garden makers. Sir Charles Kemeys-Tynte's diaries are full of references to visits by his near neighbours, especially his Hestercombe neighbour, which make it clear that Bampfylde was taking a keen interest in all the improvements at Halswell. On 17 July 1756 he records having walked with Lady Tynte 'in the wood till near twelve. Mr Prowse came before one, walked with him in the wood. Mr Bampfylde & his Lady Miss Bam ... the Hestercombe family left about seven'. On another day he writes: 'Cop Bampfylde at our return…Cop went home at midnight – a fine moonshine night'. He seems to have been free to roam around the Wood, even when Sir Charles had no idea he was there: 'Went into the wood to view the workmen who were employ'd about the Druid's Temple – and was surprised with the sight of Mr Bampfylde and his lady whilst in the wood, they stay'd with me near two, the ladies went to Hestercombe but Cop went with me to Mr Gropes where we dined'.[39] So, in addition to Henry Hoare's Stourhead, of which Bampfylde made several drawings while it was being landscaped, Halswell must have been a strong influence on what Bampfylde set out to achieve at Hestercombe. The question that has to be asked, however, particularly in the light of Thomas Wright's indictment of 'Modern productions', is whether or not Bampfylde's layout was 'defective' and lacking in meaning. Was it merely an eclectic mix of structures producing a 'Masquerade of Building', or a successful composition based on an appreciation of natural landscape enlivened, as if in a painting, by an accomplished artist? For Bampfylde was a more than competent painter in the manner of Claude Lorrain and Gaspar Dughet.

He inherited the **Hestercombe** estate in 1750, ten years after Sir Charles took over at Halswell, so his landscape improvements post-date the first phase there. He had some natural advantages as a garden maker to add to his close friendship with Kemeys-Tynte and Hoare. His brother-in-law, Edward Knight of Wolverley, introduced him to William Shenstone of The Leasowes and George Lyttelton of Hagley, two of the most important landscape improvers of the 1750s, while through his wife he was also related to Richard Payne Knight of Downton, the great Picturesque theorist. In the 35-acre combe behind his house, Bampfylde created between 1750 and 1780 a series of consciously planned internal vistas, connected by garden buildings of all styles, with views out across the Vale of Taunton Deane. Unlike the circuit at Halswell and that at Stourhead, Hestercombe appears to have no specific iconographical programme. Bampfylde seemed merely content to produce a series of framed scenes enlivened by buildings; a truly Picturesque landscape. This is nowhere more apparent than in his 1775 watercolour of the Pear Pond, where artfully contoured valley slopes cloaked with evergreen and deciduous trees are cut through to the Doric Temple and the Chinese Seat. A cascade framed by shrubs debouches into the pool, sheep graze on the open turf of the slopes, visitors saunter around the water, gentlemen fish idly, while a gentlewoman carrying a small basket walks along a gravel path taking the air. This idyllic pastoral scene was described in 1770 by Arthur Young as 'a rural sequestered vale with wood, much of the ground wild and romantic; Mr. Bampfield has filled this canvas in a manner that does honour to his taste. A walk winds around the whole in some places along the sides of the hills, at others it dips into retired bottoms, and rises again over the eminences, commanding views of the distant country'.[40]

Bampfylde's aim seems to have been simply pictorial rather than enigmatically arcane. His garden buildings were contrived to provide visual accents within the landscape, as well as offering views across and beyond it. His greatest achievement was to introduce water to the scene in two serpentine pools and a spectacular waterfall inspired by Shenstone's in Virgil's Grove at The Leasowes, which Bampfylde visited in 1762. The Great Cascade is fed by a beautifully constructed, sinuous rill that extends along the contours of the high hillside to crash out over a rocky eminence and down into a stream (*colour 10*). Bampfylde's particular skill, second nature to one experienced in painting on canvas, was in handling the perspective of a landscape scene on the ground: 'The grounds are finely thickened with wood, which is so artfully managed, as to make the extent appear vastly larger than it really is'.[41] Young criss-crossed the valley, delighting in the switch from open ground to 'wild ground', from light to shade, and up winding paths 'to a small bench, from which you have a very pretty birds-eye landscape through the branches of the trees, on a part of the vale of Taunton'.[42] Finally, 'rising the hill again', Young came to 'the hermitage or witch house, from the figure of an old witch painted in the centre panel'.[43] This had prompted a punning tribute from one of Bampfylde's friends, Dr Langbourne:

> O'er Bampfield's wood, by various nature grac'd,
> A witch presides! – but then that witch is TASTE.[44]

After a brilliant restoration, masterminded by Philip White, Chief Executive of Hestercombe Gardens, Young's walking tour can be retraced today, and the several garden buildings, some original, others either restored or evocations of those constructed in the eighteenth century, can be enjoyed again. The latest addition is the Octagonal Summerhouse, based on similar examples countrywide and also on a drawing in Richard Phelps' portfolio. Indeed, it is close in style to the octagonal Summerhouse within the grounds of Dunster Castle, most likely designed by Phelps, which suggests that Bampfylde might have used the Porlock artist for some of his ornamental buildings at Hestercombe. The possible collaboration between the two artists is difficult to decipher, as almost all the drawings and sketches in the portfolio are unsigned, though some are annotated as being by Phelps, while Bampfylde is known to have advised the Luttrells of Dunster on some Chinese-style rails for the park and on a flag for a tent, or 'Marquea', in the grounds.[45] It may be that the Dunster Summerhouse drawing, which is more highly finished and annotated with dimensions, is by Bampfylde.[46] From this high vantage point the walk extends along the hillside towards the Chinese Seat, another recent evocation, but originally framed by false acacia to give an oriental effect. The path leads up to the Valley of the Cascades, on to the Charcoal Burner's Camp in an old diorite quarry, and across the valley via a laurel tunnel to the Gothic Alcove. This first appears in Edward Knight's 1761 shorthand account of the layout recorded in his pocketbook,[47] but was taken down after 1887. It has since been recreated, based on Gothic sketches by Bampfylde, but in summer 2009 underwent another scheme of restoration. It is sited on the edge of a field commanding the Vale of Taunton. Visitors would take in the view, walk across the field and then head into the dark wood once more. The path leads to the Doric Temple (*colour 11*), from which there are views across the valley to the Great Cascade, along the path to the Witch House and down the valley to the Vale. The Witch House is a conscious evocation by Bampfylde of Kemeys-Tynte's Druid's Temple at Halswell and is also close in style to Wright's Hermit's Cell at Badminton, designed in about 1750 for the 4th Duke of Beaufort.

The Mausoleum (*22*) is accessed via a zig-zag path, and is sited on the slope below by the poolside. Visitors will have already seen it across the valley from the Chinese Seat. This is the most obscure and stylistically idiosyncratic of all the Hestercombe buildings. Its pyramidal form is suggestive of a memorial chamber, but the verse on its façade, composed by Bampfylde in Horatian mood to emulate Shenstone, is purely meditative and domestic:

> Happy the Man who to the Shades retires
> Whom Nature charms, and whom the Muse inspires
> Blest whom the Sweets of home-felt Quiet please
> But far more blest, who Study joins with Ease.

Although the present guidebook states that Bampfylde designed the Mausoleum, might it have been based on a drawing by Richard Phelps? The portfolio includes a pencil sketch of a pyramidal building (*23*) that is remarkably close in style and treatment to the Mausoleum. It has the same blocked rustication around the arch and an inscribed plaque below the upswept pediment. It could, of course, be a drawing, taken on the spot, of the Mausoleum, as it was first built, but Phelps was employed at this time by Henry Fownes Luttrell and his wife Margaret, who were restoring **Dunster Castle** in the 1740s.[48] As we have seen, the Luttrells were close friends of the Bampfyldes; letters between the families are preserved in the Somerset Record Office.[49]

In addition to the octagonal Summerhouse on the Tor at Dunster, which may be by Phelps or Bampfylde, Phelps designed other Gothic buildings for the wider landscape there. These included a castellated Bowling Green House, more Regency Gothic in spirit than mid-eighteenth-century, and a 'Broken Arch' to serve as prelude to the circular Tower of 1775, probably also designed by Phelps, for Conygar Hill opposite the Castle mound.[50] His drawings relate to the Castle Mill, which was rebuilt in 1779-2, and the nearby two-arch Lovers' Bridge. Significantly, and most appropriately, Margaret and Henry were redecorating some of the Castle interiors in Gothick and Rococo styles,[51] and a Chinoiserie bridge had been constructed on the site of the present-day Lawns Bridge. This last is shown in a painting by William Tomkins at the Castle. There were further Gothick excitements around the Castle Tor, which were seen by James Savage when he wrote up Dunster in 1830: 'The Torr is laid out in gravel walks, which encircle it from its base till they terminate in

22 The Mausoleum at Hestercombe, so called because of its pyramidal finial, has an inappropriate but improving inscription above the archway

23 This drawing by local artist Richard Phelps is almost identical to the Mausoleum at Hestercombe suggesting that he may have been the designer. Somerset Record Office, DD\L/1/22/7A

the bowling green ...There are some seats and grottos by these paths.[52]

These ornamental Gothick buildings at Dunster are matched by others, now lost, in a secret combe garden out of sight behind the great Baroque house at **Crowcombe**. The axial approach from the church to the house, its brick façade supported by majestic giant pilasters, suggests that it was once fronted by a formal garden.[53] The survival of a painting dated to about 1740[54] and a map of about 1767[55] show not only a walled formal garden with three rectangular pools down the slope to the west, but also an enclosure centred by a circular shrub directly below the east front of the house. In the distance tree avenues extend across the fields and up the rolling hills to the rear of the house. Just by the church, alongside the front drive, there is another walled enclosure with two pyramidal-roofed banqueting houses. This is annotated as the 'Old Garden' on the 1768 map and must be part of the old manorial complex around which John Carew laid out gardens in 1676. These were demolished after 1719 by his great-grandson, Thomas Carew. The Old Garden has disappeared, but there is a deviation in the churchyard wall where one of the banqueting houses must have stood, while the walled garden to the west hangs on awaiting restoration, a few old fruit trees dotted amongst the brambles in the first enclosure by the stable court, dank water in dense undergrowth in the next.[56]

In common with all these Quantocks families, Thomas Carew was on friendly terms with the Bampfyldes, the Luttrells, Henry Hoare, The Aclands of Stogursey, the Pouletts of Hinton and Sir Charles Kemeys-Tynte. The Carew Correspondence deposited in the Somerset Record Office is a fascinating record of the social round in this corner of the county. Together with some of these friends, Carew was active in compiling local historical material that would eventually form Collinson's *History*. The correspondence also includes letters from Henry Lockett, Thomas Carew's agent, which give a detailed account of work on the house and gardens.[57] Carew was often in London, away on legal business, so Lockett wrote to him regularly about the estate:

> We long for the pleasure of seeing you at Crowcombe. Everything here shall be put in the best order we can for your reception. The

people are taken off from the drains by the haymaking, after that is over they shall attend them again. Your corn is all very good. Your gardens are well stocked with peaches and nectarines, which indeed in this year, a singularity. You shore Friday last thirteen score of old sheep in fine order. In short I think your farmering all well managed.

The most informative letter is dated 25 March 1745 and shows just how close-knit and interdependent were these landscape makers:

Mr. Bampfylde's gardner was here last week and fetched away 100 of Scotch Firrs. Mr. Croft's servant of Broomfield wants 30 of the brightest green Holly – plants edged with white; and Mr. Ritherdom, servant of Langford was here for a considerable quantity of Eugh [yew] Trees; if you are willing to dispose of them they are desirous of knowing the price and first opportunity. I hear Sir Charles Tynte is making large plantations in his park and I am sure chestnuts and Firrs are exceeding proper on such occasions, of which you have a large quantity of as fine plants as any in the kingdom, which if he knew I dare say he would be glad to deal with you.

Thomas Carew was obviously a keen collector of landscape paintings, particularly of his local area, for a letter of 16 February 1739 mentions the installation of panels in the house including 'the Watchet Landskip in the parlour', and on 14 March 1742 Lockett writes that 'Mr Phelps is now here, he has brought all the painting materials but oyl for the library and best parlour'. This is most likely to have been Richard's father who, as well as producing scene paintings, was employed as a painter and decorator. He was at Crowcombe again on 22 March 1748, but was 'beginning to go blind in both eyes and wanted Thos. Carew to advise on a second medical opinion in London'. However, Thomas Carew seems to have been intent on developing the grounds around his new house, built by Nathaniel Ireson between 1725 and 1739, leaving the wider landscape to function, as it had done since the early seventeenth century under Sir John's ownership, as a deer park.

24   This Gothic-arched bridge is deep in the wooded valley behind the house at Crowcombe. An inscribed stone on its inner face records that it was built in 1776 by George Rawle, a local mason from Dunster

When Thomas died in 1766, the estate passed to his unmarried elder daughter, and when she died in 1774 it was left to her younger sister Mary and Mary's husband, James Bernard. They swept away the old-fashioned formal gardens, laid the environs of the house to lawn and created a picturesque landscape enlivened with Gothick follies up the combe.[58] A track leads up from the stable court past farm buildings, an ice house and a pets' cemetery to the wooded valley, its densely planted slopes closing in on a series of stepped pools with cascades at the lower level. Thickets of rhododendron line the pools and then a steeply-arched Bridge (24) comes into view where two pools meet at different levels, its side niches and parapet encrusted with rock-faced rustication. There is a drawing for the Bridge in the Richard Phelps portfolio (25), proving it to be of his design, while a beautiful inscribed stone on the inner face of the parapet records that it was built by George Rawle of Dunster in 1776. At this point in the walk it is important not to miss the Convent on the western side of the watercourse, as it is almost submerged under dense rhododendrons and

25 The Phelps portfolio of architectural drawings includes this sketch of the Crowcombe Bridge proving it to have been designed by the artist. Somerset Record Office, DD\L/1/22/7A

brambles. This was far more visible as late as 1933 when *Country Life* illustrated it as the 'Ruin in the Glen'.[59] There is another Phelps drawing, discovered in a loose folder in the Record Office,[60] that is close in style to the building, but with a round, rather than a square tower (*26*). Phelps' signature in these drawings and executed Gothick buildings is his use of stepped, diagonal buttresses for the angles of walls. The Convent (*colour 12*) is said to have been constructed with fragments from a chapel at Halsway Manor, but the Phelps drawing shows that it was always intended to have traceried windows. Further up the combe on the eastern slope, and almost inaccessible now, is a ruined Arch, clearly marked on the first edition Ordnance Survey. This must be yet another of Phelps' conceits and related to his portfolio drawings. Even further up are the remains of a Grotto, which suggests that Bernard conceived the walk as a simple picturesque circuit with surprise Gothick encounters as visitors crisscrossed the watercourse.[61]

Another contemporary Picturesque landscape, where Phelps might have been employed to supply Gothick buildings, survives in part at **Terhill** within Cothelstone Park, but here the emphasis is on elevated views out across to Bishops Lydeard and beyond to the Vale of Taunton Deane. High up on the slopes of Cothelstone Hill a tall statue stands guard, silently commanding the landscape. From the back it appears headless; but from the front it is revealed as an androgynous, naked figure

26 Among several drawings for Gothic ruins, this Phelps sketch is closest to the Convent at Crowcombe; in the final design a square block was built in place of the round tower. Somerset Record Office, DD\L/1/22/7A

with a dog at its feet. It looks decidedly seventeenth-century in style, so may have been re-used in the designed landscape that Thomas Slocombe laid to the east of the new house he completed in 1778, which is shown as a vignette on a map of the same date.[62] It was a low, classical building with a central loggia and generous arched windows to take in the views to the south. Its L-shaped footprint is clearly marked in red on the map, with orchards to the north, while formal gardens extended outwards to connect with a line of trees planted along a contour of the hillside.

Tracking these features on the south side is a green walk that crosses a canal, the remains of which are still visible, with a carved head of Neptune in the revetment. The walk continued, flanked by water, to its most easterly point, where a building is marked in a grove of trees. This is the Grotto that survives in ruins today; there is another building marked on the map in the field behind. The Grotto is drawn as a vignette on the map (*27*), together with two Gothick buildings, that are so close to Phelps' style as to prove his authorship. Interestingly, given the possible attribution to Phelps of the Mausoleum at Hestercombe, one is a pyramidal structure. The Grotto is built of the local friable stone and has two open arches giving onto a semicircular room (*28*). The vignette shows its façade to have been decorated with goats' and deer skulls, and guarded by a strange horned figure with a staff. This denotes ownership rather than

27 This vignette of the Grotto at Terhill Park shows the goats' and deer skulls, and the strange horned figure, which once decorated the façade. Somerset Record Office, DD\ES/18/26

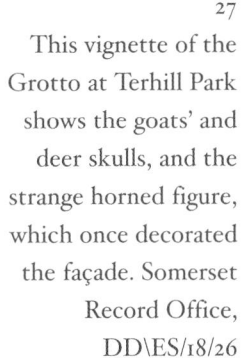

28 With its semicircular room built into the hillside, the Grotto at Terhill offered grandstand views out across the landscape; it is likely to be another design by Richard Phelps

satanic practices, as there is family coat of arms drawn on the map, which is supported by two animal figures with distinctly human faces sprouting horns. The use of animal skulls recalls Lord Orrery's fence of horses' heads at Marston Bigot and his Bone House at Caledon. Terhill also had a summerhouse and an obelisk, and the grounds were studded with ten classical statues including Venus, Minerva, Mercury, Atlas and Apollo. The statue on the hill above, thought to be Jupiter,[63] must be a fugitive from the slopes below. Backed by tall beech trees, he surveys the rural fields of this hilly corner of the county where the rivalry between a group of close friends and neighbours produced some of the most exotic and little-known landscapes, and where a gifted amateur artist created Gothick follies to strike contemporary visitors with Burkean awe.

4

Poetry, Politics and Moses' Holy Tabernacle in the Bath hinterland

▼

Prior Park · Widcombe Manor · Lilliput Castle
Batheaston Villa · Burton Pynsent

RICHARD POCOCKE, THE ARCHITECT JOHN WOOD AND MOSES ALL reappear again in the county at Ralph Allen's great mansion overlooking the Georgian city at **Prior Park**. While it is abundantly clear that Allen chose to build his house within easy reach of his freestone quarries further up the hill at Combe Down, and as a commercial gesture to promote the use of Bath stone in a magnificent Palladian-style villa, the gardens he laid out below it are not so easily readable. In essence they are Rococo in spirit, shading into the Brownian by virtue of the steep-valley site, but coded later by the overt political iconography of the Palladian Bridge. Pococke visited them in 1754, the year of Wood's death and before the Bridge had been achieved in the valley bottom. He was drawn, therefore, to the Rococo extravagancies immediately below the mansion to the west side of the combe where, with the help of Alexander Pope, who was a frequent visitor to Bath, usually sponging off Allen at Prior Park, his host had created after 1734 a woodland garden:

> I saw Mr. Allen's gardens, which are laid out in wilderness, with a piece of water in the middle, from which there is a descent, on each side of which are beautiful meadows arising up the hill; on one side is a new Gothick building, higher up is a statue of Moses with his hand striking the rock, and below it a beautifull cascade falls down about twenty feet; a little higher is the building of the Cold Bath. The center of the gardens commands a fine view of Bath.[1]

Pococke invariably reduced the layouts he visited to three distinct types: the park way, the farm way and the wilderness way, the latter being most conducive to Rococo circuits.[2]

It is not surprising, given the relatively small compass of the park in the valley, that the pleasure gardens at Prior Park were laid out there in two separate areas, while the original deer park up the hill behind the house was retained for livestock. The two garden areas are shown in detail in an engraving by Anthony Walker of 1752 (29), and there are later watercolours of the valley and its garden buildings by Thomas Robins.[3] It is clear from Walker's engraving that the gardens on the east side of the house, while laid out with a serpentine path that extended from the east pavilion of the main block as far as the circular pool in the valley, were purely functional vegetable plots. An air of politeness was suggested by the urns set on plinths at intervals along the green hedge separating them from the meadow, but behind the greenery the beds were utilitarian. However, the western garden was anything but, being a true pleasure ground of exotic architectural sensations and sounds. The National Trust has recently restored this area and reinstated some of its hidden surprises, though the statue of Moses striking the rock is yet to be recreated.[4] The first glimpse a visitor gets after the ticket barrier is an oblique view of the serpentine canal snaking off to the Sham Bridge at its eastern end, the huge bulk of the mansion towering above it and reflected in the water. The Bridge is a close copy of that by William Kent in the Elysian Fields at Stowe, though given a semicircular form.

Any sense that this was originally conceived as a classical Arcadia is dispelled by the rough stone Grotto, now under restoration, which must once have brooded gloomily over the watercourse, and the Gothic Temple, seen by Pococke, in the shrubberies below the lake. At the heart of the Wilderness is the Cascade, over which stood Moses, and there was also originally an open clearing in the woodland called the Cabinet, a secluded area where visitors could watch the gushing water, which then flowed underground to reappear in front of the Gothic Temple below.[5] This last was an ogee-arched loggia (30) derived from Batty Langley's *Antient Architecture* of 1741-2, which was re-erected in a private house nearby in 1921. Lady Luxborough visited Bath in 1752 and saw the

29 Anthony Walker's 1752 engraving of Prior Park shows the ornamental garden on the west side of the valley and the more practical areas on the east; the Palladian Bridge is yet to be built. Somerset Archaeological and Natural History Society

30 Prior Park's Gothic Temple, based on designs by Batty Langley, was removed to a neighbouring house in the early twentieth century. Somerset Archaeological and Natural History Society

Wilderness in its prime:

> The utmost use had been made of the advantages of water and quality of surprise had been achieved. Rills appeared to issue from a rock and to trickle down a precipice and the water collected below to form a winding river which flowed into a lake well stocked with fish.[6]

Pope may have suggested the grass Cabinet, as he had created several similar areas in his garden at Twickenham to 'prevent all prying from without and preserve the privacy of the interior parts'.[7] The planting around the Cabinet consisted of a matching pair of trees on either side of the Cascade, possibly willows, and was bounded by thickets of laurel and other evergreens intertwined with climbing and scented plants, such as honeysuckle and hop. With the introduction of new plants during the century, these areas became galleries in which to display exotics such as *Aristolochia*, *Passiflora* and *Bignonia*.[8] The woodland was threaded with winding paths, two of which now connect with the perimeter path, parallel to Ralph Allen's Drive, ending in the Rock Gate. This perfect Rococo conceit is a wooden barrrier on vaguely Chinese lines, hung on pyramidal piers of knobbly stones.

Daniel Defoe gave a thoughtful description of what Allen had achieved in the Wilderness in the third, 1742, edition of his *Tour*:

> Mr Allen is contented with the Situation of his House and Gardens ... instead of forcing Nature by a great Expense to bend to Art, he pursues only what the natural Scite points out to him ... He levels no Hills, but enjoys the Beauty of the Prospects they afford: he cuts down no Woods, but strikes thro' them fine Walks, and next-to-natural Mazes ... Nor does he want for fine Conveniences of Water; and as he is a Gentleman who is not enter'd into the present fashionable Schemes of ridiculing Religion and Scripture, he has a Figure of Moses striking the Rock, and the Water gushing out of it, which forms a sort of natural Cascade, when his Bason is supplied.[9]

In addition to sound biblical iconography, Moses could also denote masonic ritual, as at Halswell. Both Allen and John Wood were committed freemasons and Wood, obsessed by sacred geometry, had consciously designed the mansion with its attendant wings to occupy three sides of an imaginary twelve-sided figure – a dodecagon – centred on the combe.10 Furthermore, Allen is buried in Claverton churchyard under a pyramidal-roofed memorial resembling Moses' Holy Tabernacle in the Wilderness. Wood had explored the Tabernacle, originally a portable tent which housed the Ark of the Covenant, in his 1741 *Origin of Building*, where he gives alternative designs for stone-built structures in each of the classical orders.[11] At least two of these were built around Bath, one at the 'Lime Kiln Spaw' and the other up on Lansdown for the surgeon Jerry Peirce, to which we shall return. If the Masonic iconography in the Prior Park Wilderness was not as expressly revealed as at Halswell, the political statement on the lower slopes was hard to miss.

The focal point in the valley is the Palladian Bridge (*colour 13*), much lighter on its architectural feet than the low-lying replica at Stowe, through which a carriage drive runs, but not quite as attenuatedly elegant as the original at Wilton House, for the central intercolumniation of its colonnade has been widened to admit the view back up to the mansion. This is not just a Palladian jeu d'esprit; it was built to an intensely political agenda.[12] Allen was a hard political animal. His first move to prosperity had been a spying operation on local Jacobites. As a Whig, he was aware that rising Whig politicians were fixated on garden buildings as status symbols, and he had the wealth and the workforce to build them at Prior Park. The 1750s were the years when the 'Boy Patriots', that inner faction of the Whig party, achieved power and military glory in the wars with France. Towering above them all was William Pitt the Elder, who suffered agonies from hereditary gout, which the hot waters of Bath could relieve. Pitt was a keen gardener and anxious to become one of Bath's MPs. Allen was the power behind Bath Corporation, so they had mutual interests and ambitions.

One of Pitt's letters to Sanderson Miller, the gentleman amateur architect of Radway in Warwickshire, written on 30 October 1755, proves that Pitt and Allen were already close acquaintances. It concerns the Sham Castle above Bath:

> I shall then have one call upon your Imagination for a very considerable Gothick Object which is to stand in a very fine situation on the Hills near Bath. It is for Mr Allen, the idea I will explain to you when we meet. The name of that excellent man will render my desires to you to do your best unnecessary. I shall have a particular pleasure in procuring to him the help of the Great Master of Gothic.[13]

So in 1755 Pitt and Allen were discussing garden buildings and by 1757, after applying for the Chiltern Hundreds, Pitt became MP for Bath. Tellingly, the Palladian Bridge was built in that year of consultation by Allen's clerk of works, Richard Jones. In his rambling life history Jones records that, 'In the year 1755 he ordered me to build the bridge over the pond; the foundation stone was laid by Mr Allen May 29th, 1755'.[14] At no point does Jones claim the design of the Bridge, merely the supervision of its construction. While it cannot be proven conclusively, the complex family relationships of the Boy Patriots suggest a possible author of the Bridge.

Lord Cobham, their founder, had already built himself a copy of the serene Wilton original at Stowe, making it a symbol of Britain's imperial destiny with an iconographic frieze of 'Britannia Receiving Homage' carved by Peter Scheemakers.[15] The other leading Patriots were George Lyttelton, George and Richard Grenville, Henry Pelham and William Pitt himself. Lyttelton and Grenville built Palladian bridges at Hagley in Worcestershire and Wotton Underwood, Buckinghamshire respectively. George Lyttelton's mother was Christian Temple, Lord Cobham's sister; George Grenville's mother Hester was another of Lord Cobham's sisters. George and Richard Grenville also had a sister whose name was Hester; she married William Pitt in 1754, making another connection in the Whig political loop. Finally, William Pitt had a nephew, Thomas Pitt, later 1st Lord Camelford, a gifted amateur architect who was to design the Palladian Bridge at Hagley for Lord Lyttelton. Thomas Pitt and Sanderson Miller were equally devoted to William Pitt. In 1779 Miller set up a memorial urn to William Pitt in a grove of trees that Pitt had planted in 1754 at Radway, which Thomas had sent him from Bath. The evidence is not conclusive, but this maze of relationships suggests that the Palladian Bridge at Prior Park was built by Allen on the advice of, and to flatter,

William Pitt, and that Thomas Pitt is likely to have designed it for Jones to construct.

By the time Thomas Robins had produced his 1758 watercolours of Prior Park and Thorp and Overton had published in 1762 their *Survey of the Manors*, which includes Allen's estate, the western pleasure garden was complete and the eastern vegetable garden had been planted with trees. This is very much the view today, with both sides of the valley thickly wooded, framing the view of the Palladian Bridge, with Widcombe Manor, Crowe Hall and the terraces above the London Road forming a scenic backdrop. The tree line on the eastern side ripples in serpentine fashion along the contours, with different deciduous trees giving colour and texture to the belt. This might be the result of advice from Capability Brown, who was paid £60 for 'surveys and making plans at or about Prior Park'.[16] Brown's account was not settled until after Allen's death in 1764, and £60 does not suggest any costly contracts of work, as at Longleat and Corsham Court where he was directing landscape improvements at this time, so Brown's input at Prior Park can only be conjectural.

Robins' sketches and watercolours of Prior Park record the Cascade in the centre of the valley, which fed into the pool by the Bridge. These small-scale works may well have been studies towards a larger painting, never realised, for an advertisement Robins placed in the *Bath Journal* for 30 October 1752 offers, in addition to his services as a teacher of the 'Art of drawing and painting in Water Colours', the preparation of 'Perspects and Prospective Views of Gentlemens Seats in the correctest Manner'.[17] This suggests that Robins might have offered patrons designs for their landscapes as well as surveys of what had already been achieved. Certainly the Gothick features in the Rococo pleasure grounds at Davenport in Shropshire, which he painted in the 1750s, have close affinities to others that were eventually built at Benjamin Hyett's country seat just outside Painswick.[18] While the Painswick garden has been restored over the past twenty-five years and is now the best surviving example of a Rococo layout, the gardens at **Widcombe Manor**, which adjoin the lower valley at Prior Park, have undergone several improvements and much of the early eighteenth-century atmosphere has been lost. The two estates must inevitably have had an aesthetic impact on each other, and were also linked by Henry Fielding who wrote Tom Jones whilst staying at Widcombe; his Squire Allworthy is, of course, based on Ralph Allen. Fortunately, Thomas Robins also sketched Widcombe and, taken together with the surviving garden buildings, the original effect of the grounds can be appreciated.

Unlike neighbouring Prior Park, Widcombe's gardens were small in compass, laid out in a hollow below the house. On approaching the Manor along Church Lane the first glimpse of Widcombe behind tall gate piers and ironwork gates is of a quirkily elaborate Baroque façade and a beautiful Renaissance fountain playing in the forecourt. It was sited there by the novelist Horace Annesley Vachell after he bought the house in 1927.[19] Beyond the nineteenth-century terrace the Georgian pleasure grounds have mostly reverted to grass, but between 1927 and 1937 they were laid out in formal style by Harold Peto.[20] At the end of the south terrace there is a diminutive Summerhouse (*31*) which, in true Rococo fashion, is alive with textures: chunky grey tufa, smooth honey-coloured ashlar, blocked vermiculated rustication to the Doric columns and a Gibbs surround framing the central arched doorway. This is not visible in Robins' two main drawings of Widcombe, the first a copy of an earlier view showing the original formal gardens in front of the house, and the second taken from the south, looking back up to the house with the terrace obscured by trees. Robins did not miss the building, as it was only brought from Freshford to Widcombe in 1975, though it is entirely appropriate to the gardens. Robins' later view shows the two-storey classical Summerhouse with its ground-floor loggia in the walled garden on the other side of Church Lane, which survives in separate ownership today.

Below the Summerhouse are the roughly-arched remains of the Grotto with steps leading down to a spring, but the centrepiece of the Widcombe pleasure grounds is the rocky Cascade (*32*) set above a circular pool, backed by the Mount, which first appears on Thorp's map of 1742.[21] A Robins sketch, made before the pool had been dug and the Cascade raised, shows the Mount with a covered Chinese-style pavilion with a conical roof.[22] If this pavilion was indeed part of the Widcombe grounds, as opposed to the adjacent Lyncombe Pleasure Gardens, then it confirms the eclectic nature of the gardens laid out by Philip Bennett II in the

31 The Summerhouse at Widcombe Manor, while perfectly appropriate to a mid-eighteenth-century Rococo layout, was only introduced into the grounds in 1975

32 The Cascade at Widcombe Manor was once backed by a Chinese-style pavilion on the Mount, producing that eclectic diversity favoured by mid-century owners

33 John Wood the Elder of Bath built a bachelor pad for the local surgeon, Jeremiah Peirce, high up on Lansdown, calling it Lilliput Castle. Its grounds were laid out in true eclectic style with garden buildings and at least one rockwork arch, which survives on the site today

1750s. There were seats on the viewing platform at the top of the Cascade, where the feet of a statue of Neptune set into a dolphin's head are still just discernible.

Robins never sketched the 'Lime Kiln Spaw', for which John Wood built a 'Porticoe with the House of the lower Well' based on Moses' Holy Tabernacle.[23] Like the later spa at the heart of the Lyncombe Pleasure Gardens, it spoilt the water source it was intended to protect and did not survive long. Wood then hoped to build another version of the Tabernacle as a seal-engraving factory for John Wicksted (Wicksteed), on the other side of Prior Park Road, but the scheme came to nothing.[24] Undaunted as ever, Wood turned his mind to designing dwellings in the Mosaic style:

> Let us suppose the twelve Pillars which Moses set up at the Foot of Mount Sinai, covered over in such a Manner as to form a Cottage of that Kind…and let us suppose those Pillars made after any of the Orders; will not such an Edifice, small as it is, be beautiful, whether

the Orders be the Strong, the Mean or the Delicate?[25]

His *Origin of Building* has illustrations of three alternative domestic villas to this God-given design, stating that one, of the Corinthian order, 'is to be executed by the Person for whom these Designs were first made'.[26] In the event, it was the cheaper Doric design that Wood finally erected in 1738 on Lansdown for the surgeon Jeremiah Peirce, a fellow parishioner in Walcot and one of Wood's lessees in Queen Square. **Lilliput Castle**, or 'T. Totum' as it was nicknamed by the wits of Bath,[27] was later subsumed within the Regency Gothic Battlefields House, designed by Charles Harcourt Masters in 1802, but its cuboid shape can still be made out on the roof of the present house.

Lilliput was built as a rural bolthole where Peirce could entertain his close friends in privacy and enjoy the fresh air of Lansdown. Fortunately, Robins made sketches of the villa and its gardens in May 1760, and these are a valuable record of Peirce's bachelor pad, set far away from the prying eyes of Bath society. By this time the pyramidal roof, which was often set on fire because of Wood's typically inexpert construction, had been taken down, and a semicircular Doric porch added. On either side of the front door were niches with statues and above the porch Robins included a Latin inscription: veris amicis, suggesting that he and Peirce were intimate friends. The porch gave on to a formal lawn with a Rococo fret garden bench, while the lawn led, in turn, to a hedged and railed avenue terminating in gate piers and a claire-voie with the Lansdown Monument as a focal point in the distance. To the east of the house was a Rustic Arch that survives today (*33*) and which Robins drew, a roller propped up against it, the gates open to another formal hedged avenue with urns on plinths. There is also a Robins view of Peirce's Hermitage (*colour 14*), which was constructed of tufa-like stones with Gothic windows and a thatched roof; sadly this fanciful conceit has disappeared. It was sited at the end of another hedged avenue, its door open in the watercolour, revealing a table on which is placed a skull, behind which an inscribed board hangs on the wall. Given that Lilliput was conceived by Peirce as a venue for boisterous parties, it is ironic that the villa was based on biblical precedent, and that the Gothick Hermitage had a thatched belfry surmounted by a cross adding a further religious touch. No doubt Peirce would have enjoyed the joke, while Wood, the earnest religious fanatic, would surely have disapproved.

There is one further Robins watercolour of this Bath sequence that merits discussion, for it may well have been a landscape eye-catcher set up on the eastern slope of Lansdown to another house as yet unidentified. Robins made two watercolours of Mr Nicholas' Farm on Charmy Down (*colour 15*) and had one of them etched, which suggests that the two men were good friends. There was certainly a farm on the site in 1742, as it is marked on Thorp's map, but it is not clear when it was given a fake Gothick make-over: the wall to the left of the building with its huge traceried window is merely a screen. The farmhouse survives along a narrow track that follows the contours of the hillside to the rear of the Ministry of Defence complex at the top of Lansdown Hill. All the Gothick detail has been stripped away save for a single arched window on the south return elevation.

More survives of the pleasure gardens at Batheaston where Lady Miller, Bath poetess and social luminary, held her famous morning assemblies.[28] There is still some doubt as to exactly when **Batheaston Villa** was built, as at first sight it looks to be early eighteenth-century in date with the later addition of a semicircular bay window with a first-floor verandah and castellated parapet.[29] The tireless Richard Pococke rode out to Batheaston on 20 June 1754 to visit 'Mrs. Ravoe, who, with Mrs Riggs, a widow, has built a very good house, highly finish'd, improved the side of a hill to the road in beautiful lawn, walks, garden, cascades, a piece of water and a stream running thro' the garden, and live there in a very agreeable retirement'.[30] Could this be Batheaston Villa, or perhaps another house in the same village? Further light is shed in a letter Horace Walpole wrote to his friend George Montagu on 22 October 1766 after a stay in Bath:

> I dined one day with an agreeable family two miles from Bath, a Captain Miller and his wife and her mother Mrs Riggs. They have a small new-built house with a bow window, directly opposite to which the Avon falls in a wide cascade … Their garden is little, but pretty, and watered with several small rivulets among the bushes.

Meadows fall down to the road, and above, the garden is terminated by another view of the river, the city and the mountains. 'Tis a very diminutive principality with large pretensions.[31]

Montagu replied to Walpole's letter five days later mentioning that 'the family of Riggs and a Miss Ravant were great friends of poor Lady Babs, whose house at Bath Easttown was just by them'.[32] 'Ravant' is likely to be a mistake for Ravoe; 'Lady Babs' was his cousin, Lady Barbara Montagu, who lived at Batheaston with the novelist Sarah Scott from 1754 until her death. Lady Miller's maiden name was Anna Riggs and the DNB states that she married Captain John Miller in August 1765, thereafter building, 'at extravagant cost', a house at Batheaston. This will be the house Walpole saw a year later as 'new-built', replacing the dwelling Pococke visited in 1754. It is likely, therefore, given Pococke's description of the grounds, which accords with what is known of them in Lady Miller's time, what is recorded in watercolours by Robins and what actually survives on the site today, that the existing garden was retained.[33]

The Villa is up a narrow lane that doubles back sharply off the main road. Tall Bath stone gate piers guard a small courtyard close to the lane, making any full view of the entrance front impossible. But then the grounds open up to the side and below the garden front of the Villa, its tall bay commanding expansive horse chestnuts, the terraced slopes and the valley of the Avon beyond. The main garden is to the west side, once accessed via a tufa-like stone arch similar to that at Lilliput Castle, which was drawn by Robins. A small fern-edged Cascade overhung with a veteran oriental plane tree leads to a romatically overgrown walk that eventually reaches a small pool by an ancient walnut, above which is a diminutive Doric Rotunda open to the elements (34). Pococke, with his penchant for garden buildings, would surely have mentioned this, so it must be later than his 1754 visit. It houses a plinth, not for the celebrated antique urn shown on Lady Miller's funerary monument in Bath Abbey, and illustrated by Collinson,[34] but for a statue long since gone. Invited guests including Samuel Johnson, Hester Thrale, Horace Walpole, Coplestone Warre Bampfylde, Fanny Burney, Anna Seward and Mary Delany, who met at her literary salon once a fortnight, would place an original *bout*

34 The Doric Rotunda at Batheaston Villa is sited in deep undergrowth at the end of Lady Miller's diminutive garden.
It must have provided her literary guests with a welcome place for leisurely contemplation after the intellectual strain of their breakfast gatherings

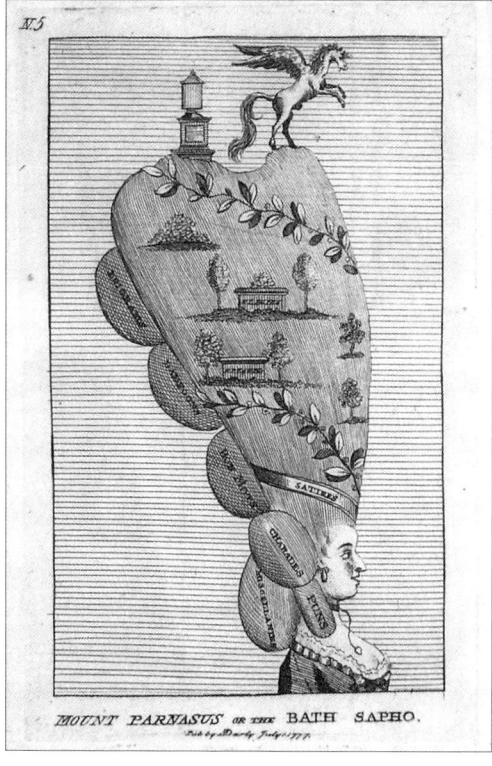

35 Lady Miller had her detractors, including the waspish Horace Walpole, and satirists were quick to deride her literary pretensions. This is a 1777 print by Matthew Darly caricaturing her as the 'Bath Sappho'.
The Victoria Art Gallery, Bath and North East Somerset

rimé in the Poetry Urn. The three best productions of the breakfast gatherings were then determined by a committee and their authors crowned by Lady Miller with wreaths of myrtle picked in the garden. Selections of these compositions were published between 1775 and 1781 as *The Poetical Amusements at a Villa near Bath*. Walpole, having enjoyed the Millers' hospitality some ten years before, dismissed the poems contemptuously in a letter of January 1775 as 'Mrs Miller's bouquet of artificial flowers', and continued: 'You will there see how immortality is plentifully promised to riddles and *bouts rimés*, and a jar dressed up with ribbands'.[35] A week later he was still moaning on about 'the miscellany from Batheaston', which he judged to be 'ten degrees duller than a magazine'.[36] Perhaps Walpole's own poetic offerings never achieved a garland.

Sandwiched between these two letters to Lady Ossory, Walpole wrote one to Henry Conway and Lady Ailesbury, which confirms again the dating of the Villa and gardens at Batheaston:

> You must know, Madam, that near Bath is erected a new Parnassus, composed of three laurels, a myrtle tree, a weeping-willow, and a view of the Avon, which has been new-christened Helicon. Ten years ago there lived a Madam Riggs, an old rough humourist who passed for a wit; her daughter who passed for nothing, married to a Captain Miller, full of good-natured officiousness. These good folks were friends of Miss Rich, who carried me to dine with them at Batheaston, now Pindus. They caught a little of what was called taste, built and planted, and begot children, till the whole caravan were forced to go abroad and retrieve. Alas! Mrs Miller is returned a beauty, a genius, a Sappho, a tenth muse, as romantic as Mademoiselle Scuderi, and as sophisticated as Mrs Vesey ... They hold a Parnassus fair every Thursday, give out rhymes and themes, and all the flux of quality at Bath contend for the prizes of these Olympic games.[37]

It seems reasonable to assume that the grounds around the Villa were already established when the Millers took over from Anna's widowed mother and that they simply adjusted them to create their own Parnassus. Not surprisingly, the Batheaston literary salon was satirised in *The Sentence of Momus on the Poetical Amusements at a Villa near Bath* (1775), Momus being the classical personification of ridicule and fault finding, and in a 1777 print (35) by Matthew Darly of 'mount parnassus or the bath sappho'. This depicts Lady Miller sporting a towering hairpiece decorated with bay leaves, tombs inscribed with the words 'Elegises' and 'Epitaphs', the Poetry Urn and the winged horse, Pegasus. This last relates to the legend of the Hippocrene Spring on Mount Helicon, which represents the source of poetic inspiration. It was created when Pegasus struck the rock so hard that a spring burst forth; Helicon and Parnassus were both mountains reputed to be the home of the Muses and of Pegasus.[38]

It is not known whether William Pitt, The Great Commoner, ever attended any of Lady Miller's 'Poetical Amusements', though by this time he had been an MP for Bath for over twenty years and lived at number 7 The Circus. He was also resident in the county at **Burton Pynsent**, where he too lived on a Parnassus, but one that commanded the vast expanse of West Sedge Moor rather than the river Avon. The tall Column he set up in memory of his benefactor, Sir William Pynsent (36), marks his estate today. The design for this has been attributed to Capability Brown, but Brown is unlikely to have had any hand in the series of garden buildings laid out along the Terrace from the house to the Column overlooking the Moor.[39] These were added to the ridge after Pitt inherited the estate in 1765 on the death of Sir William. Indeed, Pitt's payment to Brown's surveyor, John Spyers, of £10 in July 1774, must have been for minor work, as Brown usually charged in the region of £80 for a full landscape survey.[40] Even Brown's suggestions for the Column itself were not carried out faithfully, with Pitt revising the design as it was executed, substituting an urn for the proposed statue of Gratitude. Letters between Pitt's wife, Lady Chatham, and her brother Earl Temple illustrate how both Pitt's brother-in-law and the landscape at Stowe must have influenced him. In a letter of 4 August 1765 Lord Temple writes to Lady Chatham:

> I am particularly happy in the description you give of Burton Pynsent as I think it will rise into high favour and afford much rural Delectation. Sir William has already erected a monument for himself to his eternal honour in the successor he has chosen but if

in these times, Gratitude rises 114' 4" high, it will equal Lord Cobhams Pillar, statue and all.[41]

There was a close social and political relationship between the two couples and both made frequent visits to Stowe and Burton Pynsent. The letters make it clear that all the landscaping ideas for Burton Pynsent came initially from Stowe, but in return Pitt seems to have been advising

36 William Pitt set this column high up above West Sedge Moor at Burton Pynsent in memory of his benefactor, Sir William Pynsent. It was partly designed by Lancelot 'Capability' Brown, but altered in execution by Pitt

Temple on the alterations to Stowe House. As early as August 1755 Temple exclaimed: 'Where the devil you picked up all this architectural skill, what Palladio you have studied I know not, but you are an architect born and I am edified and delighted'.[42] As well as referring to Pitt as his 'gouty friend', Temple also referred to him even earlier in 1749 as 'the master of the Lakemaker and the Lake',[43] implying that Pitt had a hand in designing the new informal lake at Stowe, developed from the octagonal pool. In preparing for a visit to Burton Pynsent in November 1765, long before Spyers was paid on behalf of Brown in 1774, Temple praised Pitt's landscaping achievements there:

I shall with the greatest pleasure facilitate, as far as in my eyes, the favourite object of enlarging round Burton Pynsent, as the expence of Hayes [Pitt's other house]; and I with your estates in Somersetshire may not only rival the great Peter, but extend as wide as the sight from the top of the monumental column on the bleak promontory, which through determined purpose not blind chance, I shall most certainly see next summer, as well as the rising towers and I hope flourishing plantation which your active mind has planned and expeditious right hand already executed, so far breaking in upon Mr. Brown's department, by adorning the country which you were not permitted to save.[44]

It seems much more likely, therefore, that Pitt himself, acting as his own landscaper rather than relying on Brown's advice, was responsible for the range of eclectic temples, cottages and seats that were constructed along the Terrace to take in the views over Sedge Moor. One of these was a 'Pan's House', and Pitt had already built a Temple of Pan at South Lodge, Enfield Chase between 1747 and 1752.[45] Sadly, almost all trace of the 'portico', 'Blackbird Haunt', 'French's House', French's Seat' and 'Sheep House',[46] as well as Pan's House and an arch, has gone; they were largely dismantled after Hester Pitt's death in 1803, when the estate was sold. However, two barns with Tuscan columns survive in farms below the ridge.

What remains at Burton Pynsent is a single wing of the great classical house clinging precariously on the clifftop, its pedimented brick façade angled along the escarpment towards the Column. There are still great cedars around the skirts of the house and mature woodland, mostly of beech and oak, between it and the Column, but the North American exotic planting carried out by Pitt, and continued after his death in 1778 by his wife, was felled in the asset-stripping carried out after the 1803 sale. However, in its prime, the Terrace must have acted like that in Line Wood at Hatch Court, further west along the same ridge, where exotic garden retreats, sometimes hidden in shrubbery, sometimes set within open glades in the woods, were sited to give spectacular views out towards Taunton in the west and to Glastonbury Tor in the north-east.

Intriguingly, Brown's landscape minimalism seems to have made little impact on the county where, in the latter half of the century, Somerset gentry were still content to lay out their parks, as did Pitt at Burton Pynsent, with a scatter of ornamental buildings for playful diversion. This is in marked contrast to many counties surveyed for this series where there is a distinct stylistic break between the eclecticism of the Rococo phase and the busy Regency proposals of Humphry Repton. For aficionados of Georgian garden buildings, Somerset, by its very conservative nature, is perhaps the most rewarding county of all.

5

Somerset gentry spurn Lady Nature's second husband

▼

Earnshill · Redlynch Park · Mells Park · Barwick Park · Orchardleigh
Ammerdown · Enmore Castle · Midford Castle · Kelston Park
Nettlecombe Court · Harptree Court · Ashton Court · Ston Easton Park
Newton Park · Leigh Court

As the last chapter suggested, the later eighteenth-century landscape parks of Somerset toyed with the standard Brownian treatment of open parkscape dressed with trees and featuring a body of water, but the county's gentry seemed determined to avoid landscape minimalism by introducing garden buildings for gentle enlivenment. As a result, there is a satisfying continuum between the eclectic layouts of the 1730s and 1740s and Humphry Repton's Red Book proposals of the Regency. The county is particularly rich in eighteenth-century parks and, where contemporary plans survive, as at Earnshill and Redlynch, design intentions can be traced even if the land has reverted to cultivation.

William Pitt's Column at Burton Pynsent is a prominent feature on the skyline from **Earnshill** at Curry Rivel, an archetypal neo-Palladian house built between 1728 and 1731 for Francis Eyles, MP for Devizes, by an unknown architect.[1] A year later Eyles set up a sundial in the grounds to record the completion of work. Earnshill is a serene villa designed to Palladio's bay rhythm of 1/3/1 bays, but dwarfed by loutish additions to both flanks. These wings were added when Richard Combe, a wealthy Bristol ship owner and linen draper, bought the estate in 1758. The house is set on a ridge, just as Palladio would have advised, commanding an expansive view of the Vale of the River Isle. At some point between 1731 and Combe's purchase the brick-walled Kitchen Garden, which is such a prominent feature of the grounds today, was constructed. This is shown in a beautiful estate plan (*colour 16*) preserved at the house, drawn by

James Blackamore in 1774, and which records the landscape at that date. The estate comprised a small area of designed parkland around the house, surrounded by cultivated fields, and to the north was the adjacent 'Earl of Chatham's Land'. At Earnshill there were none of the artfully placed clumps or shelter belts associated with Brown, 'Lady Nature's second husband';[2] merely open grassland, sections dotted with trees and a shrubbery threaded with serpentine paths enclosing the Kitchen Garden, which was divided internally into four quadrants. The paths, now much

37 The over-scaled topiary at Earnshill was developed from original shrubberies, laid out around the Walled Garden, shown on James Blackamore's 1774 map of the estate

overgrown and replanted with trees, can still be walked today, although striking ornamental topiary (37) has taken the place of the original low yew hedges. Inside the walled enclosure are the foundations of the great seven-bay, pedimented classical Orangery and its attendant glasshouse and cold frame, which are shown in a vignette on the plan (38).

The decidedly bucolic character of Earnshill is mirrored at **Redlynch**, its park now mostly obliterated by hedged fields, while its significance in terms of garden history is judged today for its 1901 additions to the house and grounds by Edwin Lutyens for the 5th Earl of Ilchester. At Redlynch

38 This vignette of the Orangery in the Walled Garden at Earnshill from Blackamore's estate map shows it to have been flanked by a glasshouse and a cold frame; the footings of all these features survive in the enclosure. By kind permission of Richard Combe

too, although the house was demolished in 1913, making it difficult to conceive how the mansion interacted with its landscape, important estate maps survive recording the eighteenth-century parkscape. Redlynch Park was designed and built in 1708-9 by Thomas Fort for Sir Stephen Fox, on a site adjoining the sixteenth-century mansion. When Fox died in 1716 he was succeeded by his son, another Stephen, who took the additional name of Strangways on his marriage in 1735, and was subsequently created Lord Ilchester in 1741 and Earl of Ilchester in 1756. Work had already begun on the grounds as early as 1729, and a plan of 1738 drawn by E Grant (39) shows intensely angular groves north and south of the house and a formal 'Great Pond' to the south.[3] Many of these features were named after Stephen Fox's friends: 'Hervey's Grove', 'Digby's Walk', 'Count Coppice', after Henry Fox who was known to the family as 'The Count', and 'Charlotte Coppice', after Stephen's sister.[4] The only concession to the emergent Rococo fashion is a 'Serpentine Walk' to the south-east. Closer to the house was a Bowling Green, possibly a survivor from the earlier house, as well as a Cold Bath in the middle of an orchard. The extensive

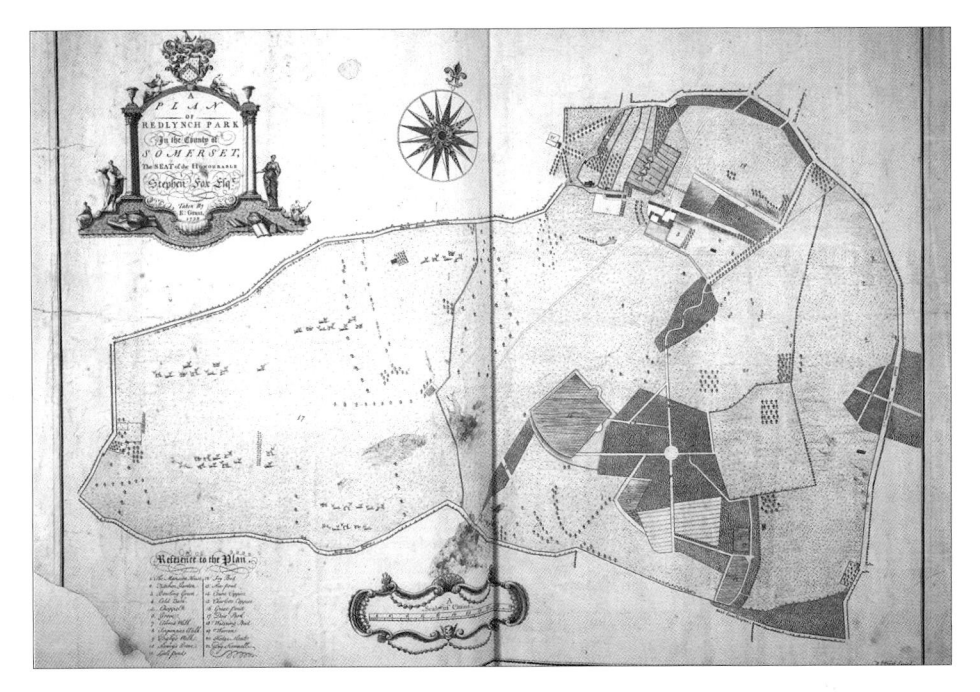

39 The 1738 plan of Redlynch Park records the angular formality of the grounds before they were softened and enlivened with flower gardens in the 1750s and 1760s.
The Bodleian Library, University of Oxford, Gough Maps 29, f.21

pleasure gardens were separated by a pale from the deer park to the west. It is not clear exactly how much of this scheme was carried out, for the park was increased in size between 1740 and 1762. However, the grove to the north, the formal pool and 'Hervey's Grove', now called Park Wood, are all shown on the 1885 Ordnance Survey map, though the Serpentine Walk had disappeared by that time.

The second phase of landscaping at Redlynch coincided more precisely with the current fashion for eclectic collections of garden buildings, so the park was enlivened with cascades on the stream below the Grove, a temple (1762), a Chinese seat (1756) and a menagerie aviary, surviving today within a farm complex as 'The Aviaries'. Also, in 1755, Henry Flitcroft, who was working on a new drawing room and other interiors at the house, designed a Gothick entrance, known as The Towers, on the west side of the park.[5] These features are all recorded on a 1762 map by Samuel Donne, which records precisely that move from geometric regularity to a more artful informality, particularly in Hervey's Grove where the axial walks have been linked by snaking paths.[6] At the northern entrance to the Grove, beside the Serpentine Walk, was a 'Ladies Garden' with a temple, which led to a 'Temple Flower Garden'. The 'Ladies Garden' was laid out for Elizabeth Fox-Strangways, Countess of Ilchester, in 1747-8, although it continued to develop well after that.[7] After 1762 she also created a new house and garden at Abbotsbury on the Dorset coast.[8] In 1750 Lady Ilchester told her husband: 'I am glad my garden looks so pretty and full of flowers'.[9] Elsewhere, the lines of the Great Pond were softened and made more irregular, and kidney-shaped beds for flowers and exotic flowering shrubs were introduced into the Grove in a clearing either side of the new south-easterly serpentine path. These new flowery introductions reflected the current taste in woodland walks advocated by Thomas Wright and anticipated William Mason's flower garden at Nuneham Courtenay, Oxfordshire.[10] Horace Walpole visited Redlynch on a tour of West Country estates in July 1762 and saw the pleasure grounds in their prime: '[Redlynch] stands above half way up a high steep hill, cloathed with old trees, commanding a pleasant view, & surrounded by a Park, & with a large piece of water in the bottom, & a small wood cut into walks, a flower garden, & a handsome menagerie'.[11]

Mark Laird has written extensively about these mid-century flower gardens and, aided by the Redlynch bills of 1758-1765 for plants supplied by Francis Kingston to the Earl, has conjured up such an accurate and evocative picture of what the 'Ladies Garden' must have looked like that it is worth quoting in some detail:

> The margins of the beds would be edged with China pinks, globe amaranth, double balsam, and sweet mignonette – 'patches' of pink, red, white cream and purple. Behind this edging, the flowers of a middle height would ascend in stages: 'bunches' of yellow and orange African marigolds, pink and purple China asters, red and yellow coxcombs, rose-coloured larkspurs, blue, white, and rose pink lupins, white and pink carnations; purple, red, and white annual stocks, and perhaps the new yellow zinnias and violet-pink phlox. At the centre of the beds they [visitors] would see the sweat peas, nasturtiums, and morning glories festooned around stakes and reaching an apex just above head height ... The perfumes of the

'Ladies Flower Garden' were no doubt also carefully chosen for delicacy, avoiding all that might cloy. In spring, there would be the gentle fragrance of hyacinths. In summer, there would be delectable carnations and the suaveolent stocks and sweet peas mingling with the more pungent perfume of the phlox. In the midst of all these flowery scents would be the sweet aroma of fresh-cut grass or sun-filled basil, brushed by a passing coat or emitted from a tending hand.[12]

Almost all the Rococo elements at Redlynch were removed in 1800, and by that time much of the western half of the park had reverted to agricultural use.[13] The eighteenth-century walled Kitchen Garden, seen by Walpole in 1762 does, however, survive close to the house, commanded by the Orangery, which is now a private house. This area of the grounds will feature in a later chapter in an analysis of Lutyens' contribution to the site.

Perhaps the best documented but least known eighteenth-century park in Somerset is at Mells. It remains unregarded because that grey limestone village of medieval and later cottages is normally associated with members of the artistic coterie The Souls, who often stayed as guests of the Horners at the Manor next to the parish church. Nowadays it is mainly visited by pilgrims who come to see the grave of Siegfried Sassoon in the churchyard, or Sir Alfred Munnings' equestrian monument of Edward Horner, killed in the Great War.

One reason the Manor has these Edwardian associations, in particular the obsessive relationship between the Pre-Raphaelite painter Edward Burne-Jones and Frances Horner, is that the Horners were forced to move back to the Elizabethan house by the church in 1901, as an economy measure after the death of Frances' mother. Until that time they had lived at **Mells Park**, a 1725 house designed by Nathaniel Ireson set within the early seventeenth-century deer park to the south-west of the village. Thomas Strangways Horner built this after a financially prudent marriage settlement with another wealthy Strangways heiress of Melbury in Dorset. He died in 1741 and was succeeded by his brother John, who died in 1746, and then by John's son, Thomas. After a period of minority, Thomas Horner succeeded to the estate in 1758 and set about remodelling the landscape. His extensive surviving accounts in the Mells Estate

Office include a section headed 'Park Improvements' up to 1799, and one of his scrapbooks contains design ideas for the park. These archives are rare and important survivals, which give a fascinating overview of how the eighteenth-century parkscape at Mells developed.[14]

The most informative document is a survey plan of the park with a key itemising suggested proposals (*40*). It is unhelpfully orientated with north at the bottom, but if it is read in conjunction with an early OS map, or indeed the present 2004 sheet, it becomes clear what Horner intended and what was eventually carried out at Mells Park. The house is marked H at the bottom of the plan, on the site of the present house, overlooking the valley in which there is a stream (B) that has been canalised (F). On the opposite side of the canal there is a site proposed for a kitchen garden (C) and the lower lodge, now called Lilybatch Lodge. Significantly, the key marks B as a valley that 'may be Esaly Cover'd with water'. This was, in fact, achieved at some point after 1758 and before Thomas Horner died in 1804. The upper lake between the Vobster Plantation in the west and the Waterfall and Stepping Stones below the house was then enlivened by a Gothick Archway on the Tor Rock with steps down to an artificial Cave (1787), and the Gothick Lilybatch Lodge of 1784. In 1775 the lower lake beyond the Waterfall was made, while at the point where a former drive hit the weir by Wraggs Mill, Horner rebuilt the Duckery (*41*), a delightful Gothick conceit linked to the park by a bridge; further up the Mells River on the north side, linking the gardens with the park, there was a Chinese Bridge.[15] There is a beautiful watercolour (*colour 17*) of the Duckery in the Mells archives that could easily pass for a Thomas Robins sketch.

On the au by the house a bastioned terrace, 230 feet long, was proposed with a central circular gazebo lit by a Y-traceried Gothick window and quatrefoils to reflect those at the Duckery below.[16] It may well date from 1781, when the accounts mention work on the terrace. This Thomas Horner scheme was never achieved; the terracing was not completed in its present form until William Sawrey Gilpin enlarged the pleasure grounds between 1825 and 1832.[17] The plan also shows two proposed treatments for the approach to the house from a point marked A: 'the place for ye temple'. The Temple Garden was eventually laid out in pentagonal form between 1760 and 1762, with deciduous trees and

40 Landscape proposals for Thomas Horner's Mells Park are shown on this map, which was drawn up after he succeeded to the estate in 1758. It includes two parallel treatments for the axial approach to the house from a proposed temple, and a fishpond in the valley that was formed into a lake. By kind permission of Viscount Asquith

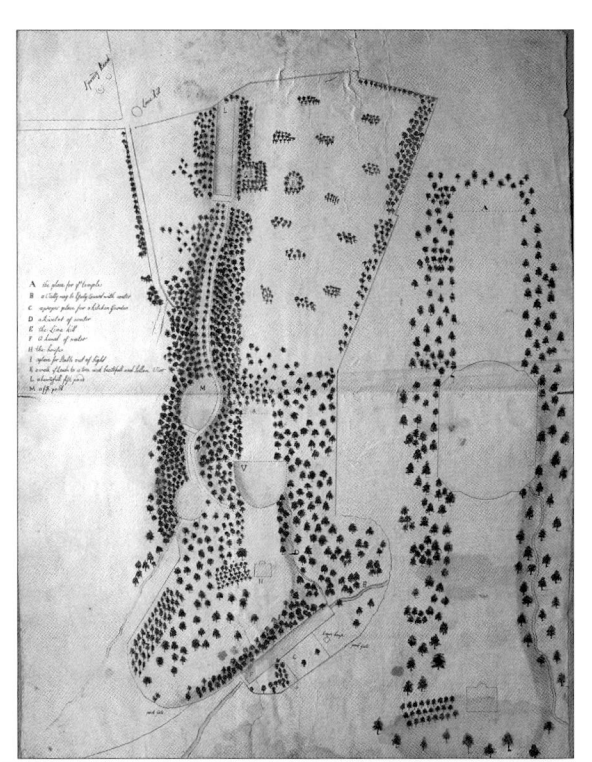

41 The Gothick Duckery at Mells Park, built in 1775, was one of a series of eclectic buildings on the west side of the lake

some yews. The 1779 manorial map of Mells shows flowerbeds within the enclosure, and by 1770 a hot house had been installed, while below it there was a grotto-hermitage and three Gothick seats cut into the rockface.[18] When the park was surveyed for the English Heritage Register in 2002 the Temple had disappeared, but it has recently been recreated. Fortunately several drawings for the building are preserved in the archives, including a detailed sheet with front and rear elevations, a ground plan and the pentagonal Temple Garden (*colour 18*).

Thomas Horner was exercised by the approaches to his estate and there are drawings for entry points with their guardian structures. A single detailed sheet has a plan for the approach from Berry Hill off the Vobster Road with a proposed lodge, ironwork gates and piers, a triumphal-arched entrance and single pedimented piers topped by talbots, the canine armorial supporters of the Horners. Another page of the 'Old Plans' scrapbook has a pasted-in design for a tripartite-arched rockwork gateway, the central arch of which was intended as 'The Gate Way Thro' which will be an Avenue to Leigh Tower'. This may have been proposed for Leigh Girth on the edge of Melcombe Wood to the southwest of the house. The left-hand archway has 'a Winding Way thro' for foot passengers', while the right-hand arch was to lead to a 'Porter's Lodge by way of Hermitage'. Nothing more is known of the hermit's dwelling or whether it was ever built. Finally, there is an estimate in the archives 'for to Build a Bath'. This was a substantial structure, 50-feet long by 20-feet wide, built of stone with a clay bottom laid on bricks. Frances Horner's *Time Remembered*, written in the 1930s, gives a clue as to where it was constructed: 'At the end of the lower lake there was a bathing house, and the water was nine feet deep. The children learned to swim, and "mixed bathing" in its infancy flourished'.[19]

In tandem with these architectural improvements in the park, Thomas Horner continued to plant trees, flowers and vegetables. Michael McGarvie gives a detailed account of the purchases between 1780 and 1793: flower roots from Hewitt (of Brompton Park); 'a large collection of ranunculus' from James Coombs; 100 Battersea Asparagus plants; hyacinths and crown imperials; thorn seeds and 2000 birch plants; two pear trees from Ford (Exeter), and 'a Capes Jessamine from Lord Digby's at Sherborne'.[20] Horner also had a close friendship with Lady Champneys at Orchardleigh. She wrote to him in 1778, hoping that he had recovered from the gout so 'that we may pursue our favourite Theme of Gardening again'.[21] Other friends sent collections of exotic seeds, some arriving at Mells from Antigua in June 1792, including yellow bell flower, stinking weed and 'Egyptian bean', and in the same year his gardener obtained 'Chinese seeds' from Lady Harriet Acland, together with two dozen cuttings for mulberry trees.[22] Even Horner's son was enlisted to purchase plants, being sent in 1793 to the nursery of William Curtis, founder of the *Botanical Magazine*.[23]

It is not clear who was responsible for contriving the landscape for Thomas Horner, if indeed he needed any design input from a professional, or who drew the designs for the garden buildings, though masons are often mentioned. Horner's plans were co-ordinated by an agent called Wickham, who was responsible for commissioning ideas about planting, building bridges and moving roads within the park.[24] A much later letter from Longleat about the use of chains to drag weeds from ponds is signed by Thomas Davis, and the archives also include a 1797 'Plan for a Fruit Garden', signed by Romeo Forbes. Horner was a subscriber to Humphry Repton's 1794 *Sketches and Hints of Landscape Gardening*, and Repton is said to have to have been consulted in the 1790s, but there is no record of a commission.[25] After Thomas Horner's death in 1804, precipitated by a stroke in 1801, his son, Colonel Thomas Strangways Horner, employed Sir John Soane between 1810 and 1815 to remodel the house and offer suggestions for an extension to the lakes with a new single-arched bridge and cascade.[26] Drawings for these are preserved in the Mells archives and also at the Soane Museum, where there is a lively correspondence between architect and client.[27] The bridge had been built by 1814, when Horner wanted it extended to a wider span; McGarvie believes that it was swept away during a great storm in August 1825.[28]

The most bizarre collection of eighteenth-century garden buildings in the county is at **Barwick Park**, just to the south-east of Yeovil. Unlike the landscape at Mells Park, Barwick is well known and its folly towers have featured in several publications, though the term folly suggests that they had no practical function. This is not strictly true, as John Newman, who

42
Jack the Treacle Eater is one of four eighteenth-century folly towers that encircle the grounds at Barwick Park. Local legend has it that the folly was raised in memory of a servant who, fortified by treacle, ran messages to the family house in London

raised the towers – the Rose Tower, the Fish Tower, Jack the Treacle Eater and the Obelisk – conceived them consciously with an eye for their landscape value. John and Grace Newman, whose relations owned the adjacent Newton Surmaville estate, built the parent house in about 1770, and then set about adding satellite buildings to be seen from it, placing them at the four points of the compass around the estate. In addition, the octagonal 1750s Summerhouse at Newton Surmaville, set on high ground to the north, acts as an eye-catcher from the Obelisk to the south alongside the A37.[29]

The Newmans' eighteenth-century house was remodelled in a bland neo-Jacobean style in the 1830s and after a succession of owners, occupation by the army in the 1940s and the conversion of the house into a school in the 1960s, the landscape gradually fell into decay until it was restored by the Lawrences after they bought it in 1992.[30] Barbara Jones saw the folly towers when she was researching her seminal book, *Follies & Grottoes*, in the 1950s. At that time they were thought to date from the 1820s or 1830s, when George and Lucy Messiter were rebuilding the house. In her second edition of 1974 Jones notes that she was shown a painting of the house thought to be of about 1780, and two family portraits of the 1770s, including in the backgrounds 'one of the two largest follies'.[31] So that dates them to the latter half of the eighteenth century. They are all built of orange Ham stone, all different, all tall, and they produce dramatic silhouettes on the skylines around the park. The Obelisk is a sharply tapered 12-metre high needle; the Rose Tower is an attenuated cone set on a base of open Gothick arches, and the Fish Tower is a survivor of two originals, the latter being dismantled about 1880, hence the adjacent Two Towers Lane. The most impressive folly, 'Jack the Treacle Eater' is due east of the house (*42*). It is a 30-metre tower set on a single-arched base rising to a circular drum topped by a cone and surmounted by a statue of Mercury. Jack is said to have been one of the Messiter servants, fortified by treacle, who ran to London with messages. If this is true, the folly must have been re-Christened after the Newmans first built it in the 1770s.

All these folly towers are sited towards the perimeter of the estate, but Barwick's most impressive park building lurks by the lake in the valley to the side of the house. Its approach is signalled on the north bank by a Rockwork Arch through which the lakeside walk leads to the Grotto at the head of the water. A deep walled and stone-paved path ends in a gaping black hole set in a mound of vegetation, its arch formed of sharply pointed stones like menacing teeth. Inside the effect is truly Piranesian (*colour 19*), as if the cavernous interiors of Giovanni Battista Piranesi's fictitious Roman *Carceri d'Invenzione* had actually been achieved in Somerset. Jones describes the Grotto aptly as 'blood-chilling',[32] and the sequence of spaces from the half-light of the first cave to the near darkness of the main chamber, its rock-faced walls rising up into a huge dome like a mini Pantheon lit dimly by an oculus, is one of the most awe-inspiring in the country. The waters of the lake lap gently into the first chamber, rippling across the pebbled floor; while the main cavern is deathly silent with a central pool and arched niches awaiting correctly proportioned classical statues. Could this be a design after Thomas Wright? It certainly has the rough-hewn bravura of the s in his 1758 *Grottos*. It is difficult to convey the precise images conjured up by the earthy, dank central cavern, but if any interior space of the eighteenth century comes close to Edmund Burke's notion of Terror, then this is it. Barbara Jones summed it up brilliantly: 'this is the most horrible place the folly builders made. The damp air chills the heart. There are not even the scratched initials of visitors'.[33] After this numinous grotto, Somerset owners waited another fifty years or so to create more caverns to feed the imagination; these will feature in the following chapter.

Until Humphry Repton's arrival in the county for a two-day visit to Ston Easton in November 1792, successive owners continued to lay out parks for productivity and enjoyment, spurning the vacancies of the Brownian tem.[34] At **Orchardleigh** the Champneys dammed up a tributary of the Frome to create a lake, flooding the site of the village. This has left the parish church of St Mary romantically marooned on an island offering picturesque views up to the new Victorian mansion, built in 1855-8 by Thomas Henry Wyatt, sited on the ridge to the north. In the churchyard there is a monument to 'Azor', Thomas Champneys' faithful dog, which died in 1796; it was originally in the park. The east end of the lake was given a romantic Boathouse with a Rotunda sited above it, both of which survive in the new golf course, and there is an ornamental Keeper's Lodge beside the main drive in from Murtry Bridge. This is an eighteenth-century building, which was later remodelled as a *cottage ornée* with decorative bargeboards and beautiful marginal glazing to the bow window overlooking the drive.

However, the main aesthetic accents are at the extremities, where a series of entrance lodges trumpets the taste and status of the family in the park beyond. The Lodges to the south-east are a lively 1820s twin-set of Tudorbethan cottages, but the great Gloucester Lodge to the north at Lullington (*colour 20*) eclipses them in style and extent. This complex of outwork towers, castle forecourt and turreted gateway with flanking round and square towers is the epitome of Regency Picturesque and entirely Tennysonian in its impact, recalling the 'Four gray walls, and four gray towers' of *The Lady of Shalott*.[35] The gateway, raised in about 1816, proudly bears the family coat of arms and the date, 1434, presumably when the Champneys first arrived at Orchardleigh.[36] While these lodges are Regency Gothic in style and date, there are two other surviving designs, one executed and the other unrealised, made earlier for Thomas Swymmer Champneys.[37] The first is for a pair of neo-Classical sentry box lodges decorated with fluted Greek Doric columns, bucrania friezes and swagged coats of arms (*colour 21*). These are annotated 'T S C 1801' and look to be the work of one of the Wyatts, possibly Jeffry, later Sir Jeffry Wyatville, who submitted plans for an extension to Orchardleigh House. The other is a watercolour of a single lodge at Orchardleigh, which is in that idiosyncratic style of segmental arches and recessed wall surfaces favoured by Sir John Soane, who was working in 1810 for Colonel Horner at Mells Park. It is inscribed 'Lodge in the grounds at Orchardley', suggesting that it was built.

There are more superb neo-Classical lodges, this time designed in 1788 by James Wyatt, for Thomas Samuel Jolliffe's unremarkable landscape park at **Ammerdown**. Wyatt had been commissioned to build a classical villa on agricultural land at Ammerdown that Jolliffe had inherited through his wife.[38] The Kilmersdon Lodges are nationally important buildings: two classical houses with elegant Ionic porticoes facing each other across a driveway guarded by incised gate piers supporting heavy cast iron gates and railings. When I first saw them in the early 1980s they were already derelict.[39] Even though this was the principal entrance to the park, the drive has been disused since the mid-twentieth century, the gate piers lie prone on the ground and the Lodges are now seemingly beyond repair.[40] They are roofless, their walls lean alarmingly, the stonework is breached, revealing rubble infill, mature trees grow out of their interiors and a barn owl has taken up residence in the most northerly of the pair. The green drive leads into the park alongside a stretch of water and once the valley below the house has been reached a tall column rears up on the ridge ahead. This was erected before 1854, in memory of their father, by his sons Colonel John Jolliffe and the Revd Thomas Jolliffe. Thereafter, pleasure grounds were laid out around the skirts of the house, and in 1901 an atmospheric formal garden designed by Lutyens was laid out, to which we shall return. The Radstock Lodges to the north-east are early nineteenth-century cottages ornées, and in 1824 there was a Cold Bath in the park (*43*), marked on the 1884 Ordnance Survey map by a semicircular pond in 'Coldbath Plantation', just north-west of the Column. Surrounded by an ornamental shrubbery and willows, its walls were covered with trellis for climbing plants.[41]

There are further late eighteenth-century landscape parks at Enmore, Midford, Kelston and Nettlecombe. At **Enmore Castle** in the north-eastern lee of the Quantocks, John James Percival, 2nd Earl of Egmont, seemed more intent on constructing an extraordinary moated castle, complete with drawbridge and underground fortifications, than with creating a designed landscape park of garden buildings to rival that at neighbouring Halswell, where the Earl and his wife were regular visitors.[42] Only a fragment of the great mock castle survives above ground today, and the banks of the scimitar-shaped lake to the west, which was dug in the 1760s by Egmont, have a 1900 Boathouse and an 1898 Summerhouse, from the Broadmeads' time.[43] It is edged in parts with a yew walk, probably dating from the eighteenth century, while beyond are the remains of rockwork cascades and pools.

Egmont's Enmore was grimly medieval, with battlements and round-arched windows, whereas, **Midford Castle** (*colour 22*) in the Bath suburbs is light-heartedly ogee-arched Gothick on a trilobal plan like an Ace of Clubs. Set above a mini-landscape with shelterbelts and tree clumps, it was built about 1775 by Henry Woolhouse Disney Roebuck, son of a Newark doctor, the design based on published drawings by the antiquary and Gothic fancier, John Carter.[44] Midford has an attendant Gothick Gateway on the main road and a romantically ruined Chapel just below the Castle.[45] Collinson reported that 'at a little distance from this [the house], under a thick mass of shade, stands a rustick hermitage on the brow of a steep descent'.[46] Roebuck also added a Gothick summerhouse.

Kelston Park, the new house that replaced the Old Manor by the church, was developed by Sir Caesar Hawkins after 1764 on a bluff above the Avon. It lacks these architectural diversions, as it is in Brown's minimalist style and was probably designed by him. He visited Kelston in 1767 and was paid £500, which implies that he acted as contractor for the work there, in addition to charging his usual fee for surveying the site.[47] Brown appears to have retained some of the formal tree avenues around the site of the Old Manor, otherwise all is vacant, though there is an ice house in a wood by the river and the main entrance on the Kelston road has a later Italianate lodge.

Nettlecombe Court at Williton, home of the Trevelyans since the mid-

43 Early maps of Ammerdown show a 'Coldbath Plantation' where this delightful bathing pavilion must have been sited. Its trellised pool and encircling shrubs are typical of the Gardenesque and an indication of its Regency date. Somerset Archaeological and Natural History Society

fifteenth century, was surrounded by a park as early as 1532, with deer first recorded in 1593.[48] At some point in the eighteenth century, but before 1787, when a view of the park was published, a designed landscape of mature tree clumps had been created. The park was subsequently enlarged, and in 1792 Thomas Veitch of Exeter provided estimates for landscaping; the stable block, which survives in a state of pleasing decay, was built at this time by John Trevelyan. His successor, Sir John Trevelyan, made further improvements to the estate about 1828. Nettlecombe was particularly famous for its oaks, some of which, together with veteran sweet chestnuts, still line the entrance drive. While the views out from

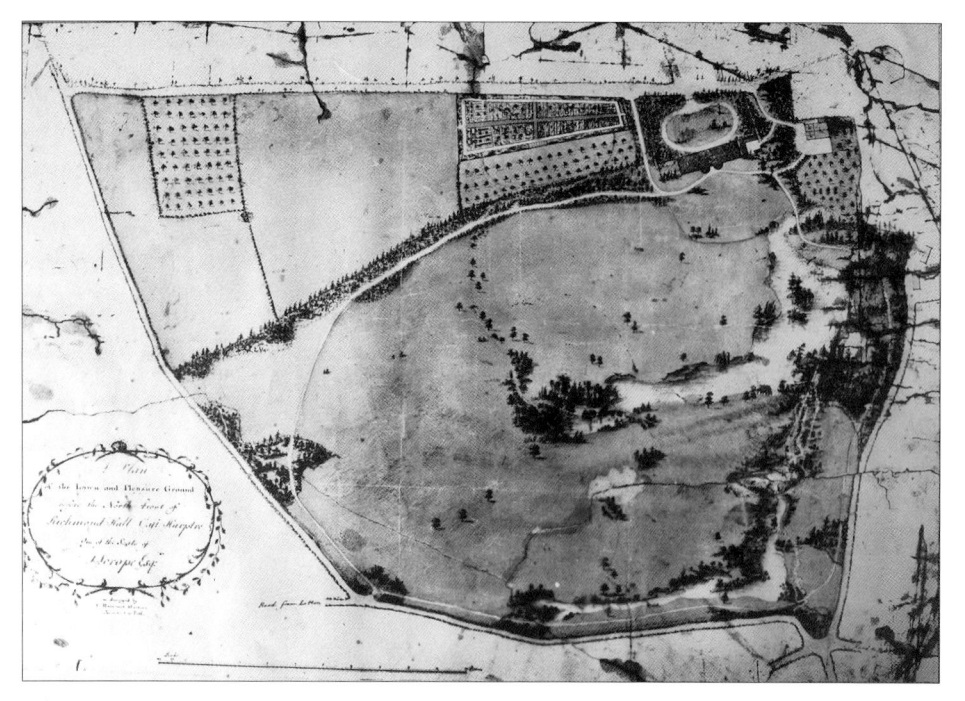

44 Charles Harcourt Masters' Reptonesque plan of his intended improvements to Richmond Hall, now Harptree Court, East Harptree. The subterranean passage and cascade survive in the grounds today. By kind permission of Charles, Linda & Mary Hill

the house to the parkland are fine, the rounded hills cloaked with woodland folding one into the other, the stream running from the house, parallel to the stable block, is the main source of interest. This was constructed in the late 1820s by Sir John Trevelyan, its stone-edged leat, enriched by a quartz cascade and quartz and millstone bridges, forming the centrepiece of a designed shrubbery of exotic trees.

With the death of Brown in 1783 and the emergence of Humphry Repton as his self-appointed successor in the late 1780s, landscape design changed perceptibly from the aesthetic aridity of Brown's large-scale agricultural landscapes to more intimate parks where garden incidents and views to and from them became the focus. This is perfectly exemplified in a plan 'of the Lawn and Pleasure Ground' (*44*), drawn up by the Bath land surveyor and landscape gardener Charles Harcourt Masters for Richmond Hall, now **Harptree Court,** at East Harptree below the Mendips; a copy of this plan is preserved at the Court.[49] It shows the footprint of the Greek Revival house with its two semicircular bays giving onto a wide

17 The Duckery at Mells Park, by an unknown artist, before its enlargement in the nineteenth century. By kind permission of Viscount Asquith

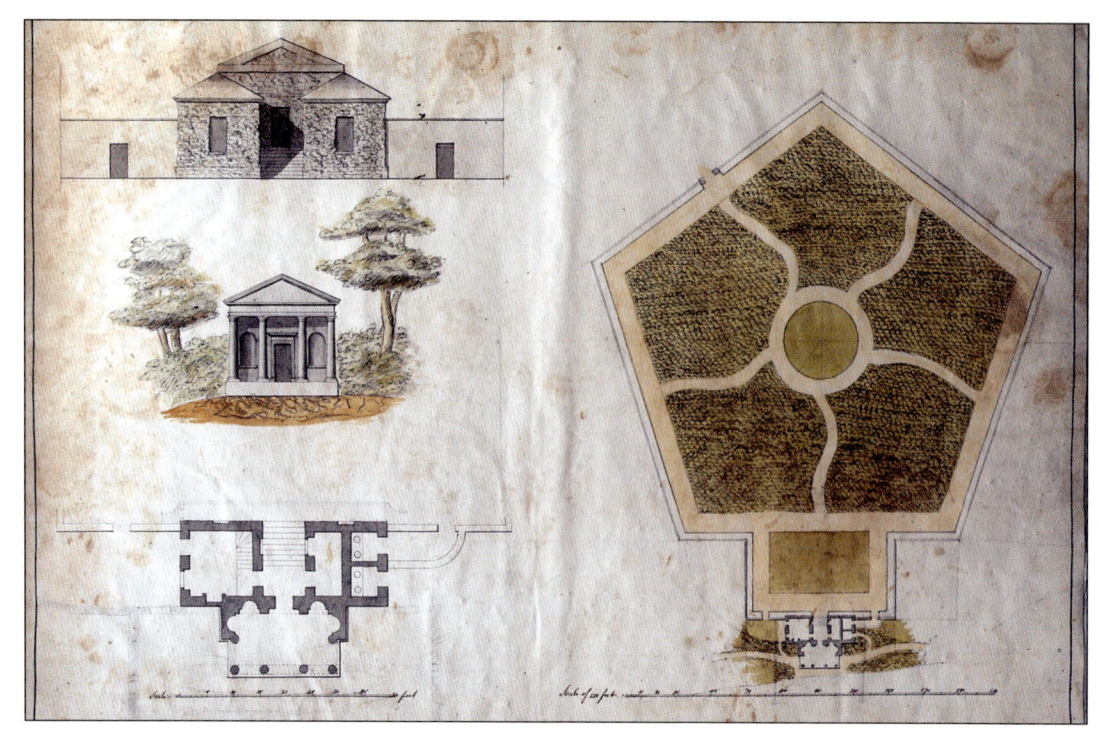

18 A design for the Temple and its pentagonal garden at Mells Park; the Temple has recently been rebuilt. By kind permission of Viscount Asquith

19 Piranesian horror in the Grotto at Barwick Park; surely the most sinister of all eighteenth-century caverns

20 A Gothick gateway and walled enclosure straight out of a Tennyson poem – the 1816 Gloucester Lodge at the Lullington entrance to Orchardleigh estate

21 This design for twin classical lodges for Orchardleigh Park by one of the Wyatts was never executed. By kind permission of Michael McGarvie

22 A minor country house, looking more like a Staffordshire china ornament, set within a miniature landscaped park – Midford Castle, near Bath

23
This extraordinarily ambitious formal layout for the grounds around Ston Easton from a 1775 map of the estate was never realised. Somerset Record Office, DD\HI\A/265

24
Humphry Repton's plan of his intended improvements at Ston Easton, from his Red Book of 1792. It shows his proposed treatment of the watercourse behind the house and a picturesque carriage drive over the valley from the Bath road. By kind permission of Mrs Kathleen Hippisley

133

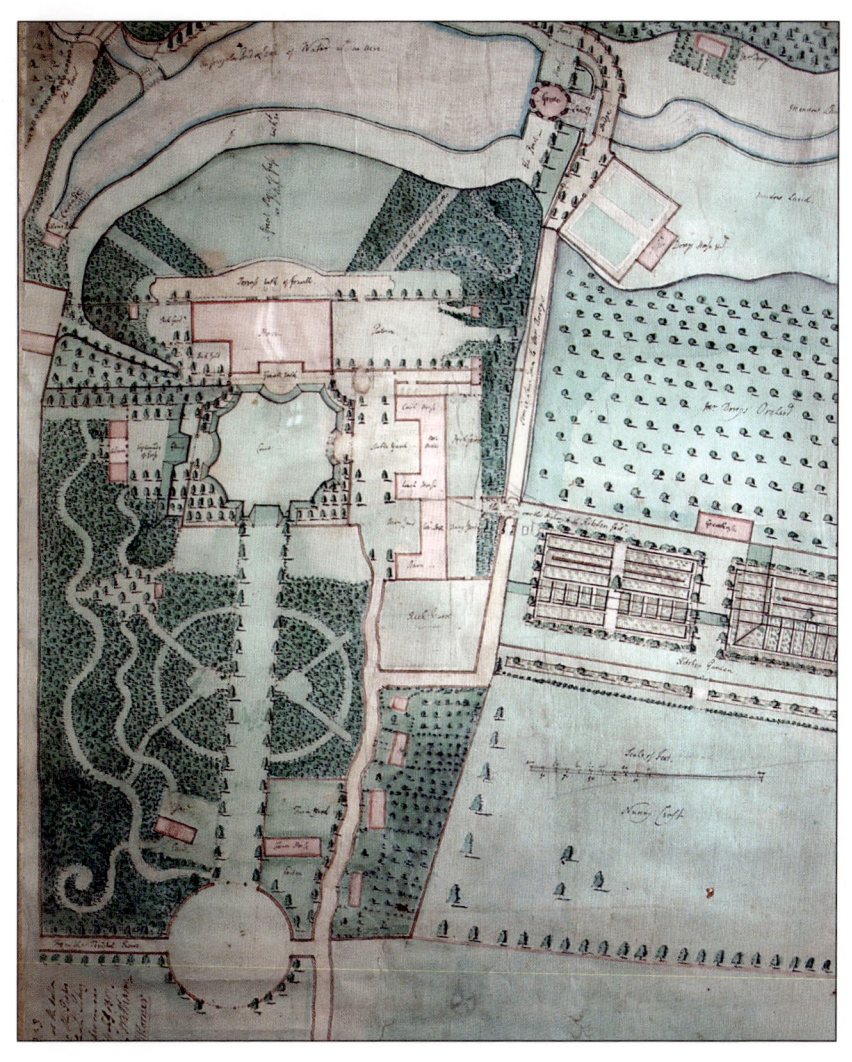

25 Capability Brown created this lake at Newton Park, near Bath, by damming the Corston Brook

26 Repton's 1814 Red Book plan for Leigh Court, near Bristol, offers few suggested improvements, but records the several viewpoints radiating out from the house.
University of Bristol, Special Collections

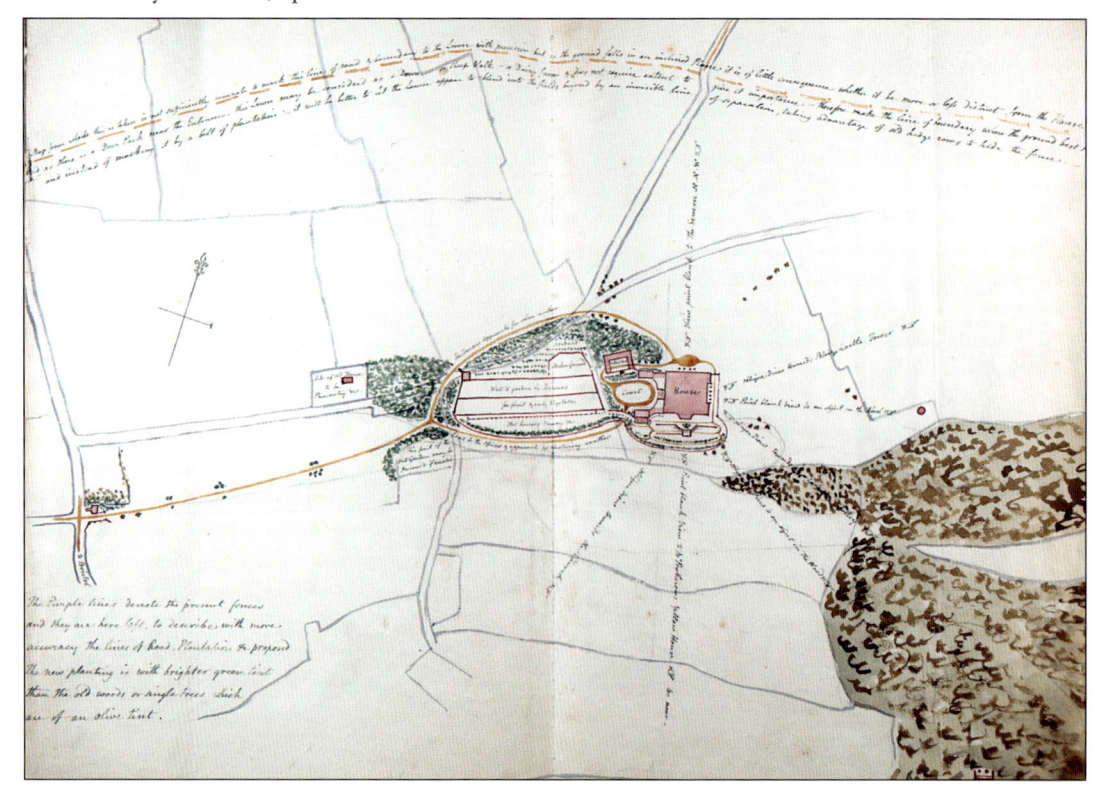

27 Repton's suggested rotunda for Leigh Court was to have been sited on a knoll in the park and framed by Cook's Folly and Blaise Castle. University of Bristol, Special Collections

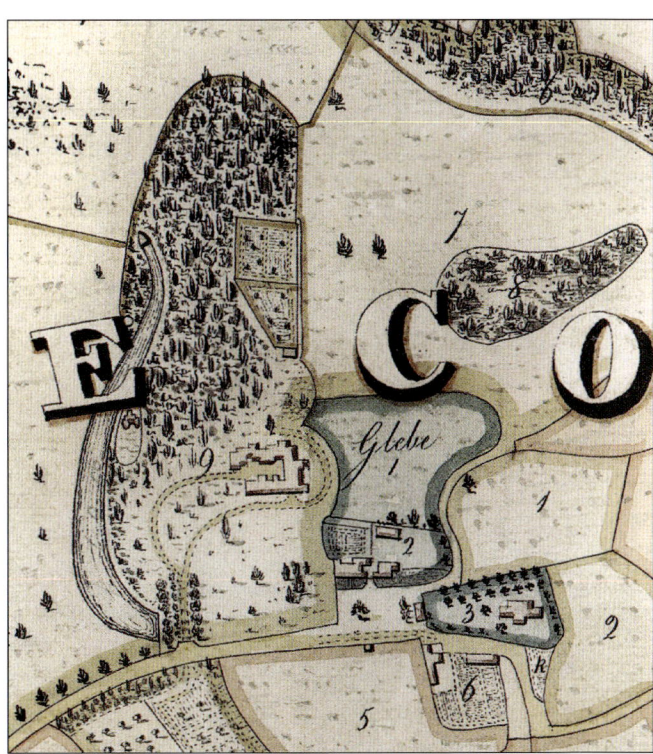

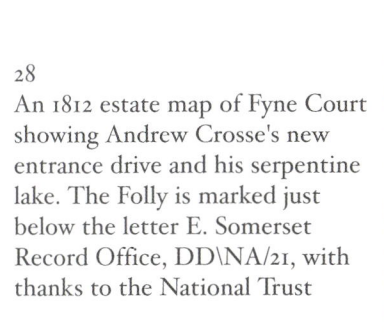

28 An 1812 estate map of Fyne Court showing Andrew Crosse's new entrance drive and his serpentine lake. The Folly is marked just below the letter E. Somerset Record Office, DD\NA/21, with thanks to the National Trust

29
The interior of Christina Balch's Grotto at St Audries is decorated with ammonites, pebbles and shells, creating the effect of an underwater sea cavern

30 James Fussell's lakeside Grotto is at the far end of the Chantry Pond on a side tributary. It includes an arcaded row of seats which commands the tunnels and the waters below

expanse of lawn leading down to a small lake. An entrance drive leads in from the Litton via two gate lodges and curves up left towards the house through a small wood and then a shelter belt, which screens the kitchen garden and orchard from the pleasure grounds. The right-hand route skirts the eastern perimeter of the estate through small woods and open glades and then turns towards the house over a bridge. Below the lake, which is wooded at its west end, is a serpentine watercourse that descends through rockworks and cascades into another finger of water parallel to the road.

Remarkably, much of what Masters proposed on the plan was carried out and recorded on a sale particulars plan of 1873.[50] By that time the estate had a greenhouse, a vinery, an orchard and peach houses in the kitchen garden area adjoining the house, while on the east return elevation of the house, in true Gardenesque style, was a wrought-iron loggia. Further out in the park, between the two lakes, were a croquet lawn and summerhouse. There were 'numerous Forest Trees' in the landscape, 'embracing nearly all the indigenous British specimens, especially some fine Elms and Horse and Sweet or Spanish Chestnuts, with some rare Foreign Trees'. Significantly, in view of what survives today, the particulars mention a 'Subterranean Passage', which was 'entered near the Waterfall' and connected with the carriage drive.[51] The ornamental bridge across the lake is balustraded, its piers decorated with paterae, and the arched passage is still visible, licked by ferns, at the lower end of the Waterfall and Cascade, which snakes down from the lake.

That hint of Gardenesque style, apparent in the Regency loggia, its piers entwined with climbing plants, is a typical Reptonian touch, seen so often in trelliswork in the 'before' and 'after' watercolour sketches in his celebrated Red Books. Due to its close proximity to Bristol, where Repton had a rich client base in the middle-class merchants of the city, Somerset has three important Repton sites and another where he offered an alternative treatment for the house, which was never carried out. These unrealised schemes are a constant in Repton's career, and his sad resignation at the lack of design achievement is palpable in the published selections from his manuscript Red Books, particularly in the 1803 *Observations* and his *Fragments* of 1816. His architectural proposals for **Ashton Court**, just outside Bristol, are a case in point. Repton had been called in by Sir Hugh Smyth to make suggestions for 'considerable additions to a very ancient mansion, without neglecting the comforts of modern life, and without mutilating its original style and character'.[52] Accordingly he produced a watercolour, dated 1802, and subsequently published it as a in *Observations* with the rueful caption: 'This was finished with the approbation of the Proprietor before I learned that the alteration here shewn will not immediately be carried into execution'.[53] His attempt to remodel the house and open up the courtyards to the park with an iron railing to admit views of the 'cheerful landscapes' beyond came to nothing.[54] Nor did he achieve that visual connection between the house and the city that he intended from a projected 'dressing-room and boudoir, lighted by a bow window ... placed at the angle in such direction as to command an interesting view of Bristol, and the river Avon, with its busy scene of shipping'.[55]

It is interesting, in view of these failures, that Repton's first Red Book commission in Somerset was for a remodelling of the grounds at **Ston Easton** where an earlier scheme, put forward in 1775, had been rejected. This was for an ambitious layout that combined both formal and informal elements and, if realised, would have been one of the most significant designed landscapes in the county. Fortunately, a beautifully drawn and coloured plan (*colour 23*) survives recording this extraordinary design, commissioned by Richard Hippisley-Coxe, who inherited in 1769.[56] By this time the neo-Palladian house that his father had begun was complete, but he determined to begin a second phase of building and to create new gardens. To finance this project Richard sold the Cricket St Thomas estate in 1775 and made Ston Easton his principal residence. The plan comprises two distinct garden elements: a formal area in front of the house either side of an axial, tree-lined drive, and a more irregular sector to the rear with a 'an irregular Pond or Lake of Water about an acre'. The formal elements include a sunken grass court by the house flanked on the west by a 'Glacis' or slope down to an 'Esplanade of Grass' leading to a columned Alcove. Further out there were to be serpentine paths set in a dense shrubbery. But the most exciting features were reserved for the valley behind the house, where the lake was to have had a bridge across a small tributary and, at the western end, a cascade and 'Bathing Room'.

The most spectacular effect was planned for the 'Pond Head' where the water was to flow through a hexagonal grotto, then out over a cascade and under a bridge before it was fed out in a serpentine channel into the wider landscape. More productive areas were to have been provided in extensive kitchen gardens and a greenhouse to the south.

It is clear from a close reading of Repton's Red Book that this ambitious layout was never achieved before Richard died in 1786 and Repton arrived in November 1792. None of the planned formality to the south of the house materialised, as by 1775 it must have seemed extremely old-fashioned, being closer in style to Bridgeman's angular designs of the 1730s. Repton was called in by Henry Hippisley-Coxe who, like his two brothers before him, had inherited an estate with severe financial problems. Sadly, Henry died soon afterwards in 1795, and his widow, Elizabeth Anne Horner of Mells, who subsequently married Sir John Cox-Hippisley, a distant cousin of her first husband, took over the financial management of the estate.[57] She must have implemented those elements of Repton's scheme, particularly in the valley below the house, that correspond with his suggestions.

Repton begins the Introduction to his Red Book with a caveat. It appears he had to spend most of his two days on the estate staking out roads, the courses of which had already been determined, so he had no time to collect 'materials to furnish a compleat outline for the whole place'.[58] This is the story of Repton's brief career: either he never had the time to do all he wanted, or owners never intended to carry out everything he proposed. The pattern of drives to the south proposed on his map (*colour 24*) was, however, carried out with two entry points from the Frome road in the south. But the most dramatic of these was a carriage drive from a new lodge on the Bath road, which would have skirted the northern contours of the valley, or 'glen' as he calls it, and crossed the 'chasm' at figure F on an arcaded viaduct with a grotto beneath (*45*). Sadly, the viaduct was never realised. Understandably, given the flatness of the approach to the south, he determined that the glen with its 'stagnant pool that fills the whole bottom of the bason' should be the 'chief source of improvement in the scenery'. To effect this and to create a 'running stream' he proposed 'to bring the stream by a subterraneous passage from

45 Humphry Repton's dramatic design for a Viaduct across the chasm at Ston Easton Park from his Red Book of 1792. As with many of his suggested architectural additions to estates, this was never carried out.
By kind permission of Mrs Kathleen Hippisley

46 At Ston Easton the pleasure grounds are separated from the Kitchen Garden by this Regency Gothick screen wall. It does not feature in Repton's Red Book, but must date from the early-nineteenth-century remodelling of the estate

the Kitchen garden, to burst out of the ground at a place where it will be most visible from the house' in a cascade. Interestingly, this was achieved, though the water now cascades under a bridge, topped by a Regency Gothick screen wall (46) separating the pleasure grounds from the Kitchen Garden, which is decorated with cruciform arrow slits. There is another stone bridge, further downstream, with a segmental arch flanked by circular openings, but this does not feature in the Red Book. Neither are two other buildings marked on the Tithe Map but having left vestigial remains: an alcove seat on the south-facing side of the valley, and a summerhouse to the north-east in Terrace Wood.[59]

The view from the north terrace of the house is exactly as Repton intended, with a beautiful stretch of running water flowing from the Kitchen Garden through the valley and out into the landscape beyond. This was achieved by draining the existing pool and removing the dam to open up the valley to the east. The planting on the northern side of the valley and around the house, particularly a majestic cedar, must be of his devising, as must the mini cascades formed by changes of level in the lakelet. This was developed from the stream by 'laying flat pieces of rock, so fitted to each other that the water in the dryest summer may always be visible, however thinly spread, and that it may not bury itself too deeply within its banks, but always glitter throughout the whole of its meandering course'.

Repton's next Somerset commission was at **Newton Park**, which is now Bath Spa University College. Whereas he found virgin territory at Ston Easton, the only encumbrances to his proposals being perceived defects in the natural scenery, the Newton Park landscape was more complex in character. The estate was owned by William Gore Langton, MP for Somerset, and had already undergone a Brownian remodelling in 1761, masterminded by the great Brown himself. Joseph Langton had commissioned Brown in conjunction with the architect Stiff Leadbetter, who was designing a new house to take the place of Newton St Loe Manor.[60] In a letter of 29 March 1761 from George Lucy of Charlecote in Warwickshire, another Brown patron, to his housekeeper, Lucy remarked: 'Mr Browne, who everyone wants, hath not yet made his appearance here, he is much wanted by a Mr Langton, who you hath heard us speak of, and will have in a short time a most magnificent place, a new house by Mr Ledbeter, Ground about it, laid out by Mr Browne'.[61] Brown's new landscape, with which Repton had to work, was achieved before Joseph Langton died in 1779, and is recorded on Benjamin Pryce's 1789 estate plan.[62] Leadbetter's house commands the valley of the Corston Brook, which has been dammed to form two lakes backed on the north side by plantations. Set amongst this wood at an oblique angle to the canted bay on the house is the Temple commanding the lakeside walk, which survives today (*colour 25*). The slope below the house is open parkland and the Castle and manor house buildings have been retained to act as picturesque eye-catchers from the west flank of the house. There are two approach drives, one from Newton St Loe village, set within one of the old formal tree avenues, and one from the main Bristol to Bath road, signalled on the perimeter by a pair of lodges.

Joseph was succeeded by his daughter Bridget, who married William Gore of Barrow Court in 1783; thereafter, Gore took the additional surname of Langton. He commissioned Repton in 1796 and the Red Book is dated May 1797.[63] His three major concerns were to connect the park with the high road, to extend the park scenery beyond its present boundary and to consider the management of the water in the valley. In short, to revisit all the elements already treated by Brown, although Repton is careful to add that 'it would appear presumptuous to suggest improvements to a spot which Mr. Brown is supposed to have finished with great attention'. Nevertheless, he has spotted 'many circumstances which would increase and heighten the interest of both the character and situation of Newton Park which will be obvious when pointed out and described'; obvious to him, of course, but not to his patron, nor to Brown. Referring to his map, he proposed to alter the present entrance with its two cottages and build instead a domed classical lodge to add consequence to the main entry point, which he asked John Nash to design for him. Next he intended to cut down most of the surviving formal avenue to open up the park and create 'natural' groups of trees. His sketch Number 3 shows the slope opposite the entrance front of the house with two woods united and enlivened with a domed temple. Neither lodge nor temple was executed.

Repton then turns his attention towards the rear of the house, where he is on shaky ground because, he admits, 'the walks round the water and towards the old tower in the garden have been finished under the direction of Mr. Brown and kept with such neatness that little is left for me to improve'. However, mindful of the current writings of the Picturesque theoreticians, Sir Uvedale Price and Richard Payne Knight, he is critical of the Brownian fashion for siting houses on bare lawns and advocates the Gardenesque touch of 'flowering shrubs under the windows as may hide part of the basement storey and spread perfume through the apartments in summer when the windows are thrown open'. He is not happy with Brown's treatment of the three pieces of water which, he feels, require 'proper management ... to produce an apparent continuity'. This could be achieved by introducing small wooded islands and a wooden bridge, and by dressing the banks with cattle. But his most dramatic improvement was to be a five-arched bridge disguised as a dam over two new areas of water. This would have opened up views of the house as carriages approached from Wells. Ordnance Survey drawings of 1808 and 1809 prove that the landscape was essentially that depicted by Pryce in his 1789 plan; the dam-bridge across the new water, like the lodge and the temple, was never achieved. 'The further improvement of the beautiful estate at Newton Park', advocated by Repton, was deemed unnecessary; it remains, therefore, a Brownian landscape of the 1760s, which is undergoing a sensitive and informed restoration by Bath Spa University.

Repton's last Somerset commission, which followed work in and around Bristol between 1795 and 1803 at Blaise Castle, Royal Fort, Oldbury Court, Dyrham Park, Brentry Hill and Cote Bank, was for the banker, Philip John Miles, who owned **Leigh Court** at Abbots Leigh. Miles had inherited a fortune from the sugar trade and was Bristol's first millionaire citizen. He demolished the old manor house by the village in 1811 and built his new Greek Revival mansion, designed by Thomas Hopper in 1814, in a more central, elevated position in the park.[64] At this late point in his career Repton had become hostile to such *nouveaux riches*, which explains the irritated tone of his Red Book.[65] Most of his suggestions were concerned with the site of the new house, in the process of building when he arrived, which had been set at a point in the landscape where the land fell away sharply to the south, giving no sense that there was a parkscape beyond. Consequently, his map (*colour 26*) is aimed at mitigating this fault by directing the owner to planned views from the house via pointing fingers: 'Oblique View towards Blaize Castle Tower'; 'Point Blank View to an object on the Knol'; 'Oblique View to an object in the Wood'; 'View point blank to the Severn N.N.W.', and so on. As these directional views make clear, Repton intended to enliven the scene east of the house with at least two buildings, a rotunda set on a hill against a backdrop of woodland and a columned portico deep in the wood, while immediately around the skirts of the house he proposed a terraced kitchen garden with flowerbeds typical of his late Gardenesque style. This last was to be in the 'more magnificent style of Italian Gardening in which Terraces & Vases & flights of Steps & Fountains' were to be 'blended with flowers & shrubs'. According to Repton 'a principal view from a Mansion requires some feature which evidently belongs to the Place & therefore with this view I should suggest a building to arrest the attention & draw it off from the less appropriate objects – This building will command most interesting views of the Avon & its rocky & wooded banks, & also will be the best Station for seeing ye Architectural East front of the House'. Repton's sketch is of a hexagonal open temple set on its grassy knoll (*colour 27*), framed by artfully placed trees under which are browsing cows. The foreground of the sketch is defined by the balustrade of a terrace around the house, dressed with flowers to add colour and interest, while in the background two Gothic towers rise up on the horizon: Cook's Folly and Blaise Castle. The view south towards the village church had potential, but there was 'a large staring yellow house, which it would be difficult to hide by any planting on the opposite bank'. Edward Protheroe, another Bristol banker, owned this 'obtrusive yellow mass of Ugliness'. Repton came up with several suggestions 'to prevent the injury of the Landscape' on this side of the Court including covering the front of Protheroe's house with slate or with green trellis. He suggested adding a bow window to the Court to provide oblique views, thereby shifting the visual focus so that Protheroe's house would not appear so obtrusively (*47*), and even proposed planting a group of three acacias on the terrace to hide 'this upstart mansion'. However, clearly

47 In his 1814 Red Book for Leigh Court, Repton was determined to hide a neighbouring house owned by Bristol banker, Edward Protheroe. A group of three acacias, seen in this watercolour, was just one solution he offered.
University of Bristol, Special Collections

exasperated, he conceded that the only expediency was 'hiding the yellow house with the finger'. There were no such hindrances on the steep slopes down to the Avon, where the 'walks in the wood on both sides the deep ravine will yield the most romantic Scenery, & these should be neither too highly dress'd nor the natural effect injured by too much interference of Art or by introducing plants unexpected in English Landscape'. A seat was hewn from the rock face overlooking this prospect, which provided a sheltered vantage point.[66]

Finally, in devising the carriage routes for the estate, Repton proposed a lodge on the Bristol road to the south-west, 'which should rather be a picturesque Cottage than any Architectural building, as more in harmony with the surrounding scenery'. He proposed raising the drive at this point on a raised terrace to provide sheds for cattle underneath. With its rustic loggia and fancy bargeboards, the lodge is in the vernacular style of Blaise Hamlet, recently completed by the Harfords, and similar to the Woodman's Cottage in Blaise woods. In the event a small lodge cottage was built, but Miles laid another more pretentious drive, entered through an imposing Ionic gateway designed by Hopper, which led several miles through Leigh Woods to the mansion. In spite of these failed proposals, the Leigh Court Red Book should be seen as an important document which charts that move from the picturesque English landscape style, as advocated by Brown, to the Gardenesque of the new century, with its flowery indulgence around the house. However, as the next chapter will reveal, Somerset industrialists had a different take on this style of formal architectural terraces, climbing plants on trelliswork, island flowerbeds, rockeries, conservatories and the rearing of exotics. They were also strangely obsessed with grottoes.

6

Science, technology, biblical exegesis and the true source of *Frankenstein*

▼

Fyne Court · St. Audries · Jordans · Ashwick Grove · Ironstone Cottage
The Chantry · Hapsford House · Pondsmead · Beckford's Ride · Oakwood ·
Ashley Combe · Banwell Caves

THE GROUNDS OF **FYNE COURT**, HIGH UP IN THE QUANTOCKS IN Broomfield parish, command virtually no outside vistas, some of the garden buildings have no clear function, and the principal feature – a serpentine Canal – is invisible, except when viewed from a walk along its dam-bank.[1] The walk leads off from the 'Folly' along the bank of the Canal to a Boathouse, and continues deep into the wooded Quantock fold above a leat, dug to feed the Canal. At a swampy area of springs and bulrushes the path bends back through an area of Savage Picturesque woodland and quarried rocks, passing two small ponds and a large Walled Garden to reach the outbuildings of the Court. The house was mostly destroyed in a fire of 1894, which has left only a service court, a Library and a Music Room. But that Music Room, built for the Arts, with its organ gallery, had also housed the Sciences and, as one of the laboratories belonging to the fifth Andrew Crosse, became the source of the wildest literary fantasy of the entire Romantic Movement. It is not, therefore, easy to isolate the gardens from the overshadowing reputation of Crosse, 'The Electrician'. His obelisk tombstone in Broomfield churchyard describes him as a man 'Humble towards God and Kind to his Fellow Creatures'; yet he was a man who, by his scientific achievements, was more challenging to the Almighty.

Crosse was born in 1784 to a line of unexpectedly intellectual squires. They traced their ancestry back to the Conquest but had been associated with Fyne Court and Broomfield only since 1634, when a Crosse bought a half share of the parish. The fourth Andrew Crosse was the fifth Andrew's great uncle. He loved music, built the Music Room, a gaunt block with long windows, and had been in control of the estate for forty years before his death in 1766. A nephew, Richard, succeeded him. He was only a life tenant by the terms of his uncle's will but he, too, controlled Fyne Court, and had opportunities to shape the grounds over a long period, until he died in 1800. Richard Crosse was a Radical in his politics. He married Susanna Porter in 1782 and the elder of their two sons was the fifth Andrew. The grounds at Fyne Court had, therefore, been under the control of a music lover from 1716 to 1766 and, from 1766 to 1800, a Radical.

Richard's influence on his elder son Andrew should not be underplayed. Richard was friendly with Joseph Priestley, author of the 1767 *History of Electricity* and the inspiration behind The London Electrical Society.[2] Andrew Crosse enjoyed a minority under his indulgent, widowed mother, Susanna, until he came of age in 1805.[3] By that time he had completed three years at Brasenose College, Oxford, and developed an interest in the electrical charges of the upper atmosphere, an interest that can be described as both obsessive and yet professionally scientific.

Until he took over, the family's landholdings had grown steadily and Fyne Court ranked alongside neighbouring Somerset houses such as Hestercombe and Halswell. The Crosses were on excellent terms with Copplestone Warre Bampfylde of Hestercombe and, especially, the Kemeys-Tyntes of Halswell, the grandest of the Quantock gentry. But the Electrician soon ended this period of prosperity and land acquisition by spending lavishly on scientific equipment that turned his wooded grounds at Fyne Cout into one complex register measuring the strength of electrical charges in the air, not just during thunderstorms but in all varying weather conditions.[4] Using a third of a mile of copper wire, threaded from poles attached to the tallest trees in the grounds, Crosse created a gathering web and connected this to a battery of fifty Leyden jars stored, apparently, in the organ loft of the Music Room. When atmospheric conditions were favourable the insurge of electrical power, literally from the heavens, was so great that the batteries would charge and discharge each time with a monstrous flash and a massive explosion of sound.

What impressed Crosse's many visitors was the easy way in which he manipulated these deadly forces with his insulated rod, directing them into his batteries and experimental jars, or out harmlessly into the earth. The 1840 *Literary Gazette* reported that Crosse's water battery consisted of three thousand pairs, which would have required a steady and reliable source of water.[5] Sir Richard Phillips writes of 'two large workshops, with furnaces, tools and implements of all descriptions' close to the main house;[6] and Crosse's wife Cornelia mentions an 'underground cellar' where experiments took place.[7] These references are the most reliable guide to the original functions of the surviving garden buildings. The battery explosions alone were enough to gain Crosse local notoriety as some kind of wizard, but in the wider world of science he was a respectable member of the London Electrical Society, working at a time when it was being suggested in scientific speculation that electricity was the primal creative force behind not only all living things, but also inanimate materials. The event that would finally seize the headlines and enrage conservative elements of society came when Crosse claimed to have produced not just mineral crystals of quartz, aragonite and malachite, but living creatures. At this point he became, inadvertently, for he was conventionally devout and no atheist, a supporter of the rationalists who were proposing that electricity was, in effect, the hand of God and the true creative spirit. This would make that airy industrial plant in the grounds of Fyne Court an integral part of wilder Romantic theorising, and Crosse himself a very real influence upon Percy Bysshe Shelley and his future wife Mary.

The unusual nature of the grounds about Fyne Court becomes apparent at the start of the entrance drive. There is no park gate lodge, only a boundary wall and Regency cast-iron gates slung upon stone piers; but catching the eye with a most effective Gothic frisson, at the far end of a straight drive cut through the woods and until recently lined with a fine beech avenue, is the Folly (48). Fyne Court itself is nowhere to be seen. It lies down to the right in a hollow, hidden by trees; so whoever planned this entry clearly intended it to focus upon the two towers rather than the Court. There can be no doubt that the Electrician was the planner. An Ordnance Survey drawing of 1802 shows the drive leading to a semi-circular area fronting the Court's east façade; this is illustrated in Nick Berry's admirable Survey Report on Fyne Court.[8] A later estate map

48 The Folly is the key to Andrew Crosse's use of the landscape at Fyne Court as a vast laboratory in which he attempted to harness electricity

(*colour 28*) of 1812 clearly illustrates the drive in roughly its present position,[9] so Crosse must have made the alteration at some expense after inheriting in 1805.

Until it swings east in two forks, this new drive runs parallel to the sinuous Canal, only a few yards distant from it on the left. Yet, because the Canal (*49*) is raised up behind the artificial bank that created it, the water is entirely out of sight, even from a carriage. Berry's careful girthing of virtually every tree in the grounds indicates that the trees along the artificial banking of the serpentine Canal date to roughly 1755-65, which is exactly what one would expect from the Rococo sinuosity of its banks. However, Robert Turner has discovered that the Canal does not feature on any estate maps until Andrew Crosse inherited in 1805.[10] With an eye on neighbouring Hestercombe, he must have constructed the leat and the lake with its two buildings, using the existing shelterbelt of trees as a shady canopy for his canalside walk.

The Folly is oddly sited, with the clumsy rear elevation of its twin towers facing the Canal walk, but there is a consciously planned water

49 The serpentine Canal at Fyne Court was dug to provide opportunities for leisurely boating and as a source of water to drive Crosse's experiments

system to the building. A rill has been constructed with a stone channel to tap the waters of the Canal and run them through both towers, then under the fireplace of the right-hand tower, emerging from the wall of the tower which faces the drive. From that point onwards its course has been lost, but, as Elaine Jamieson notes, the 1802 Ordnance Survey drawing of the estate shows 'the mansion house as an E-shaped building with a separate rectangular block to its north-west'.[11] That rectangular building occupied most of the site of the present car-park across the drive from the Folly. It has been demolished but must have been the rill's final destination: Crosse's cellar laboratory mentioned by his wife. The Folly is then a most unusual and significant garden building, part drive marker, more important to the Electrician than Fyne Court itself. For a few years the garden at Fyne Court was at the cutting edge of European physics, though Crosse was too mild and reserved a gentleman ever to project and defend his discoveries.[12]

What impact did this garden-laboratory have upon the poet Shelley and his wife Mary? Her *Frankenstein* was published in 1818, but the full title of the book is *Frankenstein; or, The Modern Prometheus*. This must have resonated strongly in the minds of the Shelleys with their half-atheistic defiance of the selfishness of Zeus and the Gods and their hero-worship of the gallant Prometheus, the true friend of men with his gift of fire. Mary Shelley's inspiration is likely to have been a lecture that Crosse delivered on 28 December 1814 at Garnerin's London lecture rooms, when he gave a vivid account of the explosive fires, which he, like Prometheus, had brought down from heaven by his copper web among the trees at Fyne Court. We have the hard reality of Mary's journal entry for Wednesday 28 December for proof that she attended Crosse's presentation: 'Shelley and Clary out all the morning. Read French Revolution in the evening. Shelley & I go to Gray's Inn to get Hogg: he is not there; go to Arundel Street; can't find him. Go to Garnerin's. Lecture on Electricity; the gasses & the Phantasmagoria, return at 1/2 past nine Shelley goes to sleep'.[13] This is not an entry pitched in the highest state of excitement, but it suggests a strong chronological link between a charismatic and stimulating Andrew Crosse and that impressionable young woman. In the course of the lecture Crosse claimed actually to have tapped and then controlled a thunderstorm. That must have seemed a case of humanity equalling or even cheating the Gods:

> When the centre of the cloud is vertical to the wire, the greatest effect consequently takes place, during which the windows rattle in their frames, and the bursts of thunder without, and noise within, every now and then accompanied with a crash of accumulated fluid in the wire, striving to get free between the balls, produce the most awful effect, which is not a little increased by the pauses occasioned by the interchange of zones. Great caution must, of course, be observed during this interval, or the consequences would be fatal.[14]

It was only a short, though brilliantly imaginative, leap on Mary Shelley's part to invent that ugly, dangerous yet tragic monster of Frankenstein's devising. She concealed Crosse's English identity, making him German, but she does, however, give one hint in her *Frankenstein* of what she owed to Crosse. Her narrator witnessed a lightning strike upon an oak tree which was 'entirely reduced to thin ribbons of wood ... On this occasion a man of great research in natural philosophy was with us, and excited by this catastrophe, he entered on the explanation of a theory which he had formed on the subject of electricity and galvanism, which was at once new and astonishing to me'.[15] So Mary Shelley's Frankenstein was inspired to undertake his destructive researches by Crosse's lecture in London on what he had discovered in his grounds at Fyne Court. Mary Shelley's subsequent book was her cynical but imaginative advance on the thunder flashes and fireballs that Crosse had produced at Fyne Court and described in his lecture. Like Crosse's electrical experiments, Mary Shelley's Modern Prometheus could be taken as a direct challenge to God. They both offered an alternative theory of creation, one that the writer and the scientist seem to have shared on that December evening in 1814.

This delight in, and obsession with, the pursuit of knowledge is characteristic of several contemporary Somerset gardens, as too is a mania for collecting plant and geological specimens. In the early years of the century this geological interest is reflected in two beautiful shell and fossil grottoes built essentially for exotic display, but at the onset of the Victorian period a more earnest and admonitory tone is struck, particularly in the Banwell Bone Caves. The grottoes are at St Audries, West Quantoxhead, and Jordans, Ashill, near Ilminster.

The approach to **St Audries** is around a hairpin bend on the A39 Taunton to Dunster road. The rebuilt St Etheldreda (Audrey) acts as a Victorian gate marker leading to a Tudor Gothic house, which was revamped at the same time as the church by John Norton for Sir Alexander Acland-Hood.[16] To the rear of the house there is a simple formal garden with a central pool of 1850 vintage which is commanded by an Orangery of Tudor-arched windows and tall pinnacles. It has the lighthearted air of the Regency rather than the mechanical Tudor vernacular of the parent house and was probably designed by Richard Carver, a Taunton architect, for Christina Balch before her death in 1824. The north-east side of the sunken garden is bordered by a stone wall with a raised shrubbery walk of yews leading to the craggy, stone-faced Grotto, which must be of the same period as the Orangery. It is mentioned in sale particulars of 1824.[17] Externally this is amorphous in shape with a recessed

50 The walls of the central room at Jordans Grotto, built in 1828, are decorated with shells and spa. The letter S, denoting the Speke family, is picked out in ammonites

seat set in the wall, Gothick windows and a Gothick-arched entrance door. Inside, the chamber is roughly elliptical and breathtakingly beautiful, its floor a swirl of patterned pebbles like a sea bed, its walls and ceiling encrusted with both British and exotic shells and ammonites (*colour 29*). It looks somewhat incongruous sited above the early Victorian parterre, but was once the focus of a more irregular, informal Gardenesque layout hinted at in the 1824 sale particulars, which describe 'A Beautiful Lawn, with Flower Garden', a 'paved Staircase, formed of Roots', leading to 'an Alcove', a 'Hermitage' and another flower garden.[18]

The Grotto at **Jordans** is more romantic in its setting, sheltering at a distance from the site of the parent house at the head of a silted-up lake, backed by dark evergreens. William Speke inherited the estate in 1791, married in 1797 and had sired seven children by his wife before she died in 1805. Thereafter his eldest son, also William, married Georgina Elizabeth Hanning from Dillington; their two sons were born at Jordans in 1825 and 1827.[19] As William senior would have been in his late fifties when the Grotto was built, it is assumed that Georgina was the driving force behind its conception, particularly as grotto-making was a favourite pastime of Georgian women. No documents survive to support or disprove this, but the date 1828 is picked out in relief on the sheep's-knucklebone flooring. Sited on its mound facing the house across the water, it must once have been the focus of a Gardenesque layout surrounded by winding shrubbery paths and dressed in front with flowerbeds and rockeries, some of which survive.[20]

On our visit the Grotto had just been vandalised and its windows were all boarded up.[21] This meant that the central room was gloomy and lacked that dappled light through stained glass which must enliven the shells on a sunny day. It is constructed of golden Ham stone and has sharply pointed Gothick windows, as well as lozenge-shaped openings higher up, and a thatched roof with a small lantern, recently restored. The Gothick porch on the main façade appears to be later, but the interior has survived relatively intact. The circular main room is dominated by a table, around the walls is a basket-weave seat, and a mirror glass flanked by the letter 'S' for Speke, picked out in ammonites, is sited centrally in a sea of shells, some English, others from the West Indies (50). The effect is dazzlingly beautiful, wonderfully exotic. As well as serving as a summerhouse, two rooms on either side were fitted up as aviaries. Their floors reveal the remains of fountains, the shell-encrusted walls are provided with nesting boxes for the song birds, iron hooks, which once held perches and swings, hang from the ceiling, and shutters close over wire mesh in the windows, under which are sliding trays for feeding the birds from outside. All the window openings, until the recent attack, were filled with early nineteenth-century painted glass, mixed together, in the antiquarian tradition of the time, with some seventeenth-century Dutch armorial glass.

Professor Robert Savage of the University of Bristol, a geologist with a particular expertise in and passion for Georgian grottoes, visited the Jordans Grotto before his death in 1988 and confirmed that all the rock and mineral specimens used were local to Somerset. His notes record that the walls are 'mostly clad in sheets of red and white gypsum from Watchet' and that the minerals are 'quartz, ferruginous quartz and other variants with one piece of Cotham marble'.[22] The West Indian shells include cowries, volutes, fungia, coral, brain corals and fan corals.

These two exquisite buildings are firmly in the eighteenth-century grotto tradition, though originally sited in Gardenesque landscapes more appropriate to the later Regency. An even more conservative landscape was laid out by John Billingsley at **Ashwick Grove**, near Oakhill, which Collinson reported 'newly built' in 1791.[23] Billingsley straddled both husbandry and manufacturing, publishing a *General View of the Agriculture of the County of Somerset* in 1797 whilst actively engaged in the family brewery. According to Collinson, his new house stood 'in a very romantic situation, in a fine fruitful vale, richly wooded with a variety of trees and shrubs on either side of the slopes which bound its extent'.[24] Sadly, the house was partially demolished in 1955, but its picturesque ruins, backed by rocky caverns in the hillside, are wonderfully atmospheric, while there are remains of the designed landscape further up the combe. These once included 'Clare's Rocks', ochre mines, a limestone grotto, quarries, a Gothic folly and a lake.[25]

The entrance to the grounds is via a footpath from the main road. The ruins of the house rear up on from its position in the valley hard against the rocks of the combe, which have been quarried out to provide caves for storage. Further along the path fragments of wall and steps lead into the valley, where the remains of a yew walk beckon. Just past this is the first Grotto: a tripartite composition of roughly hewn stone blocks with arched openings giving onto a central chamber. The path narrows, with a watercourse running alongside, and then an outcrop of limestone appears on the left with another cave quarried into it; close by is a stepped watercourse issuing from another gaping black hole and a cascade flowing from a rectangular pool, mostly silted up. It is all very reminiscent of the eighteenth-century layout at Crowcombe, yet must be Regency in date.

This innate Somerset conservatism is further reflected in an extraordinary series of even rougher grottoes, one group so large it looks like a troglodytic village, that were the particular obsession of a group of industrialists whose premises around Frome were either fed by the Mells Stream or the Fordbury Water. The Fussells,[26] manufacturers of edge-tools in the Mendip area since the eighteenth century, were the most important family, having no fewer than six flourishing ironworks in the

Mells area. One of their earliest manufactories was at Great Elm, where Maureen Lehane Wishart has made a garden around the ruins of the ironworks and its sluice gates. In the gardens of **Ironstone Cottage**, Wishart runs the annual Great Elm Festival, a Somerset equivalent of the Oxfordshire Garsington Opera Festival. At their heart is a Rose Garden with forty old roses in shades of red, pink and purple including 'Charles de Mills', 'Fantin Latour', 'Bobbie James' and 'Kiftsgate'.[27] House and garden merge seamlessly at the head of a steep-sided valley parallel to the River Mells, in which there was at least one two-storey folly. But the most impressive industrial folly complex in the area was built by James Fussell IV, who commissioned **The Chantry**, in about 1820, probably from John Pinch of Bath.[28] The house was shown on Greenwood's map of 1822, sited above the Whatley Brook, also called the Fordbury Water. Before his death in 1845, Fussell laid out a remarkable garden around the site of his Stony Lane ironworks in the valley below the house. These were powered by a lake, first built by the Fussells in 1806, which was extended by 1822; its dam was reinforced by the novelist, Anthony Powell, who came to The Chantry in 1952.

Parallel to Stony Lane on the east, a perimeter shrubbery walk lined with yews, its deep-delved stone walls licked by ferns, leads down towards the walled Kitchen Garden and the remains of the ironworks below. On the left, in thick undergrowth but visible, is the first of the grottoes: a limestone wall of craggy stonework breached by gaping holes. Inside, freestanding columns support the roofs, while passages lead in and out, their walls carved with seats. The effect is a cross between mine workings and the plastic forms of Antonio Gaudi's Art Nouveau encrustations in Barcelona, with a further hint of the druidic. But this grotto is just a foretaste of what is to come once the Chantry Pond is reached. In the distance there is another grotto brooding menacingly across the water with four craggily arched entrances, again hung with ivy. The path skirts the Pond and then suddenly veers off to the right as tall yews close in. There, completely out of sight up a small inlet set amongst winding paths and heaps of angular stones, the water flowing through them back down to the Pond, is a whole community of grotto-cells. Some of these are in underground tunnels, supported at their entrances by single menhir-like pillars; others are set into the walls of a mini-amphitheatre, lined with arcaded seats (*colour 30*), which encloses the complex. At the lake end of the inlet a rockwork bridge supports an arch, which is breached to provide a framed view back up to the grottoes through a rectangular opening.

Yet again, these grottoes are eighteenth-century in inspiration, and recall the ornamental landscapes built by Bristol merchants in the 1740s and 1760s at Goldney, Arno's Vale and Warmley.[29] However, even in Bristol there was nothing quite on this scale or of this oddity. Not surprisingly, given the close contact between these Somerset manufacturers, there are more grottoes at **Hapsford House**, just outside Mells, and also in Oakhill and Great Elm. Hapsford is an archetypal Regency *cottage ornée* with decorative bargeboards and a beautiful wrought-iron verandah, which extends across the entire length of the south front. It was built in about 1820 for George George, a Frome woollen cloth manufacturer, and later extended in the 1830s. The house is sited above a picturesque valley known as Vallis Vale and its lawns, originally enlivened with island flowerbeds in Gardenesque style, one of which survives edged with box, slope down gracefully towards the mill and its stream. The original layout (*51*) is shown clearly on sale particulars of 1874.[30] The mill leat or canal runs parallel to the Mells Stream enclosing an orchard and an open lawn between the leat and the Stream. There is a Boathouse on the canal, which survives and has been restored,[31] and at the far end of the lake, which doubles back to join the Stream at a Cascade, there is a Croquet Lawn commanded by a Grotto. This is exactly like the small grottoes at The Chantry and must surely have been built by masons employed by James Fussell. A brick-lined fireplace on the eastern wall of the southern chamber suggests that the Grotto may have been used for drying off after bathing.

The last grotto complex of this Mells hinterland is in the grounds of a nursing home at Oakhill, near Radstock. A bizarre, rock-faced Lodge, with a sweeping slate roof that must once have been thatched, guards the entrance to **Pondsmead**. Its Regency Gothic air is matched by a small Summerhouse opposite, which has also been re-roofed, but less sympathetically. Across the fields and up a slope there is a sinuous stepped Cascade falling from the dam of the first of three pools. At the far end of the pool, completely covered in undergrowth, is another dam, this time

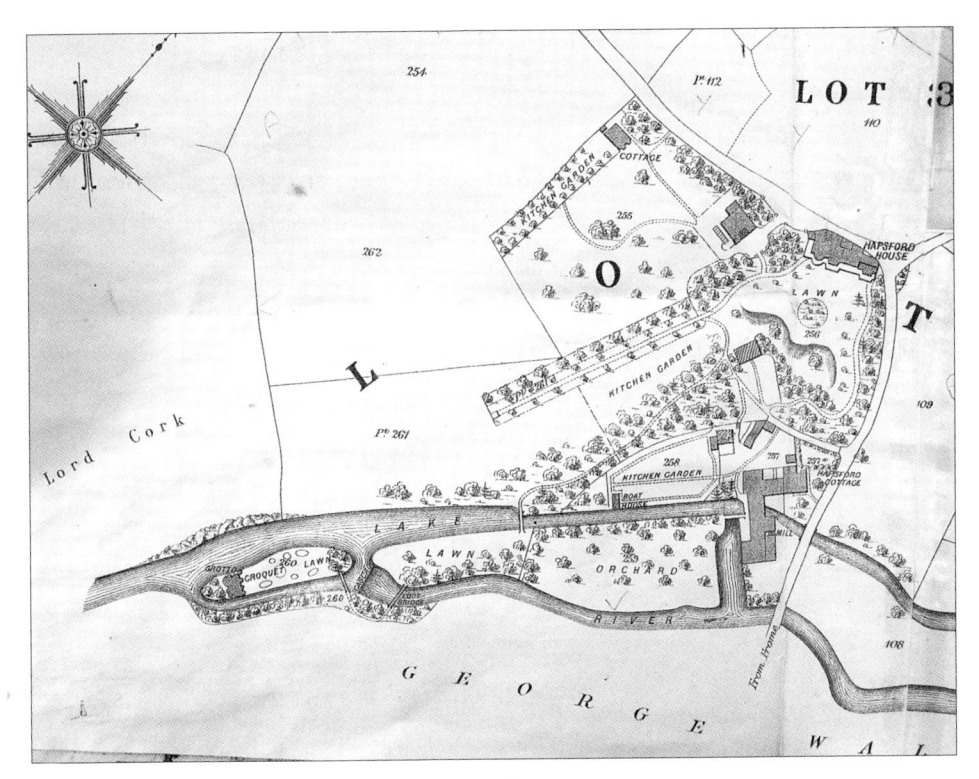

51 The original layout of George George's industrial and ornamental grounds at Hapsford House, Mells, as shown on a sale particulars map of 1874. The Grotto is sited at the end of the Croquet Lawn. By kind permission of Raj Russell

faced with rockwork screens offering wall seats (*52*), internal chambers, one room furnished with a stone table, and a stone staircase which climbs up to the level of the next pool. Needless to say, this is in the same style as the others at Hapsford and The Chantry.

The move from these deep-seated grottoes, originally surrounded by the noise and bustle of manufacturing, to the fresh airs and open fields of higher Lansdown in Bath, is a switch in culture as well as in garden design. Those Frome industrialists worked hard to amass the wealth that they then chose to enjoy in their factory gardens. William Beckford, 'England's Wealthiest Son', had no need to work and spent most of his life in sybaritic luxury, building and gardening. At just the time when George George was creating his valley paradise at Hapsford, Beckford was busy laying out a bridleway garden that stretched from his new home in Lansdown Crescent to the Tower which Henry Edmund Goodridge was to design for him as a destination belvedere. **Beckford's Ride**, as it has become known, survives fitfully within the suburban housing behind the Crescent and up Lansdown Hill.[32] The Ride began behind the Crescent with a medieval-style Gateway, originally flanked on the left by a terraced Italianate garden, and then proceeded uphill through a plantation of exotic foreign conifers, all planted around with scented herbs, via a Quarry Garden to the Dyke Garden, then into a Grotto Tunnel underneath the public lane, surfacing dramatically into the Tower Garden to reach the Tower, below which Beckford is now entombed.

The best description of the Ride, made shortly after Beckford's death in 1844, is given in John Britton's autobiography:

> In converting a large tract of comparatively sterile land to gardens, lawns, and ornamental plantations, he was intensely occupied; and in the course of three or four years, large timber trees, fertile gardens, and many sylvan beauties were brought to vigour. His old and skilful gardener, Vincent, from Fonthill, and an army of assistants and labourers, were employed for some time in these operations, whilst the idle Bathonians were constantly amused and astonished by the novelties which were perpetually brought forth. A lofty and long extent of wall was raised between the roadway and the grounds to shut out the gaze of the vulgar, but served rather to excite more intense curiosity. The lofty and commanding tower, rapidly built from the working drawings of Mr. Goodridge, an eminent architect of Bath, rose high and vauntingly above all other objects, and it still remains to perpetuate the sneering appelation which has long been annexed to tall and prominent buildings – 'Beckford's Folly'.[33]

In accord with Beckford's tastes for art and nature, the base of the Tower was planted with exotics, including *Pinus arborea*, *Osmunda regalis* and *Cistus alpina* among others, to encourage the birds, especially nightingales, linnets and thrushes.[34]

The Lansdown Tower was to set a trend in and around Bath for the Italianate style in both houses and gardens, in which Goodridge was to

52 Arched niches for rest and contemplation in the walls of the Pondsmead Grotto

play a prominent role. High up above the city on Bathwick Hill an Italianate suburb grew up in the 1820s as a direct response to Beckford's belvedere, which in turn had reflected precisely the prevailing mood of the Regency Picturesque. Jane Austen satirised this precious aesthetic approach to landscape and architecture in the figure of Henry Tilney in her posthumously published *Northanger Abbey*. The book's heroine, Catherine Morland, is subjected to Tilney's lecture on the Picturesque while they are out walking, and 'when they gained the top of Beechen Cliff, she voluntarily rejects the whole city of Bath, as unworthy to make part of a landscape'.[35] This was due to the monotonous horizontality of the Georgian terraces and crescents on Lansdown Hill opposite and the way in which they failed to connect with their surroundings. What was needed to rectify this flaw was a domestic style of building that would create organic shapes with varied rooflines, one that would respond to and integrate with its landscape setting.

Oakwood is an early example of this Italianate Picturesque style, which is essentially late Regency classicism, but enlivened by an irregular profile, loggias, French windows, shallow-pitched roofs, deeply projecting eaves, tall chimneys and, above all, belvedere towers to enliven the scene and offer views out into the landscape. Its inspiration was the architecture of the north Italian lakes, to which visitors were returning after the wars with France. Such villas display an overt awareness of topography in their conscious links between built form and landscape setting. Goodridge was the first architect to deploy this domestic style in Bath when he built his own house – Montebello – on the north side of Bathwick Hill in 1828. Later, in 1846-8, he designed Fiesole, now the Bath Youth Hostel, and a semi-detached pair of villas just below Fiesole: La Casetta and Casa Bianca, all with gardens threaded by winding shrubbery walks and stepped terraces. The writer James Henry Leigh Hunt praised Bathwick at the time as Bath's Fiesole, the hilltop village above Florence.

Oakwood pre-dates Goodridge's villas, as the first house on the site was bought in 1814 by the landscape painter Benjamin Barker and his brother-in-law, the flower painter James Hewlett.[36] It was originally called Smallcombe Villa, and between 1814 and 1817 Barker laid out the first garden there. John Britton, the antiquary and cartographer, described Barker's artistic style and his new studio-villa when composing his own autobiography in 1856. He wrote that Barker 'painted numerous small landscapes, which were very popular, and readily sold at the exhibitions of the British Institution. He saved money, purchased and possessed a very delightful villa, on the west side of Claverton Down, where his hanging gardens, trout stream, woods and paintings were calculated to command the admiration, and almost the envy, of his visitors. At this delectable retreat I spent many happy hours, in company with some of the Bath "Worthies"'.[37] Queen Charlotte visited this garden in 1817 before Barker set about rebuilding the house in about 1825, but by 1833 he was in serious debt. Selling Smallcombe Villa, he retired to Devon.

The house was then bought by Thomas Emmerson, who renamed it Smallcombe Grove and commissioned the Bath architect Edward Davis to remodel and extend the villa. The result was an asymmetrical house with a belvedere that engages so closely with the topography of the sloping site that it is more than likely Davis also re-designed the garden. The serpentine stream that threads through the valley must always have been the main focus of the garden, but more formal elements were added, including the Italianate fountain by the house and the stone bridge with its pierced balustrades lower down the garden (*colour 31*). Until the great storm of 1987 a giant cedar of Lebanon sheltered the loggia on the west front, and the terraces below the house, now decayed, were originally a series of walled kitchen gardens. In 1856 the house was sold again and renamed Oakwood. Fortunately sale particulars were prepared, and they provide the best evidence of the garden's layout with an elevation of the west façade and a plan of the grounds below it. This plan was drawn by the Bristol-based architect William Bruce Gingell (*colour 32*) and shows the cruciform fountain set within its lobed basin, the series of descending ponds linked by the stream, and serpentine walks within the woods.

The Italianate Picturesque style that flourished in Somerset between 1820 and 1850 was not confined to Bath. Bassett House, built by George Vivian in 1836 and set high above the Kennet and Avon Canal at Claverton, is a symmetrical example with deep eaves and first floor loggias providing access from the principal rooms to a balustraded promenading terrace.[38] Another example is Les Moignes at Wrington, which was built in the 1840s after designs published by Charles Parker in his 1830s *Villa Rustica*.[39] But the county's most impressive Italianate house and garden was built in 1835 at **Ashley Combe** above Porlock Weir by William King, 1st Earl Lovelace, and his wife Ada. At Ashley the several strands of this chapter – the Romantic poets, Science, pioneering technology and grottoes of the Sublime – coalesce, for Ada was the daughter of the Romantic poet Lord Byron, and she has been credited as the first computer programmer through her involvement with Charles Babbage.

Unfortunately, access to Ashley Combe was denied for this study. We got as far as Porlock Weir, opened the tollgate at the Lodge to the Combe, drove half a mile to take in the hanging woods and then doubled back. The site of the house was high up to the right as we ascended but completely hidden in the trees. As a result, the 1888 Ordnance Survey will have to suffice to explain the site and the original layout of the grounds around the house (*53*). Early photographs show an irregular house, which had grown organically, in true Picturesque fashion, from the 1799 original to the 1835 Italian villa with its round-arched windows, pyramidal roofs and towered belvedere.[40] It was set high on a promontory with terraces

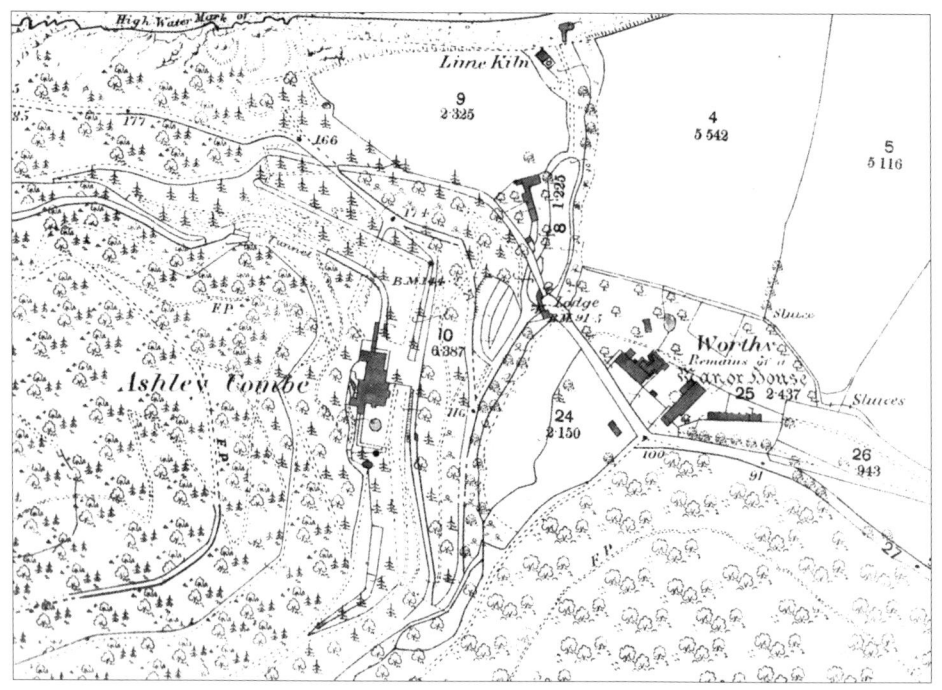

53 Ashley Combe is intensely private and access was denied for this book. This detail from the 1888 Ordnance Survey map shows the complex Italianate terraces constructed by Earl Lovelace. Somerset Archaeological and Natural History Society

to the east and north, the latter with a tunnel beneath it, while woodland walks snaked through the plantation to the west.

The landscape created by the Earl, before he married Ada Byron and converted his summer retreat into a more imposing dwelling, was described in some detail by James Savage in 1830. In view of the present inaccessibility of the site, this is worth quoting at length:

> The road to Lord King's cottage, Ashley Lodge, creeps through the woods which clothe the steep cliffs to the eastward of Culbone, and presents at every step, a variety of curious plants, the rare production of these romantic regions; *silene amoena, veronica Montana, polypodium aculeatum, poloypodium dryopteris*, bird's nest orchid, yellow rein-deer moss &c. &c. and an immense quantity of whortleberry plants, full of their cool, refreshing, delicious fruit. His lordship's house is placed, like an eagle's nest, in the cleft of a rock. The rough slope that forms the western extremity of Porlock Bay,

is the spot chosen for this singular mansion. Half way up this steep, a level platform has been made with great labour and proportionate expense, about a quarter of an acre perhaps in extent, and a small, castellated dwelling erected upon it. The thick woods which cover the face of this abrupt descent, are here cleared away, and a beautiful view opened of Porlock Bay, the town and the Bristol Channel. This indeed is the only charm which it possesses. The road to it is difficult and hazardous; the precipice rising four or five hundred feet behind it, threatens, the first severe frost, to overwhelm it with destruction; and the abrupt descent before and on each side of it, matted by impenetrable woods, confines the inhabitant to a small area of about twenty yards square.[41]

King had built the house in Gothic style and, given that there was little scope on the site to develop formal gardens around it, concentrated on planting up the woodland in the Combe. His Estate Memoranda Book gives a clear record of what he achieved between 1799, when the house was constructed for £1,300, and 1841 when the account ends.[42] In the early years of the century he was planting arbutus, cypresses, laurustinus and bays around the house, with '6 Bermuda cedars', '12 pinetus' and more cypresses near the terrace in 1804. January 1806 saw the planting of Luccombe oaks in the garden and further oaks in the plantation given by Lady Fortescue. After a lull, *'Picius lanceolata araucaria'* was planted near the open dining room in October 1826, followed by '3 Irish yews' and 'hemlock spruce' near the house in 1834, and more cypresses in the wood above the house in January 1835. But the major flurry of activity, understandably, followed his marriage, when cedars of Lebanon, deodar cedars, and monkey puzzles were planted around the house to give it that favoured proto-Victorian gloom, while the garden was turfed and more pines and larches were introduced to the woods in the Combe to take the place of old coppices to be cut. Work continued well into 1837 with a foot-bridge over the stream, a pond for the upper part of the meadow to collect water for the house and the beginnings of the 'great wood' higher up; the stables and coach house were rebuilt in 1839.

Ada was nineteen when she married William King and, like her mother

Augusta, was fascinated by mathematics. Augusta had studied under William Frend, who taught her astronomy, algebra, Latin and geometry, while Augustus de Morgan, first Professor of Mathematics at University College, London tutored Ada.[43] De Morgan wrote retrospectively about her intellectual gifts in 1834, a year before her marriage, claiming that her studies had been 'carried farther than her mother's had been'.[44] He also described her first encounter with Charles Babbage's engine:

> I well remember accompanying her to see Mr Babbage's wonderful analytical engine. While other visitors gazed at the working of the beautiful instrument with the sort of expression, and I dare say the sort of feeling, that some savages are said to have shown on first seeing a looking-glass or hearing a gun – if indeed, they had as strong an idea of its marvelousness – Miss Byron, young as she was, understood its working, and saw the great beauty of invention.

Lady Lovelace, as she became known after her husband's elevation to the earldom, continued her studies after the marriage and formed a close friendship with Babbage, out of which grew her one published mathematical work, an annotated translation of Menabrae's *Sketch of the Analytical Engine Invented by Charles Babbage Esq*. This shows her 'to have fully understood the principles of a programmed computer a century before its time'.[45] Babbage is known to have been a frequent visitor to Ashley Combe, and it is recorded that Ada discussed with him the use to which his machine could be put.[46] Apparently, in 1979 the US Department of Defence named an early, secret, software programme 'ADA' in her honour.[47]

Lacking first-hand knowledge of the grounds, this analysis must rely on local websites, but it is clear that much of the terracing and tunnels, which the Earl and his Countess created, still survive on site, albeit lost to the undergrowth after years of neglect. One early photograph shows a series of three terraces by the house, their walls enriched with round-headed arcades, while another includes images of the tunnel entrances.[48] In October 1863 the popular journal, *The Leisure Hour*, sent a reporter to Porlock who saw, 'gleaming in the wood … the turrets of Ashley Combe, the seat of the Earl of Lovelace. It is a place well worth visiting, and permission may be got from the owner's agent at Minehead. There is a fine entrance, and there is a tunnel cut through the steep hill. The absolute seclusion of the place is a great charm'.[49] We were not so lucky, but we can confirm the beautiful seclusion of a site of real importance in the history of information technology.

One last site in this early nineteenth-century overview, which also has a claim to national significance in the intellectual development of this country, is set on a high ridge of the western Mendips, where the M5 motorway slices through a cutting. Clinging to the northern side of the hill slope is an ornamental cottage, while further up, the pyramidal crown of a tall viewing tower is just visible above the trees. This is Banwell Hill, beneath which are the celebrated **Banwell Bone Caves**, first discovered by miners digging for minerals in 1757, but not re-opened until 1824. Their rediscovery caused a sensation amongst geologists and attracted the attention of George Henry Law, Bishop of Bath and Wells, who was lord of the manor. John Rutter takes up the story in his 1829 *Delineations of Somerset*:

> When the discoveries of Professor Buckland opened a new era for research, a respectable farmer named Beard, who lives at Wint Hill, a village below the south side of the high ridge, remembered hearing of this cavern when a child, and happening to meet with John Webb the miner, who now lives at the Bishop's cottage, was directed to the supposed entrance, which Webb and another miner, named Colman, commenced clearing out. After re-sinking the shaft to the depth of about 100 feet, they came to the entrance, or first landing place of the cave, where they found two pieces of candles, evidently left there by the original discoverers, encrusted with a slight coating of carbonate of lime, giving them the appearance of stalactites. The cave thus re-discovered is the one distinguished as the Stalactite Cave; and from its description by the modern discoverers, attracted the attention of Dr. Randolph, the vicar of Banwell; who, conjointly with the Bishop of Bath and Wells, resolved to improve the access to it, for the convenience of visitors from Weston and other adjacent parts, whose donations on viewing it, might increase the funds of a charity school, just then opened at Banwell.[50]

Thereafter, during further excavations to find an easier entrance, a second cave – now known as the Bone Cave – was found, the floor covered with a mixture of prehistoric animals bones including those of the wolf, bison, bear, otter, wolverine, Arctic hare, vole, Arctic and red fox and reindeer. They date from the Pleistocene Period just before the beginning of the last Ice Age; the bones would have been washed into the cave by water from rivers or melting ice. In the summer of 1827 the Bishop built the ornamental cottage as a summer retreat and enlarged it in 1833 to accommodate the numerous visitors to the caves. Rutter continues:

> He enclosed the ground, and laid it out with ornamental shrubs and plantations. His lordship has evinced great interest in the discovery and has fitted up a handsome drawing and dining room in the cottage; which also contains apartments for John Webb, who has the charge of the caverns under Mr. Beard, and who assisted as a minor, in their discovery.
>
> The situation of this cottage is pleasant and commanding, the drawing room windows over-looking the extensive valley at the foot of the hill, bounded by the Severn.[51]

Unlike the Shelleys, who were atheists and more inclined to invoke natural forces to explain creation, Bishop Law was a typical Anglican clergyman of that pre-Darwinian age which accepted without question the word of the Bible. Consequently he saw the caves as a perfect opportunity, through the new science of geology, to proselytise the truth of the biblical account of the Great Deluge by opening them to the public and displaying inscribed tablets to inform believers and admonish non-believers. When the Bone Cave was opened on 28 April 1825 he erected a board at the entrance with the following inscription:

> Here let the scoffer of God's holy word
> Behold the traces of a deluged world,
> Here let him learn in Banwell Cave t'adore
> The Lord of Heaven, then go and scoff no more.[52]

A similar plaque, now gone, was set at the entrance to the Stalactite Cave:

> O thou, who trembling, viewst this cavern's gloom,
> Pause and reflect upon thy eternal doom,
> Think what the punishment of sin will be
> In the abyss of endless misery.[53]

The entrance to the complex is through a segmental-headed arch of knobbly stones, behind which is the original Bishop's cottage, now even further extended. Its original size and proportions are shown in an engraving (*54*) accompanying Rutter's account. It was a highly decorative cottage ornée with a thatched roof and a loggia of gnarled tree trunks which offered spectacular views, then as now, towards Weston-super-Mare and Brean Down, with the Holms out to sea in the distance. Its garden was enlivened with island beds of shrubs and dwarf conifers; winding paths cut into the hillside led to the caves. In the background, the Gothick-arched Summerhouse, which has recently undergone a sensitive restoration, was sited to give even higher views. On the terrace below the house there is another inscribed stone tablet by the walk down to the caves, which prepares the visitor for the experiences to come. This was originally sited near the Summerhouse at the top of the garden:

> Reader, descending
> From this awful brow,
> Survey the wonders
> In the caves below,
> Thence mid these relics
> Of a deluged world,
> Look up from Nature
> Unto Nature's God.

This insistent use of improving poetry is reminiscent of James Mellor's slightly later 'Garden of Correspondence relating to this world and Scriptual History' at Rainow in Cheshire, where John Bunyan's *Pilgrim's Progress* is re-enacted. Both Mellor, who was a Swedenborgian, and Bishop Law

54 Bishop Law's holiday retreat at Banwell, from John Rutter's 1829 *Delineations of Somerset*, before it was enlarged in 1833 to accommodate visitors to the Bone Caves in the hillside. University of Bristol, Special Collections

55 William Beard acted as guide to the Caves and made his own bone collection in a house further along the ridge. Rutter depicts him displaying some of the animal remains that were used for religious propaganda. University of Bristol, Special Collections

were attempting to create layouts that would offer the visitor both a temporal and a spiritual journey.

The path leads down to the first of the follies: the Druid's Temple (*colour 33*), a screen wall of arched recesses and niches faced with more knobbly stones. It was built in 1834 to remind visitors of the pagan world destroyed in the Flood and has another appropriate inscribed tablet. Next to this is the Archway leading to the Bone Cave. On our visit candlelight cast the bone stacks into a ghostly relief as if we had stumbled into a TV adaptation of a short story by M R James. This animal charnel house was created by the bright-eyed William Beard (55), whom Rutter depicts presenting to the reader a vertebra and the bones of a claw. It was by his 'unremitting attention', that 'the bones were secured as they came into view, and preserved for future examination'.[54] Beard, 'in his capacity of Cicerone', was charged with taking visitors on a tour of the caves and explaining to them 'the scientific and interesting characteristics of the scenes of which he was in some measure, the discoverer'.[55] The Stalactite Cave, the entrance to which is higher up the hillside, is inaccessible today, but Rutter describes it in detail, particularly the 'Bishop's Chair', commemorating Bishop Law. 'This natural chair has considerable resemblance to the ancient stone crowning chair in Winchester cathedral. It appears to be a mass of rock separated from a corresponding portion in the roof immediately above it, which is ornamented in a similar manner, with stalactite incrustations'.[56]

At other points in the geological circuit visitors came across the Osteocion, or museum of bones, which was built in 1837 and is now under restoration, an Alcove Seat and the lofty Pebble Summerhouse. Then the path takes the contour of the ridge and leads, via the ruins of the Gazebo, which faced Banwell Moor, giving a view of Clevedon and the Bristol Channel, to the Banwell Tower, built on the site of an Obelisk. Bishop Law constructed the Tower in 1840 as a belvedere and a memorial; it is encircled by Druidic standing stones that once ringed the Obelisk. One last inscription, which might profitably have been placed here, but which was originally in one of the caves, sums up the Bishop's religious purpose in this extraordinary garden: 'Pause on this Eminence, for not the sea that stretches in its amplitude below, tho' it proclaim the majesty and might of the Creator, so distinct speakes the visible dominion and the power and might of that Creator as this cave strew'd with the debris of a world destroyed'. In another twenty years Darwin would challenge this accepted biblical view in his heretical *Origin of Species*.

7

Garish bedding, terraces and a confusion of style – the Victorians

▼

Cricket House · Nynehead Court · Parish's House · Camerton Court
Brockley Hall · Claverton Manor · Tyntesfield · Maperton House
Cranmore Hall · Clevedon Court · Hestercombe · Brympton d'Evercy
Orchardleigh · Lydeard House · Crowe Hall · Inwood House

APART FROM TYNTESFIELD, THE GIBBS' GREAT GOTHIC REVIVAL HOUSE AT Wraxall near Bristol, and Orchardleigh, near Frome, Somerset is not rich in either Victorian country houses or High Victorian garden layouts. Consequently the Italianate style of balustraded terraces, so prevalent in the early century on the hilly slopes of Bath, continued being deployed in the county well into the 1850s. This is apparent at Widcombe Manor, which was given new terracing around the garden front of the house, and, more emphatically, in the Italian Garden below Claverton Manor of the 1840s and 1850s, to which we shall return. These indiscriminately styled formal elements phased quite naturally, by their changes in level, into the shrubbery walks that characterise the pleasure grounds of this early Victorian period. The terraces also offered scope for parterres, while the lawns might be enlivened by island flowerbeds. A typical example of this somewhat fussy treatment is recorded in a watercolour of **Cricket House**, Cricket St Thomas (*colour 34*). Two conservatories front a wide terrace with balustrades and urns, while the lawn beyond is studded with serpentine beds. Interestingly, later sale particulars of 1895 describe the principal front of the house as opening 'into charming Conservatories and Italian colonnades, overlooking beautiful gardens and terrace walks'.[1] The house has retained its colonnades, but the conservatories have been returned to domestic use; below the west terrace, which has a circular pool and flowerbeds, there is a sunken garden, now used by the hotel as a croquet lawn, commanded by a detached Orangery.

The most stylistically inventive parterre of this period is at **Nynehead Court**, near Wellington.[2] Its precise date is uncertain, though it seems to be associated with the construction in 1844 of the Great Western Railway line, parallel to the old Grand Western Canal out in the wider parkland to the south. The parterre appears to have been laid out under the south façade of the house at the same time, when the south drive, which originally passed through the pleasure grounds, was re-routed. The approach to the garden from the east entrance courtyard is wonderfully picturesque, sweeping through a yew tunnel by the parish church. The parterre has a central circular bed from which radiate further box-edged beds divided by grass paths (*colour 35*). So much, so typical of parterres designed at this time, particularly by such exponents as William Andrews Nesfield, whose name has been associated with the feature at Nynehead. But here the outer edges of the parterre are defined by swirling guilloche patterns, giving it an almost sculptural quality. The ingenious elaboration is perfectly complemented by open lawns that spread out beyond the formalities, dramatised by an avenue of majestic sweet chestnuts and studded by other mature trees including a Lucombe oak. To the east, behind a brick-walled enclosure, are the spindly evergreen shapes of the pinetum, providing another visual counterpoint to the intricacies of the patterns.

This combination of formality around the house easing into less manicured nature in shrubberies further out, advocated by Humphry Repton in countless Red Books prepared before his death in 1818, is exemplified in two Somerset houses with Reptonian connections: **Parish's House** at Timsbury and nearby **Camerton Court**. The Parishes at Timsbury were close friends of the Jarretts at Camerton; both men had been captains in the Royal Navy, both had interests in the Somerset Coal Canal Company and the Conygre Colliery and both planted extensively around their estates. While Parish's House was almost certainly designed by Thomas Baldwin of Bath in about 1816, George Stanley Repton built Camerton Court for John Jarrett in 1835.[3] Each house had formal terraces around its skirts, while the grounds beyond were laid out in shrubberies with winding walks and planted with specimen trees. A glimpse of the social round of this close-knit community of like-minded retirees is given in the

Revd John Skinner's diaries:

> We drove to Timsbury to dine with the Parishes and met a large party: we had music after Tea ... Mr. and Mrs. Hammond, Captain and Mrs Parish, Mr. and Lady Elizabeth Repton, Mrs. Brooks, Mr. and Mrs Jarrett ... formed our dinner party...Poor Anna was destined to feel many mortifications, for the pastry and good things she had prepared were burnt by the inattention of the cook ... After all this, however, we found our Company very pleasant and disposed themselves to be pleased with our efforts ... The evening was spent looking over the coal fossils, and Shakespeare prints by Boydell. Lady Elizabeth Repton seems to inherit her father's strong sense, if one may judge from casual remarks. Mr. Repton, her husband, is a pleasing, gentlemanly man.[4]

It is reasonable to assume, therefore, that G S Repton had an influence on the garden layouts at both Camerton and Parish's House. Although primarily an architect, working in John Nash's office during his father's lifetime, G S was involved in Repton's work as a landscape gardener from an early age.

One of the most important Picturesque gardens in the county, combining shrubberies leading to a wider landscape treatment which took advantage of topography to create consciously planned views, was laid out after 1824 by John Hugh Smyth-Pigott and his wife Ann at **Brockley Hall**, near Bristol.[5] The house has been converted into flats and its grounds have been turned into an affluent residential estate, so it is difficult to envisage how it must have looked in its prime. Fortunately we have a valuable description of Brockley, published in 1829 by John Rutter, which gives a good account of both the pleasure grounds and the surrounding landscape. After itemising the family's collection of paintings, which included two landscapes by Poussin, as well as works by Claude, Titian and Salvator Rosa, Rutter moves to the exterior: 'Brockley Hall is surrounded by shrubberies and pleasure grounds, extending a considerable distance ...The park as well as the rest of the grounds is luxuriantly wooded, not a tree has been allowed to be cut for several generations; amongst these trees is a noble cypress, which in size and beauty, equals, if not surpasses, those of the luxuriant climate of Italy'.[6] He then describes the carriage drive that extended more than three miles:

It commences at the bottom of the glen, through which it pursues its way, turning to the right, to the high ground above, which has been extensively planted. It continues its winding course along the very edge of the cliffs, on a level with the tops of the trees, which grow on its precipitous sides, through which are caught some fine views of the opposite rocks,

56 These twin sphinxes guarding a subterranean passage at Brockley Hall are the only survivors of the statuary-crowded pleasure grounds laid out after 1824 by John Hugh Smyth-Piggott

rearing their naked heads above the surrounding foliage.[7]

Smyth-Pigott, influenced possibly by his old master paintings, intended to enrich this savage scene with a copy of the Temple of Vesta at Tivoli. A model for this had been brought from Italy by 'a Mr. T. Shew of Bath, under whose direction' it was to be built.[8] Sadly, the classical rotunda was never achieved, but the carriage drive still offered a panoramic view of the surrounding country 'including Brean Down, Worle Hill, Cleeve Toot, Cadbury Hill, Yatton and its church and the coast of Clevedon, crowned by the ruins of Walton Castle, beyond which are the waters of the Bristol Channel'.[9]

Close to the house there is a subterranean tunnel under Brockley Lane guarded by two stone sphinxes (*56*) with a tablet inscribed in Latin over its dark entrance. The verse translated reads: 'Whoever enters here, what seems horrid to you is pleasant to me. If you like it, stay, if it bores you, go away; both are equally pleasing to me'; there is an identical inscription at the Villa Farnesina in Rome.[10] The tunnel leads to the Walled Garden, now in decay, but originally 'containing from two to three acres of ground, divided by a cross wall into three portions, the centre one being intended for the erection of spacious conservatories'.[11] Smyth-Pigott filled the Walled Garden with sculpture and statuary including lead cupids, stone Greek vases, pineapple finials, a copy of Bernini's Neptune for the central pond, and a statue of The Three Graces.[12] More statues were sited in the pleasure grounds around the house. There was a copy of the Bristol High Cross, as well as busts of Shakespeare, Voltaire and, most appropriately for a garden, Francis Bacon.[13] Most of the statues were sold off in the 1950s, apart from the sphinxes and a strange odalisque sculpture in the tunnel.

While Smyth-Pigott was influenced by the picturesque qualities of Brockley Combe and by his collection of artworks, the contemporary garden at **Claverton Manor**, overlooking the Limpley Stoke valley outside Bath, was the result of foreign travel and response to the current fashion for things Italian. The original manor house by the parish church, which Ralph Allen had bought from the Skrines in 1758, was demolished after its subsequent purchase by John Vivian in 1816. Thereafter, Jeffry Wyatville was called in to design the new mansion, now the American Museum, on a site higher up the hill. The grounds around the new house were substantially remodelled after Dallas Pratt founded the American Museum in 1961 when two new gardens were made: the George Washington Garden with its box-edged rose beds, and the Mount Vernon Garden with an octagonal pavilion based on Washington's school house.[14] But these were laid out within the structure of the earlier garden, which is terraced in the fashionable Italianate style of the 1830s with balustraded walls topped by urns, steps and yew topiary, now much overgrown. Early photographs published in the *Gardeners' Chronicle* show it to have been sharp-edged in its lines, with a statue of Hermes on the lower terrace.[15] The terraces must have been laid out by George Vivian, John's second son, who inherited in

1828. George was an amateur artist and inveterate traveller – he returned from a Balkan tour in 1818 and went on another during which he met Byron not long before the poet's death at Missolonghi in 1824 – before malaria forced him to give up travelling and painting.[16]

Although George spent most of his enforced retirement in London, he must have exercised a guiding hand in the development of the garden. The small Grotto above the garden might be eighteenth-century in style, but the terracing below is Italianate. In this he was probably advised by the architect and landscape designer Alexander Roos, who was working with Charles Barry on the imperious Italianate garden at Shrubland Park in Suffolk.[17] Helene Gammack has discovered a connection between Roos and George Vivian in letters written between 1843 and 1850, now held in the Scottish Record Office.[18] There is also a drawing by Roos in the Shrubland archives which is for a gate pier 'at Mr Vivian's Lodge, Claverton, 1839'.[19] This suggests that the towered Keeper's or Alpine Lodge at Claverton might be by Roos rather than Wyatville.

The letters also contain references to Roos' contemporary work at **Tyntesfield**, where he designed a small terrace on the west front of the house. Unlike the Italianate terraces at Claverton, which accorded well with the severe neo-Classicism of the Manor, those at Tyntesfield look decidedly incongruous, despite the pierced quatrefoils in the retaining walls, below the turrets and pinnacles of the south elevation of John Norton's Gothic house. William and Blanche Gibbs were responsible for the present layout, which has not been significantly altered since the 1850s. The top and lower terraces, the Broad Walk, the lake and Paradise – an arboretum of specimen trees at the end of the Broad Walk – were all created in the 1850s with plants supplied from James Veitch, the Exeter nurseryman, and advice from Roos.[20] In addition to the terraces around the house, there was a huge Conservatory on the west façade; its onion-shaped dome was based on the dome of St Mark's, Venice, and it extended as far as the now dilapidated Aviary.[21] The great Conservatory replaced an earlier Gothic conservatory attached to Tyntes Place, the previous house on the site.[22] Further out to the west, there is a sunken Rose Garden (*colour 36*) with twin vernacular-style Summerhouses, designed by Norton. All these features lack any sense of stylistic coherence, and it is the carefully contrived planting in the wider landscape, offering framed views up Bendle Combe and out towards Blagdon and the Mendip ridge, that are the real excitements of Tyntesfield; those and the Walled Garden, designed by Walter Cave in 1896, which will feature in a later chapter.

The Tyntesfield Conservatory was demolished in 1917; fortunately the Conservatory at **Maperton House**, in the far south-east of the county near Wincanton, survives, though in need of restoration.[23] While this scimitar-shaped Ionic glasshouse, which projects from the side elevation of the main house, is mid-century in date, Maperton House was rebuilt in a severe Greek Revival style in about 1805, its garden façade originally softened by a canopied, wrought iron porch, shown in photographs taken in 1970.[24] The Conservatory has a canted glass roof supported on elaborately carved brackets. It terminates, like a basilica, in an apse decorated with shell-headed niches that encloses a circular pool (*colour 37*). The interior is decidedly Italian in feel, whereas the exterior is in a severe Ionic classicism that accords well with the earlier house. A more stylistically appropriate approach was taken in 1869 at the Tudor Gothic **Cranmore Hall**, near Shepton Mallet, where John Moore Paget added a Jacobethan Conservatory connected to the main house by a round-arched Arcade, which overlooked a formal garden of flowerbeds punctuated with stone urns.[25] It is known that Edward Kemp advised on the planting in the wider landscape, which included cedars, pines, beech, and a 'rookery of lofty elms and limes', so he may also have designed the formal areas.[26] Cranmore is now All Hallows School and the Conservatory, which has been subdivided, serves as a study area. The main room seems to have had a section at the back for the display of plants and a sitting area at the front overlooking the south garden. The Summerhouse on the outer terrace has swept ridges to its pyramidal roof and is likely to be Edwardian in date.

Elsewhere in the county this record of Victorian improvements continued with typically garish bedding schemes, either set within ill-conceived architectural frames, or simply imposed on existing terrain with little feeling for the overall visual impact. At **Clevedon Court** a great fan-shaped formal garden was laid out in 1857 in the semicircular lawn to the rear of the house, with bedding plants punctuated by yews; there were more beds and single bushes further up the slope.[27] The square beds along the Pretty Terrace below the retaining wall were remodelled in the 1880s by Dame Agnes Elton; understandably, Gertrude Jekyll condemned this as 'quite indefensible. The foot of one of the most noblest ranges of terrace walls in England is too good to be given over to the most commonplace forms of bedding'.[28] Mercifully, all these beds were swept away in the 1960s. Viscount Portman laid out another such bedding garden on the top terrace of his new house at **Hestercombe** in 1872, which survives, though restored. At least this has the focal point of a fountain to distract the eye from the brightly insistent ranks of salvias, perlagoniums and verbena.

Lady Georgiana Fane, daughter of the 10th Earl of Westmorland, was more circumspect in her interventions at **Brympton d'Evercy** when she took over in 1857. She confined herself to raising a terrace on the south front of the house (*colour 38*), making a lake on the site of the old parterre, and supervised extensive tree planting in the wider landscape, which was already well established.[29] Reginald Blomfield illustrated the terrace in his *Formal Garden in England*, commenting that the 'general effect is very good, though the detail is poor, and the balusters are crowded and too short'.[30] While these are valid criticisms, the terrace helps to anchor the long seventeenth-century façade, and its balustrade is topped with lively pierced finials and a sundial. Blomfield was more impressed with the balustrading on either side of the forecourt at Brympton, which is understandable, as it is of seventeenth-century vintage.

William Duckworth laid out a High Victorian garden of far more consequence at **Orchardleigh Park**, after he bought the estate in 1854.[31] As we have seen, the old house was badly sited, close to the church in the valley by the lake. Duckworth intended to build his new Orchardleigh on the elevated ridge above and commissioned Thomas Henry Wyatt to design it and William Page, whom he had employed previously at Beechwood in Hampshire, to contrive the landscape setting. As well as specifying trees for the wider parkland, Page laid out the terraces in front of the house, which by August 1857 were 'brilliant with flowers and the conservatory, only ten days old, quite cheerful with creepers'.[32] Orchardleigh also had that staple of Victorian features, a rock garden.[33]

57 The parterre at Orchardleigh, laid out after 1854, was originally planted with snaking flowerbeds, specimen shrubs and mushroom-clipped Portuguese laurels. Needless to say these have all disappeared, though the stone urns and basic structure survives today. Reproduced by permission of English Heritage. NMR

Early photographs show manicured lawns, the pierced Jacobean-style balustrades topped by vases full of spiky yuccas, naked cherubs supporting tazze planted with geraniums, the terraces studded with mushroom-shaped Portuguese laurels, the stone-edged flowerbeds (57) alive with snaking floral patterns.[34] Sadly, all the planting has gone and the Conservatory is roofless and windowless, but the architectural bones of the garden still survive. It is to be hoped that the consortium which now owns Orchardleigh, running it as a wedding venue, will appoint a manager intelligent enough to appreciate the value of a restoring a historic garden.[35]

Fortunately, private owners are often more sympathetic towards their historic inheritance, and this is the case at **Lydeard House** at Bishop's Lydeard, due west of Taunton. Since March 1998, Vaun and Colin Wilkins have effected a most sensitive restoration of both the house and the grounds, using documentary and historical evidence.[36] The exact date of the layout is unclear, as some elements may be eighteenth-century to accord with the house, which was built for a local lawyer, John Coles, in 1740. However, the formal garden to the rear of the house is stylistically of the mid-nineteenth century, and the Pergola flanking the stream is perhaps of the 1890s. Coles' daughter Frances Hamilton supervised additions to her father's house in 1787, while during the nineteenth century the west wing and clock tower were added; so garden improvements must have taken place during those periods. Indeed, Frances Hamilton's daybooks record extensive works being carried out in the grounds between 1787 and 1788.[37] In August 1787 the walks were mown and there were 'men in the garden the whole day'; in September a door was made for the 'Sankey Temple', a garden building sited in the Sankey Field marked on the tithe map; in November a Mr Lethbridge brought cauliflower plants; in December the workmen 'finished the bigger court and then planted box, cleared the little garden', and in January 1788 vines were planted on the fence 'in the little garden' and also in 'the border near the Chinese gate near the Apricot tree'. The 1840s tithe map shows plantations, walks and fishponds, so Lydeard must have had a significant eighteenth-century mini-landscape to the east and north of the house.

However, the impact today is decidedly Georgian, with an overlay of nineteenth-century Victorian embellishment. The approach is directly from the main village road beside a high retaining wall crowned by diminutive balustrades, through gatepiers of alternate purple and sand-coloured blocked rustication, which are flanked by similar arched pedestrian archways with Arts and Crafts gates. This Victorian delight in textures and colour banding is picked up in the forecourt, which is constructed of patterned pebbles. There are further walls and balustrades around the clock tower and the Victorian wing. The house itself is a typical example of local Georgian vernacular, its proportions a little leggy for the width of the main façade. Basement windows, just visible below the level of the forecourt, suggest that the entire front area has been raised to provide a safer and more enclosed entrance court. At the same time, presumably when the west wing and clock tower were added, the perimeter wall was built with a raised terrace and provided with stone seats at either end. There was originally a four-bay heated conservatory in

58 The formal nineteenth-century parterre at Lydeard House, Bishop's Lydeard is enclosed with balustraded walls which ingeniously incorporate stone seats

the angle between the main house and the Victorian wing.

Similar seating provision was made in the walled formal area behind the house, where there are stone benches at the angles of the pierced stone walls; there is even a circular stone table at one corner. An angular box-edged parterre forms the centrepiece of this walled enclosure, which is criss-crossed by crazy-paved stone paths and punctuated by stone urns on plinths (*58*). The Parterre Garden is overlooked on its west side by a three-bay Conservatory, which must have been built at the same time, attached to the service range of the house. Next to this is a roofless structure, which was once a Fernery.[38] Further out, to the east, the stream, which begins as a small lake crossed by two small late eighteenth-century bridges, narrows into a canal flanked by the Pergola. This last looks later in style than the Parterre Garden and it is not marked on the first edition Ordnance Survey; its rustic square pillars are more Arts and Crafts in feel than High Victorian. It was restored in 2003 and replanted with roses from Peter Beales, using cultivars that were in existence in the 1870s. From the house end, the colours begin with purple (*R.* 'Mannington

Mauve') and range through velvety crimson (R. 'Etoile de Hollande') to pale pinks, peach, apricot, yellow and finally to white (R. 'Rambling Rector') at the woodland end. At this end there are two statues: a Venus and a diminutive river god, affectionately called the dribbling man. Vaun and Colin have continued to develop the garden, planting the new Long Border below the east wall of the Parterre Garden and building a new walled kitchen garden on a ridge to the west of the house.

The most breathtaking landscape view in the whole of Bath, with Prior Park as its focus, can be enjoyed from another Victorian garden of indeterminate date. Whether on the formal terrace of **Crowe Hall**, or high up in the fields above the house, visitors can survey the entire combe, with the Palladian Bridge in the middle distance and John Wood's majestic Palladian villa strung out along its ridge on the horizon. The garden is essentially the creation of Sir Sydney Barratt and his wife, who came to Crowe Hall in 1961 and, latterly, of their son, John Barratt, although the structure of the layout, and particularly the sunken garden to the southwest, must date from the Tugwells' ownership. In 1804 George Tugwell of the banking family bought the 1770 house, built here on Widcombe Hill 'by someone called Crowe', and began a campaign of alteration.[39] The bow window on the south-west front dates from this early period; there were later, more extensive additions about 1870 when Henry Tugwell built the grandiose hall and portico, and added a room with French windows giving on to the garden.

This then is the likely date for the formal terraced garden which early photographs show was originally an extraordinary floral amphitheatre.[40] It was busy with ranks of pot plants, which lined the central area of crescent-shaped beds surrounding a circular pool (59). This last has been replaced with a rectangular pool with apsidal ends centred by a lead statue of a cherub supported by dolphins, while the rest is now laid to lawn. On the level below, the path leads to another Barratt enclosure with a Moorish-style quatrefoil pool and a brooding terracotta bust of Hercules set below a canopy. Then the path snakes down the hillside, with the roofs of Widcombe Manor just visible through the trees, via Victorian grotto tunnels to the productive kitchen garden area. In the brick-walled enclosure the Sauce Garden, which is enclosed by wooden lattice screens containing a rectangular rill, was laid out by John Barratt in memory of his mother Isabel Vaughan Barratt, who died in 1988. From here there are views down to the Cascade in the grounds of Widcombe Manor and across to Lyncombe.

The wildest and most exotic Victorian garden of this lacklustre showing in the county is that laid out around **Inwood House** at Henstridge by Thomas Merthyr Guest, who bought the estate in 1876. This is a Victorian garden like no other, signalled by the first edition

59 This amphitheatre of busy mid-Victorian planting at Crowe Hall in Bath has completely disappeared. The garden is now laid to lawn, and even the central pool has been altered. By kind permission of the Barratt estate

Ordnance Survey map of 1884, which must be unique in its marking around the pleasure grounds of no fewer than twelve statues. The layout is predictable for the time: a linear pleasure park of open glades and winding walks through shrubberies, bordered on the north-west by a wood with axial rides and on the south-east by open fields. Before his death in 1904, Guest had enriched both his house and grounds with bought-in eighteenth-century lead statuary, much of which had come via his wife's family, the Westminsters. There were little musical *amorini* on his new porch, sited as decorative finials to piers supporting Italian ironwork screens; cherubs held fruit platters on either side of his 'Italian Gate' and the 'Minstrel', the 'Forester' and the 'Dancer', more French in style than Italian, posed on stone plinths in the pleasure grounds.[41] Miraculously, many of these survive in the care of Richard, Count de Pelet, who inherited Inwood in 1993.

A tour around the grounds is like a visit to one of the most desirable architectural salvage businesses in the country, with exquisite lead figures around every corner. It has to be said that the house is a bizarre confection of Dutch-style shaped gables in dull grey render overshadowed by a garish red brick tower, dated 1881, which was built as an observatory. The carriage drive is lined with stepped Italian ironwork screens, punctuated by stone piers with elaborate lead urns. The *amorini* still play their instruments, but a semicircular entrance has been added to the porch since the 1901 *Country Life* article. This has a beautiful sundial, its gnomon in the form of a sharp-beaked heron. Around the corner to the rear of the house is a box parterre, its low stone walls rich with statuary, a pointing Mercury at its heart. Then, out across the open lawn, where statues lurk in every hedged recess, there is a copper-domed Turkish tent (*colour 39*), which looks as if it has been magically transported here from some Eastern European park like Potsdam's Sans Souci. It is, without question, the most exotic garden building in the entire county, its undulating copper canvas supported on wrought-iron columns topped with dragon rainwater heads, their long tongues protruding to convey the water to the ground, while Rococo-style cartouches enliven the ogee curves of the roof. It must post-date Merthyr Guest's period of ownership and may have been added by his wife, Lady Theodora, before her death in 1924.

But the most sensational piece of sculpture at Inwood is sited close to the Japanese Garden, planted on the site of tennis courts next to what was originally a triangular Herbaceous Garden, which is entered by the Italian Gate. The Japanese Garden is a leafily numinous area of pools guarded by bronze cranes. Across the forecourt, close by the service ranges, there is more statuary, including a dancing shepherdess and an Atlas groaning under the weight of a globe. Set against a brick wall, a stone Doric canopy shelters a great bronze sculpture group of the Laocoon (*60*), which was

60 William Beckford of Fonthill once owned this great statue group of the Laocoon, now displayed at Inwood House

originally owned by William Beckford and purchased at the Fonthill sale of 1822. The writhing figures of Laocoon and his two boys, gripped in the coils of vengeful serpents, rise from a stone plinth carved with lines from the *Aeneid*. Nearby, there is a tall eighteenth-century Gothick water tower, its circular walls heavily buttressed against collapse. Even allowing for the saccharine effulgence of early *Country Life* writers like H Avray Tipping and Arthur Oswald, the 1901 article ends with a fitting tribute to these memorable grounds: 'We have surveyed many fine and beautiful gardens, and we must conclude by saying that that which Mr. Guest and Lady Theodora Guest have adorned, ranks with the fairest of them, and has a distinction quite its own'.

8

Where stone flowers at least as vigorously as the plants – the Edwardian gardens

▼

Barrow Court · Montacute · Tyntesfield · Milton Lodge · Wootton House
Lytes Cary Manor · Hinton House · Nailsea Court · Ammerdown House
Redlynch Park · Mells Manor · Hestercombe Gardens · Barrington Court
Mells Park · Glencot · Wayford Manor · Burton Pynsent · The Old Court
Widcombe Manor · Barley Wood · North Cadbury Court
St Catherine's Court

THE EDWARDIAN PERIOD IS, WITHOUT DOUBT, THE GREAT HEYDAY OF Somerset historic gardens. Somerset ranks alongside only Dorset as a county where, in the late nineteenth and early twentieth centuries, new money found inspired expression in a series of effortlessly satisfying garden layouts attached to existing houses. However, it outranks Dorset in one important respect: all the major designers of the period are represented. While Dorset can claim two of Francis Inigo Thomas' schemes at Athelhampton and Chantmarle, neither comes close to the architectural sublimity of the grounds at **Barrow Court**, surely one of the most evocative gardens of its time. And while Dorset has its fair share of gardens by Thomas Mawson, and lesser known figures like Percy Morley Horder and Philip Tilden, Somerset has great layouts by Edwin Lutyens and Gertrude Jekyll; several important gardens, mostly created for members of his family, by Harold Peto; other works by Reginald Blomfield, Alfred Parsons, Walter Cave, Henry Avray Tipping and Hugh Mackay Baillie Scott; and Thomas Mawson's least known, but perhaps most atmospheric, garden which was laid out in 1910 around the house once owned by a Georgian feminist. But this survey must begin chronologically with that most patrician of landscape designers, Francis Inigo Thomas, and his masterpiece at Barrow Court, Barrow Gurney, to the south of Bristol.

As we have seen, William Gibbs of Tyntesfield, visible across the valley from Barrow Court, had made a fortune out of nitrates from bird droppings on the islands off the coast of Peru. With the family's wealth his son Henry bought the run-down Tudor house at Barrow Gurney in 1882, restored it, together with the parish church in its lee, and then began to create the gardens.[1] The man he entrusted with the design was both an architect and landscape designer. Thomas was initially articled to the Gothic Revival architectural firm of G F Bodley and Thomas Garner, and had spent much time in the years between 1889 and 1894 travelling in France, Germany, Holland and Italy.[2] His first successful commission was the layout at Athelhampton, which had been bought by Alfred Cart de Lafontaine in 1891.[3] Soon afterwards, he supplied the pen-and-ink illustrations to Reginald Blomfield's 1892 *Formal Garden in England*. Their book came out two years after J D Sedding's *Garden-Craft Old and New*, which also advocated the adoption of the 'architectural garden'. This was essentially the extension of a house into the landscape by means of strategic walls, steps and yew hedges. The aim was to shape a series of surprise avenues and hedged enclosures beset with summerhouses, gazebos, pigeon cotes, moon ponds and statuary: a stage set of Renaissance England, whether Elizabethan or seventeenth-century, entwined with honeysuckle and homely wild flowers. A generation accustomed to Beerbohm Tree productions of Shakespeare, and with a taste for maximum consumption in a gentlemanly manner, fell for such gardens in a big way. That elite Edwardian group, The Souls, led by Arthur Balfour, frequented them because the substantial garden buildings were perfect for assignations and for the gently adulterous love affairs, accompanied by birdsong, that were their speciality.[4]

Thomas' design for Barrow Court dates from 1892-6 and expresses this mood at its fantastic height; not that the High Church Gibbs family indulged in any such bohemian or licentious activities. Unlike his scheme for Athelhampton, which expanded upon the medieval theme of the *hortus conclusus* with a series of rectangular walled enclosures around the house, Thomas was more daring at Barrow, providing two distinct areas, one public and the other secretive. Thomas' first garden, which flows axially down from the terrace alongside the house with its parterres, is a formal scheme with wide-open views across the valley. Predictably, the Tennis Lawn succeeds the Terrace but then, at a limiting line of balustrade, gatepiers and gates, the composition swings unexpectedly to the left in a movement of inspired poetry. Just below the West Court on the Terrace, entered by Ionic gateways (*61*) and furnished with wooden settles, twelve terms representing the months of the year stand in an open Exedra commanding meadowland (*colour 40*). Each is set on a high pier and carved with sensitive realism to show a stage in the life of one woman, the twelve making up a sequence from childhood to old age (*62*). They stand, acting as a life clock, and the kindest possible *momento mori*. The carved portraits are of William's wife, Emily Ann Gibbs, to whom he gave Barrow Court as a wedding present.[5] The terms were carved by Thomas Drury, a contemporary of Alfred Gilbert and William Goscombe John, the fashionable sculptors who were rebelling against the cautious Victorian establishment style of insipidity. Both Drury and Thomas are equally responsible for the strange atmosphere of a place where stone has flowered at least as vigorously as the plants.

Logically, the garden should end here, at the threshold of farmland; in fact, Drury and Thomas had only just begun. At right angles to the main axis, beyond the East Court, which mirrors its twin on the west, is a second, secret garden of dark hedges and alleys cut through thickets of flowering trees, now wildly overgrown. If there is any focus, it is the church tower, but that pulls the composition together only from certain viewpoints, and never seems the intentional goal. The area is relatively small, little more than an acre, but into these rectangular jungles of bloom have been crammed enough major garden buildings to stock a full-sized park twice over. On one axis are three massive structures: a pyramidal-roofed Palladian Gazebo, a second Exedra (*63*) embracing a lead statue of a winged victory and a towering set of gatepiers guarding the walled courtyard of the colonnaded Garden House.[6] Everything is exuberantly carved: stone fruit tumbles from heaped urns, swags loop and scroll, and the overscaling has an *Alice in Wonderland* effect, as if the gardens had been laid out for lazy giants confined to wheelchairs. The Exedra is at least twenty-five feet high, and that scale is standard. The surprises come

61
Francis Inigo Thomas' elaborate Ionic archway frames one of twin Gazebos at Barrow Court

62
The Exedra at Barrow Court is made up of twelve stone terms representing the months of the year, each decorated with the head of Emily Ann Gibbs as she progresses from childhood to old age

63
The central vista of the woodland garden at Barrow Court is terminated by this wildly over-scaled Exedra centred by a lead statue of a winged victory

geometrically, and their historical reference is compressed: Tudor, Jacobean, Palladian; all with a fruity dash of Beaux Arts. Turning a corner, the visitor climbs a flight of steps into an open dining room where a heavy wooden table waits to seat six for an *alfresco* banquet. The possibilities for fantasy are as rich as those in a garden of the Italian Mannerists. It is a place to visit in order to understand the origins of the First World War. No ruling class that indulged in such gracious games of make-believe could ever have anticipated the harsh reality of the Flanders trenches.

Thomas' literary partner, Reginald Blomfield, made one significant appearance in Somerset: at **Montacute**, where the existing East Garden with its banqueting houses provided the stylistic impetus, and the walled enclosure to the north gave scope, for a new architectural feature. Blomfield's sketchbooks show that he had been visiting Elizabethan and

31 This Italianate Picturesque garden at Oakwood on Bathwick Hill above Bath was designed in the 1830s by Edward Davis when he was extending Benjamin Barker's original house for the new owner, Thomas Emmerson

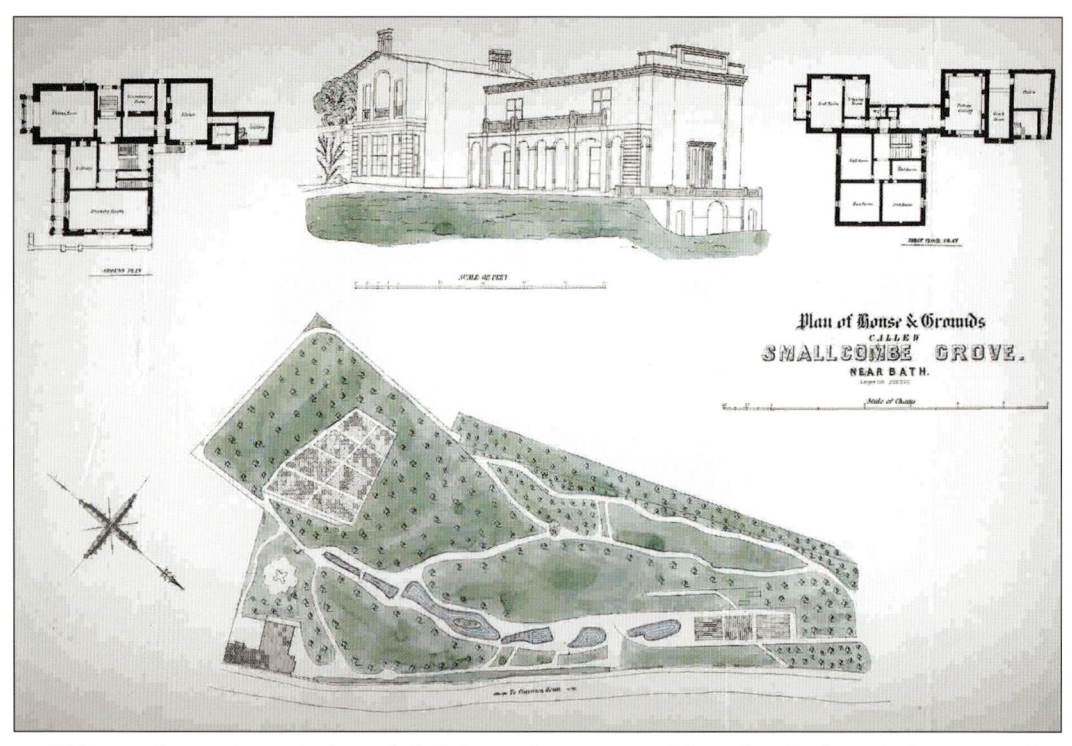

32 This map from sale particulars of 1856 shows the mixture of formal and informal elements within the terraced gardens laid out below Oakwood in the 1830s.
By kind permission of Michael and Vera Forsyth

33 The 1834 Druid's Temple at Banwell reminded visitors to the Bone Caves complex of the pagan world destroyed by the Great Flood

34 Garishly bright island flowerbeds, typical of the Gardenesque, at Cricket St Thomas. Somerset Archaeological and Natural History Society

35 This early Victorian parterre at Nynehead Court, worthy of William Andrews Nesfield, is dramatised at the edges by swirling guilloche patterns

36 One of a pair of rustic Summerhouses in the Rose Garden at Tyntesfield; another instance of the stylistic uncertainty of the mid-Victorian landscape

37 This scimitar-shaped Conservatory at Maperton House, near Wincanton, has an Ionic-columned apse more appropriate to a basilica

38 This mid-Victorian architectural terrace at Brympton d'Evercy was illustrated in Reginald Blomfield's 1892 *The Formal Garden in England*

39 Unquestionably the most exotic and bizarre garden building in the entire county – the Turkish (or is it Chinese?) Tent at Inwood House. Regency in date, it was introduced into the gardens in the 1920s

40 A garden building as *memento mori* – the Exedra of the twelve months of the year at Barrow Court, Barrow Gurney. Each month is represented by the carved face of Henry Martin Gibbs' wife Emily Ann Gibbs as she passes from youth to old age

41 Alfred Parsons' signature planting, held in place by cow dung, used to soften walls in the grounds of Milton Lodge, Wells; the Summerhouse was built in 1909

42 The Long Border at Lytes Cary is a 1980s recreation, by Biddy and Jeremy Chittenden, of Graham Stuart Thomas' original planting of 1954

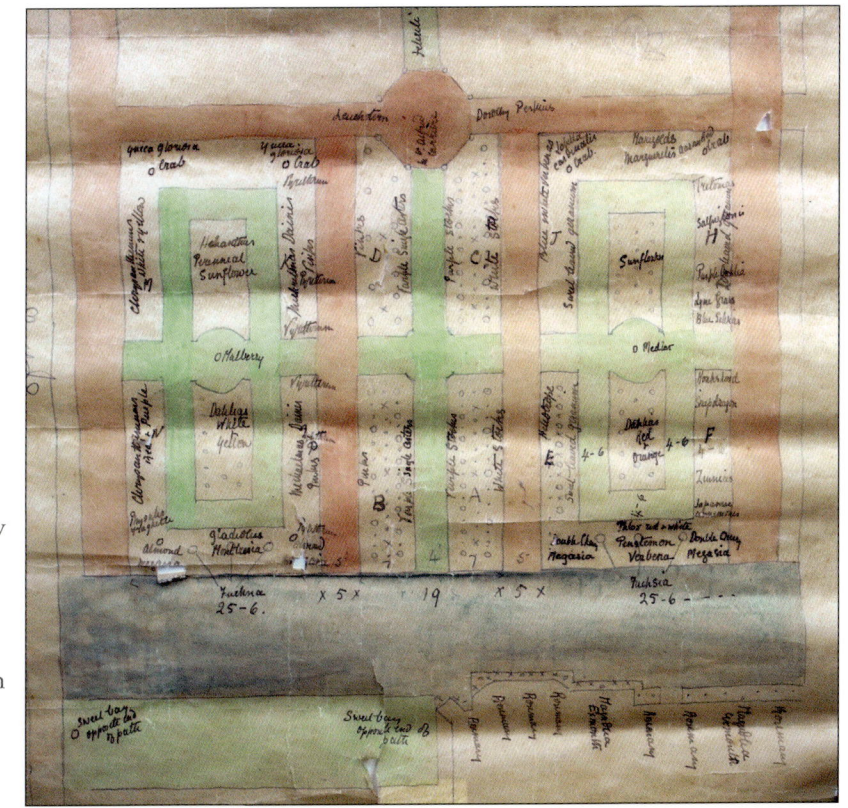

43 Archival proof that the South Court Garden at Mells Manor was designed and planted jointly by Frances Horner and Norah Lindsay. By kind permission of Viscount Asquith

199

44 The walled Edwardian *hortus conclusus* at Mells Manor, now planted in spring with tulips; the sundial is an original feature

45 Architecture and planting in perfect accord at Hestercombe – the Great Plat, designed jointly between 1904 and 1906 by Edwin Lutyens and Gertrude Jekyll

Jacobean houses since the 1880s to research details for his Formal Garden. Several of the pencil sketches in his Sketchbook 11, dated 1889, are of the architectural enclosures at Montacute, which show the Fountain in the North Garden.[7] There are further, later, sketches by R Shekleton Balfour showing the feature in place in 1894, with each quadrant of the lawn centred by a circular flowerbed and the present line of yews flanking the east terrace.[8] The basin takes the form of the fountain that was originally in the East Garden, which was in turn designed on the ground plan of the banquet houses, enlivened with obelisks copied from the roofline of the house. It is not clear whether Blomfield was responsible for the Fountain in the North Garden, as the present National Trust guidebook hedges its bets, and the contemporary *Country Life* articles,[9] while illustrating the feature, give no designer, merely confirming the seamless merging of house into garden that was the principal aim of these landscape architects: 'It will be observed that the architecture does not end with the house. It has its place in the garden also. This is as it should be, for thus are house and garden made one'.[10]

Blomfield is the link again, this time with **Tyntesfield**, where he designed the Chapel. The visual and architectural connection between the house and grounds was mishandled in the 1850s, but Blomfield's pupil Walter Cave was commissioned by Antony Gibbs to revive the kitchen garden there, and his scheme more than makes up for the stylistic incoherence of the features around the house. Set apart, at some distance to the north-east of the house, the Walled Garden is entered through a wrough-iron gateway whose elaborate overthrow of proto-Art Nouveau sinuosity contains the family motto, the Gibbs monogram and the date 1896. The date tells it all: the kitchen garden was re-designed in part to commemorate Queen Victoria's Diamond Jubilee in 1897. Cave subdivided the walled enclosure into the Lady Garden and the Jubilee Garden, adding a loggia, garden offices and a bothy; the Orangery in the Jubilee Garden looks to be earlier in style, though of the same date, but confirmation of this must wait until the Trust gains access to the family papers for a firm attribution.

Cave's brand of muscular classicism is in direct contrast to the hit-or-miss Gothic of the earlier garden architecture. The gateway leads into an insistently buttressed brick-walled court, terminated by a pedimented Ionic Loggia of golden Ham stone. There are glimpses through the rear colonnade of the Jubilee Garden beyond, but glimpses only. This space was sometimes referred to as the Old Orange Garden, so the surviving stone plinths might have been used for the display of orange trees in the summer.[11] The visitor must go through the Loggia, either rest awhile on the oak settle inside, or turn right and enter the next enclosure. Here there is a raised area which has a sundial set up to mark Victoria's sixty-year reign, now absent and awaiting restoration; the octagonal base is inscribed: 'I am a shade/a shadow/too art thou/I mark/the time/say gossip/dost thou so?' It is overlooked by a stone bench with tall piers topped by ball finials. There are further pilaster buttresses, ball finials and pediments on the office range (64), which forms the division between the Jubilee Garden and the Lady's Garden beyond. The Ionic Orangery was under restoration on our visit in the summer of 2009, so it was not possible to inspect it closely, but the Trust information boards claim it to be by Cave, and Judith Patrick has noted similarities between the details here and at Cave's Colherne Court on the Gunter Estate at Brompton, London. However, the nearby Bothy definitely has his signature elements of overscaled brick piers, delight in mixing materials and a typical Doric porch set in the angle of the two ranges.

Every good landscape architect has these design signifiers, none more so than Alfred Parsons, whose work, like his paintings, is characterised by an almost garish profusion of colourful plants. His only commission in Somerset appears to have been at **Milton Lodge**, just outside Wells,[12] where he worked alongside Charles Clement Tudway, a merchant with interests in Antigua, who was a minor partner in the garden design partnership of Parsons, Partridge and Tudway, formed in 1899.[13] The family owned The Cedars, an eighteenth-century house in the middle of Wells, but had remodelled Milton Lodge in the late nineteenth century in preparation for a move up the Mendip hill to overlook the city.[14] Tudway's work for the firm consisted of 'financial organisation, practical assistance, wall work, specially as regards the planning for plant and fruit culture under glass'.[15] He was later persuaded to start a nursery, which he ran from the old house in the city, supplying plants for the use of the firm when

64 Walter Cave designed the Jubilee Garden at Tyntesfield to commemorate Queen Victoria's Diamond Jubilee of 1897

carrying out landscape designs.

The reference to 'wall work' indicates exactly what Tudway had to achieve on the vertiginous slopes of 'the hanger' above the Old Bristol Road, which was begun in 1900.[16] Perched between the hanging beech woods above and falling meadow below, some hard landscaping was required to create a formal garden around the house. Tudway constructed a series of four elongated south-facing terraces on which to fashion sheltered hedges, walks, borders and open spaces for the Edwardian sporting pastimes of tennis and croquet.[17] In 1899 Alfred Parsons suggested that Tudway begin raising seedlings of some plants given him by the nine-tenth-century horticultural polemicist, William Robinson: purple-leaved holly, an orange-berried shrub and *Cotoneaster horizontalis*. In typical entrepreneurial fashion Parsons went on to suggest that they make use of a stone carver, whom Tudway knew in Wells, to manufacture some vases and sundials to sell on to their clients.[18] The sundial at Milton Lodge, sited on the axis where terrace and steps meet, was probably a result of this initiative. Despite disagreeing frequently on the terms of their business partnership, at some point Parsons was drafted in, thanks to his extensive plant knowledge, to help Tudway with the design of the terraces. His signature schemes of yew hedging on top of walls is still evident between the Sundial and Pool Terraces, as is the wall planting which he advocated to soften the stonework, which was held in place with cow dung (*colour 41*). No plans exist of this planting, as discussions were almost always held over a convivial dinner and a glass of port when Parsons was passing by on his way back to the family home near Frome. But by 1901 Tudway was having financial concerns, and work may have stopped until the Summerhouse was built in 1909, which served as a shady space from which to admire the views. The three partners swapped design ideas up to 1913, with Parsons giving detailed suggestions for a series of steps, a low wall and piers 'on the west side near the garden house'.[19]

As with so many gardens that remain in the family, the layout has not altered in over a century. The approach, winding up the hill past Walcombe, gives a good impression of the eighteenth-century landscape that was once part of the wider gardens of The Cedars. The cedar theme continues with a specimen of *Cedrus atlantica* planted in the late eighteenth century, coeval with the main core of the house, in front of which is a stone path and lawn. Below, specimen trees such as *Ginkgo biloba*, *Diospyros lotus* and *Morus nigra* (another of Alfred Parsons' favourite trees) break up the horizontal lines. The path leads away west to the arboretum, which was predominantly planted in the 1960s by David and Elizabeth Tudway Quilter. It includes an interesting variety of acers and prunus, among others, all under-planted with spring bulbs.[20]

The Central Terrace is reached via steps from the upper terrace or by returning towards the house from the arboretum. This space is the most informal of the four terraces and has a sloping lawn, lined with shrubs, herbaceous planting and a thicket of *Rosa* 'Frensham' covering the low wall. At the eastern end a lily pond and stone seats are set on a gravel terrace, giving spectacular views of the Vale of Avalon, Wells Cathedral and, in the distance, Glastonbury Tor. Another set of steps leads down under a spreading Japanese cherry to the Sundial Terrace, the narrowest of the four, predominantly planted with old roses and ground-covering geraniums, forget-me-nots and dead nettle, which are allowed to colonise the stones. The path ends with a stone menhir in its own carved yew niche before a final flight of steps descends past the Summerhouse, which now commands an alarmingly turquoise swimming pool. The remainder of the Pool Terrace is simply lawn enclosed by a solid yew hedge. It is only at this point, when the visitor looks back up to the house, that the extent of the hillside can be appreciated. Unlike most Edwardian gardens, those at Milton Lodge are outward-looking beyond the confines of the yew hedges, blending the gardens into the surrounding landscape of rolling slopes and mature trees.

Another minor layout of this period was designed by Henry Avray Tipping, later the architectural writer for *Country Life*, for the Acland Hoods at **Wootton House**, Butleigh Wootton, near Glastonbury. They were involved in politics and the railways, as was Tipping's father; Mrs Acland Hood attended Tipping's funeral in 1933.[21] The house is a grey Regency affair with a delicate ironwork loggia, its garden front offering views across the fields to the Hood Monument on Windmill Hill.[22] On either side of the loggia are rectangular blocks of yew topiary shaped into domes, while in the angle between the house and service buildings Tipping laid out a simple Rose Garden, similar to one he created in about 1900 at Mathern Palace, Monmouthshire.[23] This has crazy-paved paths and rises to a terraced lawn, perhaps intended for croquet. An archway through the ancillary range leads to the rear of the house, where there are two Pergolas for climbing roses supported on blockish rectangular columns.

A few other gardens designed in this first decade of the new century deserve a mention before the great Somerset gardens of Lutyens, Peto and Mawson are discussed. Perhaps the most perfect example of an Arts and Crafts garden grafted on to an old manor house is that laid out after 1907 by Sir Walter Jenner and his wife Flora at **Lytes Cary**.[24] The Jenners found the fifteenth-century manor house run down, with the great hall being used as a cider house. Their programme of restoration included the creation of a garden that would complement the parent house and extend it into the grounds, as Sedding and Blomfield had advocated. The walled enclosure to the front was given an axial path aligned on the Dovecote in the field beyond and flanked by yew topiary topped with pyramidal cones. Through a gateway in the wall the visitor reaches the Long Border, originally designed by Graham Stuart Thomas in 1954; Sir Walter had died in

1948 leaving the house to the National Trust. Biddy and Jeremy Chittenden, who were tenants at the time, replanted this in 1996, using a mixture of new and existing plants but following Thomas' original colour scheme. It is a horticultural *tour de force* of brilliant colour, which grows more intense as the Border extends eastwards (*colour 42*). The Border is planted with plum-coloured berberis, purple pittosporum and pink roses, while ceanothus, clematis and solanum cloak the wall behind. The path leads through a yew-hedged White Garden to the Raised Walk, lined with beech on its outer side, which overlooks the Orchard.

The Orchard is bisected by diagonal paths meeting in a sundial at the centre, each path with a weeping ash arbour at its head, while in the meadow there are mulberries, pears, quinces and walnuts. After this open sector there are further enclosures, in true Arts and Crafts style, which include the Long Walk, the Pond and Seat Gardens, the Croquet Lawn, the Lavender Garden and the Private Garden, once for the use of the tenant, but now open to the public. The gardens are beautifully maintained by Head Gardener Simon Larkins, who has celebrated the herbal tradition of Henry Lyte by planting a border of herbs against the south wall of the house. Another house border is a blend of pinks, mauves, blues and whites, consisting of poppies, achillea, salvia, echinops and day lilies. One of the few remaining plants from the Jenners' planting is the small pale-pink cupped *Rosa* 'Macrantha Raubritter', now entwined with a *Clematis* 'Perle d'Azur' against the wall of the house. Simon's collections of pot plants enliven the dull inner courtyard, and his welcoming blackboard charts the garden jobs for the week to inform visitors of daily progress in the gardens. These are welcome personal touches, and set Lytes Cary apart from other National Trust gardens that are often too corporate in their impact.

At **Hinton House** the great seventeenth-century south façade, which had languished overlooking open lawns since the removal of the early eighteenth-century formal gardens, was finally given an appropriate architectural setting of balustraded walls and piers (*65*) when the 7th Earl Poulett created the Sunken Garden in 1913.[25] Sadly, the distinctive oval roundels no longer hold their Ham stone baskets of fruit. These were photographed in 1968, when the statuary was auctioned off before the death of the 8th Earl in 1973. The photographs, now deposited at the NMR, record statues of Bacchus, Samson and a Greek athlete that were either in the niches around the house or set within the grounds.

Of similar date is the Walled Garden which fronts **Nailsea Court**. Charles Evans had laid this out before Henry Avray Tipping visited in 1912 to write a *Country Life* article on the house and grounds.[26] This shows the Jacobean porch, once at Upper Langford Manor on the Mendips, in the lower garden at Nailsea, and also the Walled Garden newly planted

65 The long seventeenth-century front of Hinton House was given a much-needed architectural frame when Earl Poulett created the Sunken Garden in 1913 on the eve of the First World War

with standard roses lining the central path. The porch has disappeared, but the walled garden survives much as shown in the early photograph, its tall roses now interspersed with yew globes. Tipping described the enclosure as 'a little walled pleasaunce of old English flowers, for Mr Evans limits the list of plants to those species contained in Parkinson's *Complete Herbal*'.

In Sylvia Hope Evans' *Book of Nailsea Court* the enclosure is called 'The Ladies' Pleasaunce' and its planting up is covered in some detail. The obvious problem in using Parkinson as a guide is that he would have arranged his plants in formal beds or knots. While some Edwardian gardens, such as that below the terrace at Barrow Court, recreated knots and parterres, most relied on open lawns edged with floral borders. This was also the case at Nailsea, where the flowers, apart from the rose standards, were confined to the borders, with roses at the top and stocks and larkspur at the bottom in spring and summer respectively. To retain colourful interest at all times the plants were designed to bloom alternately on each side of the enclosure:

> Early daffodils on the right opened the game, and Wallflowers on the left made the next move. Later, the right hand challenged with Peonies, Lupines and Columbine, and the reply came in Sweet Williams and Snapdragons. The right-hand bed held chiefly herbaceous plants, with the gaps filled by Love-in-a-Mist, French Marigolds, Greek Valerian, and Lungwort, which last West Country Folk call 'Faith, Hope and Charity'. By the wall on the left were clumps of Hollyhock, yellow Foxgloves, Peach-leaved Bellflowers, white and blue, and Steeple Bellflowers.[27]

In its prime, the Pleasaunce at Nailsea must have resembled a painting by Helen Allingham, and would have delighted William Robinson. However, architectural gardens are more characteristic of the period, and with the Italian Garden at **Ammerdown** we come to the great Edwardian heavyweight: Edwin Landseer Lutyens. The 3rd Lord Hylton and his wife, née Lady Alice Hervey, commissioned Lutyens in 1901 to devise a formal garden that would connect James Wyatt's house with the eighteenth-century walled garden and its Orangery, also by Wyatt, some way off. Lutyens chose to project his new axial path from the south-east corner of the house, via two flights of semicircular steps, to a circular hub from which six paths would radiate out, towards the park on the south and east, and towards a Rose Garden and the Orangery on the north (66). This inspired geometry was enclosed, and further elaborated with box parterres, within huge walls of yew hedging.[28] Inside the house there are several pastel paintings by Alice, Lady Hylton, which were done in the 1930s and record the gardens in their prime.[29] One shows a view of the Orangery from the Italian Garden with the caption: Women on the land

66
Edwin Lutyens delighted in geometric games when designing both houses and their gardens. Here at Ammerdown he devised a series of axes radiating from the Italian Garden to the park, the house and the eighteenth-century Orangery. By kind permission of the Hon Andrew Jolliffe Grange. Copyright Abbey Gate College

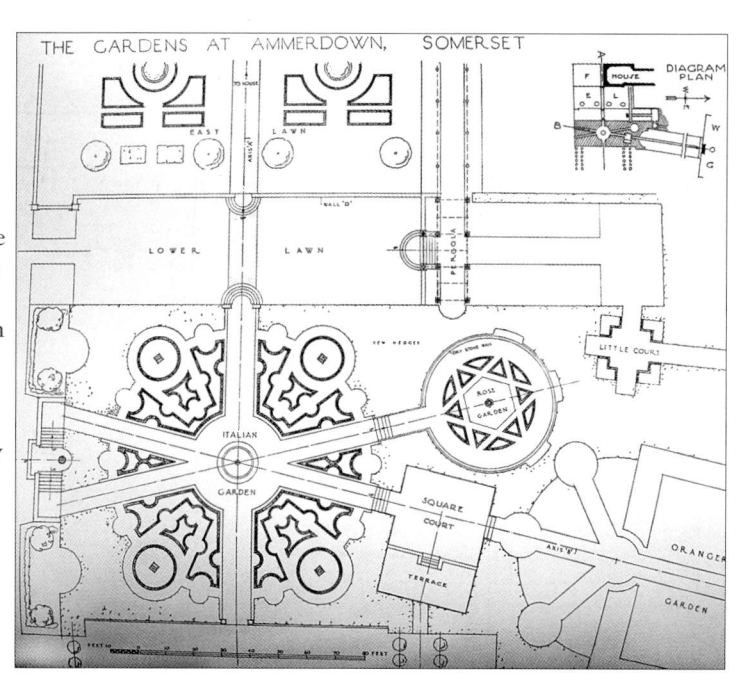

working during the War 1916. Another scene of the family playing croquet is entitled: George Lord Hylton planted yew hedges to Sir Edwin Lutyens designs in 1901; this is illustrated on the back cover of this book.

Any tour of the grounds must begin with the extraordinary fountain on the forecourt, which is set within a rectangular pool with semicircular extrusions. It is encrusted with lively *rocaille* decoration, but looks more seventeenth-century than eighteenth in date. Behind it, a tell-tale Lutyens porthole window is set into the wall bordering the South Parterre. From the top of the steps by the south-east corner of the house open lawns descend, now stripped of the parterres shown in a *Country Life* article of 1929, but with umbrella-clipped Portugeuse laurels.[30] To the left is a Pergola of concrete Doric pillars, extended to the west by timber beams and backed by a solid barrier of yew, which gives access on the north side to the 'Little Court', in which there is a trapezoid sundial dated 1725. But the insistent main axis leads down to the Italian Garden (*67*), each of its quadrants commanded by 'Thomas Samuel Jolliffe's artifical stone deities, set on a concrete plinth made by the Wharf Lane Concrete Company, Ilminster'.[31] They preside over box-edged enclosures, which in 1929 were ablaze with scarlet planting: geraniums, zinnias, gladioli and begonias 'in succession with the scarlet mignon Dahlia Coltness Gem at the base of the statues'.[32] Elsewhere, the grey of the statues was picked up in the beds with strips of artemesia and clumps of tall grass.

The Rose Garden is similarly enclosed within tall blocks of yew above a drystone wall plinth; the original Star of David pattern of paths has been altered and the astrolabe which once centred the space has disappeared. The enclosure was planted with pink *Geranium* 'Clorinda' and polyantha roses, and masses of that old cream rose 'Felicité Perpétue'.[33]

67 Lutyens' 1901 Italian Garden at Ammerdown contains further internal geometries in the stepped yew walls and the box-edged parterres; the concrete deities were moved to this site in 1925

On the adjacent axis the Orangery is reached via a Green Theatre and more yew barriers that break to offer views out across the park. The path to the Orangery is still lined with the box globes and standard lilacs present in 1929, though the rosemary which originally lined the steps has been subsumed within the yew hedges. The *Country Life* article illustrates a stately avenue running east to west below the Italian Garden, framed by pylons of *Cupressus macrocarpa*, terminating in a statue of Mercury which has now been sited in front of the Pergola. Finally, a forlorn sundial stands in an expanse of grass on the south front; it was once the central feature of the South Parterre, which featured box-edged compartments filled with those stalwarts of Edwardian planting: pink penstemons, antirrhinums, mallows, stocks, heliotropes and pink and purple asters. The southern setting has now reverted to the eighteenth-century landscape treatment of lawns sweeping right up to the house, but the formalities beyond still provide that important connecting link between the house and its garden.

Much less survives of Lutyens' contemporary work at **Redlynch Park**, where the 5th Earl of Ilchester commissioned him to convert the eighteenth-century service range for residential use and to remodel the gardens.[34] The estate was sold on in 1912, a fire started by Suffragettes seriously damaged the service range, and the eighteenth-century mansion was demolished at the same time. After a period serving as a school, the house and stables were converted into apartments. Consequently, only the Summerhouse, set high up above a sunken lawn on the approach to the Shrubbery, is likely to be by Lutyens, designed as part of the formal gardens he laid out across the east front of the former stables. Certainly the geometry of the adjoining terrace with its exedral-shaped feature is reminiscent of Lutyens' style, and the entrance gateway to the terrace and one to the walled garden are unmistakably in his inventive classicism.

Less architecturally successful, both stylistically and practically, was the music room with its external loggia and outdoor sleeping balcony (*68*) that Lutyens added to **Mells Manor** in 1904. Lutyens appears to have been approached in 1900 for advice on remodelling the house and laying out gardens. It has been wrongly assumed that, because Lutyens and Gertrude Jekyll often collaborated on projects, she advised on the planting at Mells. There was also a family connection by marriage between the Jekylls and Horners, which has perpetuated this mis-attribution.[35] In fact, the Manor garden plans, which are dated 1904, are from Lutyens' practice, but Norah Lindsay devised the planting much later, in 1924, in collaboration with Frances Horner.[36] Not only is there a plan at Mells for the South Court by Norah Lindsay, with plant annotations by Frances Horner, but Frances describes their creative partnership in her 1933 *Time Remembered*:

> It is said some people are born to garden, others have gardening thrust upon them. I was in the latter class, for when we came to live in the Manor House, it stood among somewhat bare surroundings, with no shining magnolias clothing its walls, no herbaceous borders brightening its green courts, no rosemary spreading round its pavements. Fortunately for me, I had a friend with unrivalled taste and knowledge, Mrs. Harry Lindsay, and it is to her I owe most of the beauty which the garden boasts of today. If any of the flowering shrubs flower, if the annuals come up as they are meant to do, if the valerian ramps on the walls, and the aubretia hangs everywhere in purple masses, it is chiefly her doing. She is an artist and the garden is her paintbox.[37]

Norah Lindsay's own garden at Sutton Courtney in Oxfordshire was well established by the early 1920s, but in 1923 the house was rented out and Norah and her estranged husband Harry lived a peripatetic life, country-house hopping between their aristocratic friends: Diana and Duff Cooper, Lady Ottoline Morell, Philip Sassoon, Emerald Cunard and Clemmie and Winston Churchill. In 1924, after a protracted stay in Rome, Lindsay returned to England, only to find that Sutton was again let, so she sought refuge with the Horners at Mells, where for eight days she and Frances virtually lived in the gardens.[38] The fragile plan of the South Court garden (*colour 43*) shows a grid layout of beds, with perpendicular gravel walks bisected by an octagonal sundial plinth and interspersed with rectangular grass walks for the main frame. Rosa 'Madame Alfred Carriere' and R. 'Dorothy Perkins', both popular in Arts and Crafts gardens, were planted around the dial. The remaining spaces between the walks are large herbaceous borders, designed to be viewed from all sides.[39] It would have been entirely in character for Frances to fill in the planting recommendations on a tem, as she so often did with embroidery patterns designed for her by Burne-Jones.[40] Underneath the windows of the house were beds of rosemary, while Magnolia 'Exmouth' were trained against the walls. Each bed either side of the central axis was planted with dahlias and sunflowers, centred by a mulberry on the east and a medlar on the west, while the flanking strips were awash with

68 Edwardians often preferred to sleep in the open air, so in 1904 Lutyens designed an outdoor sleeping balcony above his music room for the Horners at Mells Manor. It is accessed by an oak ladder also designed by Lutyens

purple and white stocks and purple asters. On the extreme periphery to the west there were purple dahlias, blue salvias, zinnias and snapdragons; to the east, red, purple, white and yellow chrysanthemums brightened the border. Evergreen structure was provided by *Yucca gloriosa* and sweet bays, while crab apple trees provided vertical accents along the central path. This informal approach softened the bones of the geometrical layout, replacing the 'crayon-coloured flowers that existed in the beds with flowers of butter yellow, soft blues and milk whites'.[41] It was one of the first gardens to be opened for the National Gardens Scheme, and this is essentially the layout that exists today (*colour 44*), planted in spring with tulips.

Where Lutyens and Jekyll did come together to create a garden of breathtaking beauty was at **Hestercombe** which, unlike many of their gardens in Surrey that are still privately owned and, therefore, difficult to visit, is wide open to the public and maintained with erudition and sensitivity. This is due in part to the stewardship of the Somerset Fire Brigade from 1952, then Somerset County Council after 1977 and, latterly, under the inspired direction of Philip White, of the Hestercombe Gardens Trust, which was established in 1997. The whole site, comprising the eighteenth-century landscape and the Edwardian garden, is one of the most rewarding and imaginatively presented in the entire county. It is not hyperbole to state that the great garden, which Lutyens and Jekyll laid out for the Hon Edward Portman between 1904 and 1906, is the epitome of their brilliant partnership, where the architectural framework is complemented perfectly by carefully colour-coded planting. Where Lutyens devises a strong stony accent, Jekyll allows it to makes its impact, then softens it with swathes of texture and colour. His sharp-edged vision and her gauzily impressionistic planting, the result of her myopia, combine to make a walk around the Great Plat, the East and West Water Gardens, the Pergola or the Dutch Garden a constant revelation of sights, scents and sounds. It is as if Reginald Blomfield and William Robinson, the two opposing garden writers, had called a truce and devised the ideal Edwardian garden; but it took Lutyens and Jekyll to achieve this ideal.

So much has been written about the layout that a detailed analysis of the gardens is perhaps superfluous,[42] but its link with both Mells Manor and Ammerdown is worth mentioning. Here again, as at Ammerdown, Lutyens uses his favourite geometrical trickery, with the Rotunda court acting as the fulcrum of the layout, connecting the Great Plat to the Orangery Terrace and the Dutch Garden. The Plat itself is a giant *hortus conclusus* like the South Court at Mells, but here the walls are on three sides only. The fourth is formed by the massive Pergola, 230 feet long, which offers expansive views out across the Vale of Taunton Deane, but also commands the Plat from a considerable height. The East and West Water Gardens also act as raised terraces for views down to the Plat, Lutyens varying the levels ingeniously as the visitor walks the garden. It is a most sophisticated and subtle form of architectural manipulation, with Jekyll's planting enlivening every open vista and every close arbour. For, despite its openness, each corner of the Great Plat has secret areas for rest and contemplation. And, not content with such a profusion of architecture and planting, Portman commissioned what must surely be

69 One of the two rills Lutyens devised for Hestercombe between 1904 and 1906 reveals his obsession with geometric form, its strong lines softened by Gertrude Jekyll's planting of irises

one of the great classical buildings of the twentieth century: Lutyens' Orangery, a rare synthesis of Serlian forms and 'Wrenaissance' detail.

In terms of planting, the first restoration of the soft landscaping took place in 1973 when the Fire Brigade, aided by the discovery of some of Jekyll's plans in the potting shed, initiated a complete re-planting of the Great Plat.[43] Further research led to another set of plans in the University of California at Berkeley, where they had been deposited by Beatrix Farrand. This meant that, for its time, the restoration was particularly well informed and scholarly, and this approach has continued as more information has come to light about the planting. As a result of new research, the Great Plat was subsequently replanted in 1998. Its cruciform pattern of paths is given horticultural solidity 'by the thick surround of *Bergenia cordifolia* enclosing pink roses and lupins',[44] and Jekyll's favourite plants – lilies, yuccas, lavenders, santolinas and stachys – are now precisely where she planned them to be. Nowhere is this more apparent than on the Grey Walk, where her indebtedness to the impressionistic painter, Hercules Brabazon Brabazon, and her own affliction with myopia, created a silvery horticultural canvas worthy of Cèzanne.

All great gardens continue to pose questions. Are the iris rills of the two Water Gardens (69) merely a development of that at Deanery Garden, or are their owl-like extrusions consciously modelled on the strainer arch in the nave at Wells Cathedral? Lutyens delighted in architectural games, hence the form of his Chinese Gate in the Dutch Garden. The circle containing a square hole is the design used for Chinese coins. Could this be another of Lutyens' jokes, aimed at Portman whom he found parsimonious?[45] Is Hestercombe then the greatest of all Edwardian gardens? My only caveat would be that it lacks garden buildings for leisure, as opposed to productivity. Perhaps Lutyens thought there were enough of those in the landscape garden that is glimpsed through his gateway. Henry Avray Tipping summed up its design succinctly: 'above all, it is reticent. There is nothing restless or overdone. It is an architect's garden certainly, but it leaves scope for the gardener'.[46]

That scope for elaborate planting schemes was even more in evidence at **Barrington Court**, where Jekyll, this time working without Lutyens, was responsible for the formal gardens to the west of Strode House, the former seventeenth-century stables that had been converted into domestic use for the National Trust tenant, Colonel Arthur Lyle. In 1917 he had commissioned JE Forbes to prepare a masterplan to turn Barrington into a model Arts and Crafts estate with workers' cottages, farm buildings and extensive walled gardens.[47] Lyle's wife visited Jekyll at Munstead Wood to discuss the planting schemes which, even though the house was occupied by a boys' preparatory school in the Second World War, were maintained throughout the twentieth century. The Lyles held the lease until Andrew Lyle, who had continued to develop and restore the gardens with Head Gardener Christine Brain, gave up the lease in 1991. Since then the gardens have been managed by the Trust.

Forbes devised the structure of the garden enclosure, constructing new walls and incorporating earlier sections; he also formed the artificial moat, which encloses the gardens on west and north. The whole area is subdivided into four sectors, entered by a timber door designed by Lutyens. Indeed, there are several gates and doorways at Barrington, all individual in design, which create different associations as the visitor enters or leaves each garden area. This individual character is repeated in the brick paths: bold herringbone in the Lily Garden, stone inlaid with slivers of brick in other enclosures.

Jekyll's White Garden (*colour 46*), originally centred by the figure of a dancing faun, which was stolen in 2008, is a symphony of white, cream and silver-flowering plants: annuals in the central beds and herbaceous perennials in the outer borders. Jekyll designed it as a rose and peony garden, but by 1986 the roses had gone over, so new planting was supplied for the wheel-shaped arrangement of beds. The idea for an all-white garden had been proposed in Jekyll's 1908 *Colour in the Flower Garden*; this one was created with a mixture of plants including tulips, white pulmonaria and forget-me-not, arabis, lilies, iris, lychnis, crambe and phlox.[48] The walls are festooned with white wisteria, actinidea and the climbing roses 'White cockade' and 'Iceberg'.

Her Rose and Iris Garden has been planted with old varieties of bearded irises interspersed with herbaceous plants, purple sage and antirrhinums, while the Pergola Walk, designed in her style by Andrew Lyle and Christine Brain, is wreathed in honeysuckle, jasmine, wisteria, hop and clematises, particularly 'Perle d'Azur' and 'Nelly Moser'. Finally, the Lily Garden, which is the largest enclosure, has been planted, again in her style, to create those rising and falling crescendos between pale shades and fiery colours. This effect is achieved by azaleas, bergenias, yuccas, day lilies, heliotropes and *Crinum x powellii*, the last and only survival of the original planting.[49]

Lutyens' last garden commission in Somerset saw him return to **Mells**, where the eighteenth-century house, for which he had been planning additions, was gutted by fire in October 1917. He was subsequently commissioned in 1922 by Reginald McKenna, a former Chancellor of the Exchequer, to design a new house on the site, and to lay out gardens around it. The new Park he devised for McKenna is a rather grim affair with unremitting Doric pilasters and a hipped roof. To the main garden front facing the Temple and the return elevation he provided two simple sunken gardens edged with drystone walls topped with yew hedges; he enlivened one of them with a rectangular pool. The pool enclosure has small borders planted with irises, and in each corner is a tall circular evergreen globe, breaking the insistent geometry. There are further low squares of box on the paved garden terrace. That is all. Infinitely more impressive and satisfying is the recently planted box parterre within the arcaded courtyard of the old house, which survives to the rear of Lutyens' addition.

Like almost all these Edwardian garden designers, apart from Alfred Parsons who was essentially an artist, Harold Ainsworth Peto began his career as an architect, working first for a firm in Lowestoft, then moving on to a London practice before setting up in partnership with Ernest George in 1876.[50] It was a thriving firm with a sound country house portfolio, and Peto is recorded as having been particularly good at handling clients. During the 1880s he made several trips abroad to Italy, America and Spain, recording his travels in a series of diaries and storing up design ideas for future commissions. In 1892 Peto dissolved his partnership with George on the understanding that he would not work as an architect in Britain. It is probable that he had already determined to practise instead as a landscape designer. In 1896 he moved to Landsford House, near Salisbury, which was owned by his eldest sister, acting as a kind of house sitter when she was in London. He was also closer in the country to Chedington Court, Dorset, where his eldest brother, Sir Henry, lived. This desire to maintain close contact with his family is apparent in many of the commissions he accepted after 1900, when his landscape business took off, as several of his Somerset gardens were designed for family members.

Peto's work in the county may well have begun with the garden at **Glencot House**, near Wookey Hole, where the partners built a new country house in 1887. Robin Whalley, the current expert on Peto, has discerned certain features at Glencot, including the statue of St Cuthbert on a bridge over the stream that threads through the grounds, which are 'uncannily in the mode of Peto'.[51] He would later raise a statue of Britannia on the bridge at his Wiltshire home of Iford Manor; the Glencot Bridge is dated 1901. Further out across the lawn at Glencot there is a spring surrounded by a strange architectural frame and deep rill that recalls, according to Whalley, some of the Pompeian-style fountains that feature in Peto's later work. In the distinct spirit of exoticism that pervades the current hotel at Glencot, the fountain is lit from a tree above by a hanging crystal chandelier.[52]

Glencot is by way of a mild introduction to Peto's most accomplished garden, at **Wayford Manor**, near Crewkerne, and a lesser layout at **Burton Pynsent**, both drawn up for sisters. As one of fourteen children, it is not surprising that Peto was called upon by his family to give advice on garden schemes. Helen Peto had married Ingham Baker in 1885, and they bought Wayford Manor in the late 1890s. Her brother Sir Henry was only five

70 The forecourt of the Manor, with its Jacobean loggia-porch, offered Harold Peto the first enclosure at Wayford that he could turn, with the addition of clipped bay trees and grass plats, into a secluded garden room

miles to the east at Chedington in Dorset, while Helen's sister Edith moved to Seaborough Court, a few miles from Wayford, in 1904. Yet another sister, Sarah, having married into the Crossley family, moved to Burton in 1909. All three sisters were very close and visited Peto regularly at Iford; it was probably Helen who was with Peto when he died.[53]

Peto's distinctive architectural style is signalled at the water fountain on the village street, long before the visitor reaches the Manor. This has a bronze puma's head identical to one by the Casita at Iford. The entrance path to the Manor leads, via cascading magnolia blooms on the left and razor-edged yew hedges and rounded topiary on the right, straight into a barrier of yew.[54] At this point the visitor turns left to take in the entrance forecourt of the Manor (*70*) with its clipped bays and loggia-porch, or right to a yew enclosure sheltering a Byzantine font from Ravenna, and then obliquely to the Iris Garden, its crazy-paved paths bordered by beds of bearded irises leading to a bronze copy of Giambologna's statue of Mercury. The close proximity of the farm buildings and the original Italian cypresses complete the Tuscan feel of this area. The effect of these garden rooms is purposely claustrophobic and confined, a conscious preparation, after the yew hedge, for the openness of the Long Terrace, which stretches across the whole width of the garden and offers grandstand views out over the River Axe to the Dorset landscape.

At one end of the Long Terrace, Peto devised an arcaded Summerhouse in imitation of the Jacobean loggia on the entrance front.[55] This connects the Terrace with the Kitchen Garden and is decorated with sculptures in much the same way that Peto enriched his Cloisters at Iford. From here the view along the Terrace, which is walled to the forecourt and balustraded to the gardens, is centred by a sundial on a gadrooned stone base and climaxes in two stately horse chestnuts. Sundials are ubiquitous in Arts and Crafts gardens, signifying, as Blomfield puts it in his *Formal Garden*, 'the human interest of the garden, [and] the long continuity of tradition, which has gone before, and will outlive us'.[56] The dial itself is dated 1630 and inscribed with the words: 'As the long hours do pass away/So doth the life of man decay'. Parallel to the Terrace on the north is another yew-hedged enclosure, with a rectangular pool guarded by a fountain of an *amorino* holding a dolphin; another Peto memory of Pompeii. This area is commanded by a small, rustic Garden Seat, covered in stone slates. At the west end of the Terrace steps lead down into a high-walled Water Garden, overshadowed by *Acer palmatum* and bordered by a herbaceous planting of hostas, foxgloves, hypericum and rodgersia, interspersed with ferns and irises. Here there is another *amorino* fountain; this time the cherub holds a bird that spouts water. Behind him, set within a semicircular recess, is one of Peto's favourite Pompeian exedral seats, while alongside is another puma fountain, its jet spouting into a rectangular trough.

An archway in the wall leads out onto the main lawn, with views back up to the house and the Long Terrace (*colour 47*) and, on the east, to the Pergola, which was built in 2000 in imitation of Peto's style. At the southern end of the lawn Italian pencil cypresses, planted by Robin Goffe, mark the boundary between the formal elements and the Wild Garden below. A beautiful *Magnolia x Soulangeana*, dating from Peto's scheme, prepares the visitor for the exoticism of the Japanese planting beyond.[57] This is a bosky area, alive with birdsong, threaded with winding paths, streams and pools shaded by camellias, rhododendrons, forsythia, magnolias and acers. At its heart is a small Japanese Garden (*colour 48*), with a stone sculpture and a lantern, set within a rocky, pool-entwined slope overhung with acers. The planting in the Wild Garden, especially the *Betula Maximowicziana*, first introduced from Japan in 1893, could be Peto's, as could the tall pines.[58] These last might, however, have been introduced by Helen's son, Humphrey Baker, who owned the house when it was the subject of a 1934 *Country Life* article.[59] Wayford is a dexterous mix of both formal and informal elements; the original variety of trees has been greatly enhanced by the Goffs.

Peto's layout at Burton Pynsent, designed for his sister, Helen Crossley, was less ambitious, comprising a balustraded terrace laid out in front of the east façade to take in views across the escarpment above Sedge Moor towards Sir William Pynsent's Column. Peto retained some of William Pitt's great cedars to the north of the house, but felled others to open up the view. The house was given a new door, and a bisecting axial path was designed to lead through a wrought-iron gate into the lower garden. He also laid out a transverse path across the garden front of the house, lined with clipped Portuguese laurels and fastigiate yews, while a rudimentary brick Loggia headed a path connecting the formal gardens around the house with a yew-hedged panel garden, now laid to lawn. Parallel to this, on the south side of the yew hedge, is a Lime Avenue, which was illustrated in its pleached form in 1934, but which is now pollarded. Sarah Crossley died in 1938, four years after her house and gardens were photographed for *Country Life*.[60]

There is one further Somerset layout which might have Peto family connections, though this is not proven. Now in divided ownership, **The**

Old Court at Misterton, near Crewkerne, was owned in the 1920s by Anthony Crossley, a relation of Sarah's through her marriage with Clement Crossley.[61] 1930s photographs reveal a typical Edwardian mix of open lawns, shaped topiary and stone walls. In one side of the grounds, owned today by Peter Facey, there is a pyramidal-roofed Summerhouse of Arts and Crafts style, and a small woodland garden with a pool, which has a Japanese feel. In the other, owned by Pam and Roger Entwistle, open lawns lead, via a circular well surrounded by paving, to a low-walled Topiary Garden (*71*) backed by a Loggia. This is centred by a clipped peacock, flanked by box-edged beds in the quadrants planted with heathers.

Peto's last commission in the county was at **Widcombe Manor**, where he laid out a simple formal garden below the Italianate terrace for the novelist Horace Annesley Vachéll.[62] The first stage of this survives, accessed via blockish stone steps decorated with distinctly Art Deco stone urns, connecting with a walled and yew-hedged enclosure containing a crescent-shaped pool and short pergolas. Beyond this is now open parkland, but originally two flights of steps led down a grass slope to another sunken area, this time rectangular with a central stepped octagon containing an Italianate wellhead.[63] An area of clipped topiary centred by a stone statue has been laid out approximately on the site of this earlier formal garden. We have no precise date for the Peto garden, though Arthur Oswald reported in 1937 that 'the terraced gardens on the steeply shelving slope west of the house have been laid out in the last ten years'.[64] Given that Peto died in 1933, it must have been one of his last commissions.

Barley Wood at Wrington is not normally associated with the Edwardians, as it was the home from 1802 of the social reformer and educational pioneer, Hannah More.[65] Hannah and her sister built a typical Regency *cottage ornée* with a thatched roof and a latticework verandah. On the terrace, which offered views out towards the sea at Weston-super-Mare and across to the Mendips, they placed commemorative urns to the Wrington-born philosopher John Locke and to Beilby Porteous, Bishop of London. In the wider grounds the sisters planted laurels, larches, cypresses, chestnuts and other trees, and laid out shrubbery walks.[66] They even indulged in a 'Druidical Temple made of knots of oak',[67] so by the

71 The Topiary Garden at The Old Court, Misterton, a possible Peto design, has survived remarkably intact, though the heathers are a later planting

time Henry Herbert Wills, of the great Bristol dynasty of tobacco barons, took over the house and grounds he acquired a mature designed landscape.[68] Sir Ernest George enlarged the house for him between 1900 and 1901, and built the walled vegetable garden across Long Lane. When he was later commissioned to remodel the grounds for Wills in 1910, Thomas Mawson determined that 'no alterations of the poetess Hannah More should be removed', rather that there should be some 'touching up here and there where the original intentions had been lost'.[69] Mawson's main contribution was the sunken Rose Garden, which survives, albeit decayed. Mawson located this 'quiet panel rose garden at a part of the site and in such an unobtrusive way' that he 'felt the illustrious authoress would have approved'.[70]

The Rose Garden is certainly unobtrusive, as it is set well below the entrance drive, parallel with Long Lane and connected with the yew-enclosed lower terrace beneath the house by Mawson's typically robust moon steps, which are book-ended by stone benches with scrolled arms. The path down leads to the open loggia at the rear of the Garden House with its sweeping hipped roof and classical columns. There is just a

72 Thomas Mawson devised this Garden House as a link between the formal terraces of Barley Wood and the 'Rosarium', with its expansive views of the Mendips. He laid the garden out in 1911 for Henry Herbert Wills, the Bristol tobacco baron

glimpse of the angular hedges and pool beyond, but no wider view at this level. Once the Garden House (*72*) is reached, a Latin inscription on an inner doorway records the creation of the 'Rosarium' by HH Wills. A flight of steps descends to a sundial set on a classical baluster with a further inscription: 'Hora Fugit/ Caritas Manet', accompanied by the dates 1886 and 1911 and the initials of Wills and his wife. It is only then one looks up and a breathtaking view unfolds (*colour 49*), with the Pool Garden in the lower foreground, the Walled Garden in the middle distance and the Mendip ridge above Churchill, Burrington and Blagdon on the blue horizon.

Mawson's hard landscaping features are apparent everywhere: blockish paving, axial terracing, rock-faced rangework mixed with chunky smooth ashlar for walls and sturdy stone benches, all complemented by tall yew hedges, cut through with straight-arched entrances, surrounding lawned garden rooms. The rooms lead axially across the slope towards the east, where there is another change in level down to the Pergola, which runs along the retaining wall between the garden and the road below. This is built of rock-faced masonry on the garden side and brick piers on the other, connected above head height by oak beams. The Pergola is wonderfully atmospheric today, smothered in a mass of undergrowth, but it once commanded views out between the piers across the roofs of the Walled Garden to the Mendips beyond. It was, without doubt, inspired by Lutyens' similar feature at Hestercombe, though Mawson often introduced pergolas into his designs, most notably at The Hill, Hampstead. The future of the house and grounds at Barley Wood seems unclear, as they were deserted on our visit in the summer of 2009. It is to be hoped that the historical and architectural importance of both are soon recognised by a sympathetic new owner.

Mawson's other commission in the county was at **North Cadbury Court**, where in 1912 he 'replanned the gardens in such a way as to permit the scheme being realised by annual instalments' for Mr and Mrs Langmuir.[71] Apparently the Langmuirs spent much of their time in Canada, where they had property interests, so Mawson determined to have the alterations carried out during their absence. Apart from an expansive view over open lawns towards the mighty Iron Age Cadbury Camp, little survives of Mawson's scheme at the house today. The terraced lawns extend across the garden front of the Regency house, terminating in a typical exedra of receding and projecting yew blocks. On axis with this is a grass walk, crossed by two runs of Ham stone walls and dumpy piers topped by ball finials, which leads to an eighteenth-century walled garden. There are further, blockish yew hedges closer to the house, and some topiary shapes by the entrance front, but that is all.

St Catherine's Court, hidden up a valley to the north-east of Bath, could not be a more fitting place to end a chapter where the architecture of the past has been the catalyst for new garden layouts. Nestling close to its parish church in the tradition of English manors, the fifteenth-century house phases almost seamlessly into its architectural environs and even into the churchyard itself, whose wall is the northern boundary of the entrance forecourt. In the sixteenth century the manor was owned by Sir John Harington of Kelston, who sold it to the Blanchards of Marshfield in 1591. On the north front of the house they added a porch which acts, like the one at Wayford Manor, as a proto-garden building with seating

73 Hugh Mackay Baillie Scott's double Pergolas during their reinstatement at St Catherine's Court in the summer of 2009

niches for viewing the gardens. The terraced gardens, which climb the steep slope above the house to the west, were laid out at that time. These were given Jacobean-style balustrades by Colonel J H Strutt after he bought the property in 1841. Strutt and his daughter Charlotte Elizabeth, who took over on the Colonel's death in 1845, also added the massive yew hedge which separates the terrace from the gardens above. This is now a series of overgrown yew trees shadowing the Bowling Alley. Up above is a romantic Bathing Pool, entirely enclosed in yew for privacy, with two changing rooms of yew denoted by carved stone tablets with the words 'Adam' and 'Eve'. Its date is uncertain, but it is likely to have been installed in the 1920s by the Hon Richard Strutt.

Charlotte died in 1897, and the following year *Country Life* featured the gardens in a lavishly illustrated article, which records precisely what she had achieved all around the house. Further *Country Life* articles of 1903 and 1906 feature the Grass Stairway and the complex terraced gardens laid out to the south of the house. The main difference between these archival images and the gardens today is that originally they were alive with clipped yews, shrub and herbaceous borders, pencil thin conifers, grasses and island beds: all typical late Victorian features. These were deplored by Gertrude Jekyll, who wrote in the 1906 *Country Life* article that:

> the quiet lawns of these old places should be jealously guarded, especially from the intrusion of specimen conifers. Fifty years ago many a beautiful lawn, whose velvet-green expanse had endured for centuries, was cruelly cut up to make gardens for bedding plants. They were often without any design, a shapeless sprinkle of stars and crescents, diamonds and circles, to be filled with garish plants, ill-assorted, whose presence has destroyed the character of many a fine old garden. Happily we know better now, and the vandalisms of the last generation are no longer practised.[72]

Most of the beds and the conifers have gone, but the Grass Stairway survives, albeit eroded to a series of gently undulating curves, with its herbaceous border replanted by Head Gardener Alison Jenkins (*colour 50*). She has injected new life into all the borders with a vibrant combination of traditional herbaceous and modern prairie planting. The pale walls of the Croquet Lawn and Grass Stairway are clothed in the vivid purple of *Cotinus coggygria* to off-set the planting in the borders below, which consists of massed perovskia, purple sedums and heucheras sharply contrasting with the acid yellow of golden marjoram. Every month the borders subtly change in their texture, structure and colour to provide seasonal interest.

By 1912 the estate was owned by the Hon Richard Strutt, who began a campaign of building and gardening. He built the library, added the orangery and redesigned the approach to the house and gardens.[73] The steps by the church were given a new balustrade and an arched fountain was built underneath them as a welcoming feature. In the entrance forecourt he created a stony sunken garden, centred by an octagonal pool, and then turned his attention to the south front. The 1906 *Country Life* article shows a terrace along this elevation with no central access to the slopes below. Strutt called in Hugh Mackay Baillie Scott to rectify this and to connect the south side of the Manor more closely with the landscape. Baillie Scott produced a pastel painting of the house and gardens, which was published in *The Studio*.[74] Unfortunately this shows the terraces descending to the Croquet Lawn and the entrance front of the house rather than the south garden, where he designed two pergolas striding out from a new terrace and steps.

These pergolas have had a chequered history. Richard Strutt was succeeded by his second son, Geoffrey St John Strutt, and the estate was sold to a Christian Charity Trust in 1975. The following year the Christophers bought the estate and attempted to restore the gardens back to their Tudor origins.[75] In order to do this they proposed to demolish what was left of the ancient gatehouse and east wall on the approach to the house, to return the sunken garden in the forecourt to a more appropriate design and to remove the pergolas. The Ancient Monuments Society raised the alarm, but no other organisations objected. The District Council granted permission and the gatehouse was demolished along with the pergolas, while the sunken garden was filled in.

The Christophers were well intentioned, if ill-advised, for their time, but an owner more sympathetic to the Edwardian garden features bought the house from the actress Jane Seymour in 2008, and is embarking upon a brilliant recreation of the Baillie Scott pergolas. Fortunately, the circular bases of the columns were still in place when Helene Morling carried out her research on the site in 2005, and these have provided the basis for a complete reconstruction (73), which was taking place when we visited in the summer of 2009. Furthermore, Alison Jenkins is re-planting the area between the two new pergolas with ranks of box cones and mounds, interplanted with diagonal lines of feathery grasses. In May the tall heads of *Allium* 'Purple sensation' contrast with the structural greens. The kitchen garden has also been brought back into productivity, and in the wider landscape a vineyard is in the process of being planted. It will shortly be appropriate for *Country Life* to visit again to record the revival of this seminal architectural garden.

9

Twentieth-century plantswomen take centre stage

▼

East Lambrook Manor · Brympton d'Evercy · Tintinhull House · Montacute
Greencombe · Barford Park · Hadspen House · Cothay Manor
Lady Farm

THE LAST CHAPTERS IN THIS SERIES HAVE TENDED TO BECOME SURVEYS OF those gardens created in the twentieth century that might possibly be considered historic in the near future. When specific designers of national and international repute have been commissioned the choice has been an easy one; what has been more difficult is to predict the longevity of gardens where plants alone have driven the design. Fortunately this has not been a problem in Somerset, which must rate two chapters on the last hundred years: one to come, which includes gardens as unexpected as the Geoffrey Jellicoe-Russell Page layout at the Caveman Restaurant in Cheddar Gorge; the other here, centred on a series of gardens achieved by a group of redoubtable plantswomen, most of whom made the county their home. In no particular order of importance they are: Phyliss Reiss at Tintinhull House, Violet Clive at Brympton D'Evercy, Margery Fish at East Lambrook Manor, Sylvia Crowe at Barford Park, Joan Loraine at Greencombe, Judy Pearce and Mary Payne at Lady Farm, the unlikely TV personality Mary Ann Robb at Cothay Manor, and finally Penelope Hobhouse at Hadspen and Tintinhull, who has now returned again to Hadspen to create yet another new garden.

It is hard to believe, when walking around the suburban site at **East Lambrook Manor**, that its principal creator, Margery Fish, was a woman ahead of her time who was to alter the style of post-war gardening. She was one of those remarkable women who took to gardening in her forties and managed to combine sensitivity of design with a vast knowledge of plants.

Margery Townsend set herself apart from many middle-class women of her generation by carving out a career in Fleet Street after completing her secretarial training in 1911. Her hard work and determination were recognised by Lord Northcliffe, owner of the *Daily Mail*, who insisted that she accompany him as his personal assistant on his British War Mission to the United States in 1916, for which she was awarded an MBE. Working for a series of editors, she eventually married Walter Fish, three years after he had retired from the paper in 1933. Like the current owners, Mike and Gail Werkmeister, the Fishes began to look for a home away from London. Similarly, they both considered the Manor and initially dismissed it, eventually returning and buying the crumbling old farmhouse and two acres of land in the village of South Petherton.[1]

Walter and Margery Fish came together late in life, more for convenience than passion. They would certainly have been prime candidates for the 'marriage guidance' so often sought on Radio 4's *Gardeners' Question Time*, as their views on the garden did not often coincide. Walter's experience of gardening led to his decisive layout of 'the four essentials': lawns, hedges, walls and the gravel paths, which he assiduously maintained,[2] whereas his wife's approach was more relaxed. She advocated trial and error and sheer hard work. Although she referred to her husband as a philistine in his relationship with plants, she admitted the debt of knowledge she owed to him. Fish believed in creating winter interest by planting evergreens, such as the *Chamaecyparis lawsoniana* 'Fletcheri' (re-planted 2000), which she fondly referred to as her 'pudding trees', whereas Walter was more interested in the flamboyant summer colours of delphiniums, lupins and dahlias. Following Walter's sudden death in 1947, Fish was free to continue her experiments in unusual planting combinations: mixing rare and everyday cottage garden varieties, allowing seedlings to grow where they would, and creating collections of snowdrops, primulas and iris. But it was her friendship with the plantswoman Valerie Finnis that increased her knowledge and encouraged her to experiment with new varieties, giving rise to *Artemisia absinthium* 'Lambrook Silver' and *Polemonium* 'Lambrook Mauve' to name but two.[3] However, where Tintinhull and Cothay offer formal, enclosed layouts, due to their owners' sweeping changes, the garden at East Lambrook evolved as Fish gained confidence in tackling new areas.

Today, the garden is reached across the road from the scar of a carpark, insensitively carved out of a field by the previous owners. On entering the driveway at the Barton, the visitor is beset by a variety of notices offering information, teas and art exhibitions in the Malthouse. Following a plan of this garden is unnecessary as the scale is diminutive, and there is no chance of getting lost. From the grandly named Sundial Garden and Green Garden with its meandering paths, past the Wooded Garden, carpeted in winter with hellebores, around the cowhouse, the visitor reaches the Ditch (*colour 51*). This is now a dry area covered in self-seeded forget-me-nots, *Anemone nemorosa*, and other woodland plants, and was clearly influenced by the writings of William Robinson. It is punctuated by starkly pollarded willows along the gulley, which are reminiscent of withies. On the opposite side is The Strip, a bare area that would benefit from being returned to a simple lawn to offer a breathing space from the busy planting, as in the Theatre Lawn at Hidcote. The water garden, or Lido, as the Fishes named it, provided damp shade for her treasured groups of iris, meconopsis and Asiatic primulas, but soon after they planted it the source dried up, and she was left with a bog-planting scheme devoid of water.[4] A narrow path leads to the Top Lawn, which is dotted with specimen trees of *Magnolia x.soulangeana* and *Cercis siliquastrum*, enveloped by a low hedge of Fish's favourite *Lonicera nitida*. In the White and Silver Gardens herbaceous perennials cluster together tightly. It would be interesting to know how many visitors to East Lambrook realise that cottage garden favourites such as *Stacchys byzantinus* (bunny's ears) are only so prolific because Fish rescued them from extinction. Finally, a snaking narrow path cloaked with frothy plants leads back to the Front Lawn and the Barton.

After Margery's death in 1969 the garden was bequeathed to her nephew, Henry Boyd-Carpenter. Overwhelmed by the profusion of plants and their need of intensive gardening, he eventually enlisted the help of his parents, and the garden has since had a succession of owners, all of whom have tried to continue the spirit of Fish's original conception. As is so often the problem when the designer dies, the essence of the garden dissipates over time. However, the constant gardeners in this period have been Head Gardener Mark Stainer and volunteer Maureen Whitty, who both worked with Fish, and their knowledge should be documented to keep this garden from losing its identity. As John Sales has commented, East Lambrook might not have gained its reputation without Fish's self-promotion through books and lectures.[5] Often, those gardeners who document their achievements are the best remembered, but Fish should also be admired for her ability to create texture, good ground cover, unusual planting combinations and colour throughout the year. In post-war Britain, when labour was scarce, this was the key to a successful cottage garden.

As any keen gardener will know, begging, borrowing and stealing cuttings and seeds is *de rigueur* between owners, but in the rationing days of the 1950s it was essential to start or maintain any garden. Fish's friendships with neighbouring Somerset garden owners, especially Violet Clive at **Brympton d'Evercy**, ensured that there were always supplies. Clive inherited Brympton in 1915 from her grandfather, the cricketing enthusiast Sir Spencer Ponsonby Fane.[6] After the early death of her husband, Captain Edward Clive, she faced a long future as a widow. Clive filled the next thirty years with travel and gardening, often combining the two by plant hunting, storing specimens in the ideal damp conditions of her sponge bag.[7] At Brympton she removed the formal bedding of the previous century and, anticipating the emergent cottage style, planted wide beds of mixed shrub and herbaceous plants, combining texture, colour and structure to form the archetypal floriferous border. As yet, there is inconclusive proof of her influence on the gardens at Sissinghurst, but if the new owner's claim to having a plan of a rose garden for Brympton by Gertrude Jekyll is true, this would put Clive's gardening associations in a new light.[8] The 1927 *Country Life* article on Brympton illustrates a rose garden, and Jekyll included a picture of Brympton's dovecote in her 1918 *Garden Ornament*, so it is likely that she visited. In the spirit of make-do-and-mend, Violet also used reclaimed materials from Yeovil Town Hall to create a classical temple with pediment and Corinthian columns at the eastern point of the south terrace.[9] She also planted a small vineyard on the upper terrace, since replanted with fruit trees. As she grew older, her travels dwindled, and she was happy to remain at Brympton, bringing elements of foreign gardens to her own with the inclusion of Japanese artefacts and plants from her brother Richard Ponsonby Fane's garden in Kyoto.[10] One of the stone lanterns still sits at a jaunty angle on the island in the centre of the lake.

The American born designer, Lanning Roper, had visited the Fishes at East Lambrook whilst still serving in the US naval reserve during the Second World War.[11] As their friendship grew, he was introduced to many of Somerset's gardening fraternity, including Clive at Brympton, where he noted her unusual colour combinations, as well as at **Tintinhull**, which Phyllis Reiss and her husband had bought in 1933.[12] Although Roper's own style would later become more modernist, he revelled in the cottage garden planting of the Somerset villages, and particularly Tintinhull.[13]

Phyllis Reiss was the sixth child of Colonel and Mrs Alfred Lucas of Hobland Hall, Norfolk, a family of noted amateur gardeners. Although Reiss never received any formal horticultural training, travels in Italy influenced her style and taste for compartmentalised gardens that extended the structure of the villa's rooms to form a cohesive whole. In addition, the early years of her marriage were spent at Dowdeswell Manor in Gloucestershire, a near neighbour of Hidcote, where she absorbed ideas of the grand cottage garden style laid out by Lawrence Johnston between 1907 and 1914.[14] When she arrived at Tintinhull with Captain Reiss they found a smaller garden laid out around the west and north sides of the house, with strong architectural elements of garden rooms and paths but on a flat, two-acre site. This had been created in 1900 by the tenant, Dr S J M Price, an eminent botanist, possibly with advice from Harold Peto.[15] He had laid out the flagstone walk of the Eagle Court and Middle Garden, their compartments leading down to the Fountain Garden at the west end; he also planted the two rows of clipped box domes edging the path.[16] No doubt this simple formality appealed to Reiss, who then set about increasing the garden by bringing an old paddock into the grounds to form the Cedar Court to the north. Alongside the existing cedar of Lebanon she planted a second, remarking a month before her death: 'I'm so glad I thought of putting in that little cedar. I feel it's part of me'.[17] At the end of the war, the tennis court was removed and the rectangular space used to form the Pool Garden which is overlooked by a classical Summerhouse.

Possibly through Lanning Roper, Reiss became firm friends with Margery Fish, with whom she learnt more about plants and how to tend them in the often soggy Somerset climate. They were, however, diametrically opposed in their chosen styles. Whereas Fish loved individual plants for their own characteristics and was an inveterate collector, Reiss used plants to create the space and structure that her garden required. Strongly disciplined, she would not give in to pretty new specimens unless they had design merit; this meant that her borders retained a simplicity and ease of maintenance. Through her father, Reiss met and became friends with Sylvia Crowe who wrote: 'One of Phyllis's strengths was that she knew just what plant was right in a particular place and would not be seduced by novelty or extra colour'.[18] In fact, in the post-war era, funds and new specimens were in short supply, and Reiss's use of repeated plants probably stemmed from her need to fill spaces with plants taken from cuttings and collected seed. She lived at Tintinhull for twenty-eight years, donating it to the National Trust in 1954 before her death in 1961. During her tenure she had only one gardener, George Mapletoft, who appeared to come with the gardens; this length of service suggests that Reiss was a generous employer and an inspiring garden lover.

After her death the house was taken over by a Miss Bevan and a Miss Ware who were less interested in the gardens, before they were revived in 1974 by the National Trust's tenants, Penelope Hobhouse and her husband, Professor John Malins. Although she met Reiss only twice, Hobhouse's strong design instincts and passion for plants enabled her to continue in the spirit of the Reiss gardening ethos. In 1979 all the beds were sterilised and returned to Reiss's designs, based on original photographs. Graham Stuart Thomas, who had been a good friend of Reiss, was enlisted to seek out particular plants and re-instate them. But whereas the Reisses had always holidayed in Scotland during August, the gardens were now open to the public in this difficult gardening month, so Hobhouse started to fill the gaps with the help of advice from John Raven.[19]

The high wall adjacent to the road gives no hint of what lies behind, and on entering the courtyard there is a collection of old farm buildings, draped with wisteria in a vernacular cottage garden style. The garden proper can be approached either through a door in the north wall, or more appropriately through the Drawing Room of the house, a route recently re-instated by the National Trust. This gives the visitor a considered view of the formality created by the elongated path, punctuated by the box domes and with framed views to the west. Steps give access to the West Terrace, on which pots are filled with Reiss's traditional *Lilium regale*, but also tulips for spring interest and, most disconcertingly, a motley collection of succulents.

74 The borders of the Eagle Court at Tintinhull were first planted by Phyllis Reiss, then revived in 1979 with the help of early photographs by Penelope Hobhouse; sadly, her planting has not been maintained by the National Trust

The Eagle Court (*74*), named after the pair of eagles on top of the tallest gate-piers, is edged with borders against the eighteenth-century brick walls. It is immediately apparent that these are filled with structural mounds and shapes of small trees and various shrubs: *Malus hupehensis*, *Prunus* 'Ukon', *Ceanothus* and *Itea ilicifolia* with its creamy green tail-like racemes. The north and south borders, although planted differently to suit their conditions, are both given a repetitive treatment setting a rhythm, whilst hybrid tea and floribunda roses are allowed to mingle with *Clematis viticella* 'Etoile Violette' ensnaring the eagles. The path leads on through the Middle Garden, a shadier space thanks to a pair of *Quercus Ilex* dominating the south side, where an urn creates a focal point from a cross vista. The curving beds here are planted in a more naturalistic woodland style, but the path and box domes carry the formality through into the Fountain Garden. This circular pool is edged with clumps of Angel's fishing rods (*Dierama pulcherrimum*) and white agapanthus, while the white theme is continued in the beds around the pool, which take on a luminous quality against the dark yew hedges. Vertical accents are provided by the silvers of *Salix helvetica* and the recently introduced *Cornus controversa* 'Variegata'.

From here the grounds take an unexpected turn, arriving at the Kitchen Garden, which is meticulously maintained, abundant and beautifully labelled. With the public's interest in all things 'below stairs' the National Trust has made much more of its productive areas, and at Tintinhull this has the feel of a potager with billowing sprays of blue starry chicory flowers and paths edged with *Rosa* 'Nathalie Nypels'. A gap in the yew hedge leads to the Pool Garden with its much-needed watery elements. A plaque in the Summerhouse records Reiss's creation of this garden in 1945, in memory of her nephew Michael Lucas. The rectangular Lily Pond is flanked by grass, which in turn is edged with wide borders: the west side is filled with crimson, reds and yellows, whereas the east border is cooler, with pink, mauve and blue plants. Pots around the pool echo the planting colours and were introduced by Hobhouse.[20] Finally, the paths lead to the Cedar Court, where high brick walls enclose a large lawn dotted with magnolias and edged with crazy-paved paths that line borders. Up against the yew hedge is the first bed that Reiss planted: the Purple Border with its structure of purple-leafed berberis and cotinus and filled with other shades such as *Penstemon* 'Sour Grapes', *Sedum telephium* subsp. 'Atropurpureum' and *Rosa* 'Frensham'. Although one of the cedars was diseased and had to be removed, the Trust planted another specimen to maintain the pairing that Reiss had felt so important.

Since Hobhouse's departure the house has not had gardening tenants, and it shows. Whilst hard work, goodwill and much volunteer enthusiasm keep the gardens going, there is a lack of cohesion in the borders and a spottiness to some of the more ephemeral planting; this is in complete contrast to the massed blocks of colour created by Reiss. If the Trust can recreate historic interiors at will, why not restore historic planting? However, with its six contrasting garden areas, Tintinhull still provides that combination of architectural formality softened by varied planting which, in turn, offers ideas for today's gardener.

Unlike Margery Fish, Phyllis Reiss was not a writer, and as far as we know did not even leave any planting plans for Tintinhull. However, her importance as a gardener was recognised by the Trust, who asked her to re-plant the borders of the East Garden at nearby **Montacute**, previously laid out by Vita Sackville-West. Reiss designed the new planting with her signature blocks of strong colours and large groups of foliage plants to provide colour throughout the year. The main planting is clematis and vines on the north and south walls, red 'Frensham' roses, 'Orange Triumph' polyantha roses, delphiniums, lupins, dahlias and achillea, berberis and cotinus. Spikes of acanthus and yucca echo the vertical accents of the roofline of Montacute.[21]

Whereas those women came to gardening later in life, Joan Loraine enjoyed the natural flora of the Somerset countryside from an early age when her mother moved the family from the London Blitz to Hartrow Manor.[22] Shortly afterwards she bought Greencombe (*colour 52*), a solid 1930s house now heavily covered in wisteria, perched on the hillside above Porlock Bay. Around the skirts of the house Horace Stroud had laid out the usual combination of lawns, borders and an Italianate pool on the lower northern terrace with a gazebo for taking in the views. Above the house, on the vertiginous southern side, Loraine designed a formal vegetable garden, entered by a brick and stone arch, reminiscent of a moon gate. At the outset she enlisted the help of local gardener Norman Haddon to create a garden on the site of a thirteenth-century deer park, known as the 'gut', of which sections of the pale can still be found in the woodland. When Loraine was not away teaching in Uganda, Turkey and Italy, she was collecting plants and arranging them in her hidden woodland garden.

The 3.5-acre grounds now have four national collections: erythronium, gaultheria, polystichum and vaccinium. From the western lawn sinuous paths lead through the woodland, rich with ericaceous leaf mould and

75
Tom Preater's carving of a woman and child, from a sweet chestnut grown in the garden at Greencombe, encapsulates perfectly Joan Loraine's strong Christian beliefs and her passion for plants and trees

planted in Robinsonian style with a colourful collection of shrubs, including vibrant camellias and azaleas. Loraine's passion extends both to 'sizzling colours', which light up the green glades, and to more delicate specimens, such as *Rhododendron lindleyi* with its intoxicating fragrance.[23] The woodland is thick with Spanish chestnuts, beech and a magnificent champion holly tree, gnarled and multi-stemmed, while tiny plants carpet the ground. The planting appears effortlessly natural, which is how a woodland garden should be, but which belies the immense amount of work carried out by both Loraine and her garden helpers. Wandering along the paths, brushing through swathes of blossom, the visitor eventually reaches a surprising new addition. This is a circular Chapel – Our Lady of the Secret – designed by the Revd Dan Olive to commemorate the Millennium. It contains a moving sculpture of a mother and child (75), carved from a sweet chestnut grown in the garden, by the Taunton artist Tom Preater. The Chapel, intended to 'rejoice in his incarnation' supports Loraine's strong beliefs and was blessed in July 2001.[24] The bench seats inside offer a restful stop for reflection on the combination of nature and woman that have united perfectly to create this beautiful and subtly designed Arcadia. But Loraine did not stop at the Millennium. In 2009 she built the Garden Registry adjacent to the house, which has been designed as an educational resource for visitors. Made of green oak from the gardens, it was opened in May of that year by her friend Patrick Taylor, when the triptych by local artist John Hurford was unveiled. This impressive painting displays the staggering range of plants to be found in the garden as if they were all in bloom together.

Sylvia Crowe's commissions in Somerset encompassed vast landscape projects such as Wimbleball Reservoir,[25] and the considerably smaller scheme at **Barford Park**, a perfect mid-eighteenth-century house. In 1957, new owner Michael Stancomb commissioned fruit-tree nursery specialists, Scotts of Merriott, and they asked Crowe to remodel the old walled Kitchen Garden behind the house. Quite what modernist design she suggested is not known, but eventually Stancomb decided against it and implemented his own scheme based on four quadrants.[26] The garden is rectangular with curving corners and consists of low walls facing the house, rising higher at the sides; the wall facing the house has two eighteenth-century pedimented loggias. The planting areas within the enclosure have now been minimised to four curved areas at the corners of the garden and consist primarily of structural phormiums, columnar yews and shrubs. However, the herbaceous planting comes into its own in May, when Barford hosts an annual plant fair. On our visit in early February 2009, Michael Stancomb was coming to terms with the loss of several limbs from the great cedar of Lebanon in front of the house. His clever trick of lighting a bale of straw on the ground below to prevent damage from the snow's weight had failed, because like most of western Somerset he had been completely caught out by the second round of snowstorms.

Prior to her tenancy at Tintinhull, Penelope Hobhouse began her gardening career in earnest at her first husband's family home, **Hadspen House** at Pitcombe, due east of Castle Cary. She set about restoring the neglected and overgrown eight acres around the house, working her way eastwards from a terraced slope on which her husband's grandmother, Margaret, had created steps, walls and a fountain, and had planted several specimen trees including Scots pines, copper beeches and a tulip tree.[27] Venturing further out she replanted the formal Victorian terraced Pool Garden with its rectangular lily pond (76). This sheltered enclosure produced conditions reminiscent of the Mediterranean, making it suitable for more tender plants. Up against the mellow walls *Abutilon*

76 The Victorian Pool Garden at Hadspen in its current state of precarious decay

vitifolium and *Hoheria sexsylosa* mingled with old fruit espaliers, of which several lead labels remain, including 'Peach Grosse 1908 Mignone' and 'Peach 1903 Early Alfred'. Finally, she came to the walled Kitchen Garden, sloping away to the south, which provided the site for a small nursery that she ran with the help of the hosta specialist Eric Smith.[28]

After her move to Tintinhull, the garden at Hadspen became neglected until the house was leased in 1987 to the Canadians Sandra and Nori Pope, who created the most English of gardens within the walled Kitchen Garden. The Popes had a successful garden design and nursery business in British Columbia, but leapt at the new challenges Hadspen offered. Their planting combinations took Gertrude Jekyll's colour themes to vivid new heights. This transformation of Hadspen and their particular design ethos are beautifully recorded in their books – *Colour by Design*, *Colour in the Garden* and *Planting with Colour* – where the whole spectrum is covered, colour by colour, along with practical advice on how to create textural and colour groupings all year round. The naming of a plant after a designer's work is an impressive accolade, and the Popes are rewarded by *Astrantia* 'Hadspen Blood' and *Lobelia x speciosa* 'Hadspen Purple'.

After the departure of the Popes in 2005, Niall Hobhouse took an active role at Hadspen, and his mother Penelope returned to live on the estate. Every new owner wants to put his or her mark on a house and landscape, usually by creating a new avenue, commissioning new buildings or sculpture, or bringing an area of wilderness into the designed grounds. Very rarely do owners take a bulldozer to a much-loved garden and raze it to the ground, as Niall Hobhouse did in 2006. The shock waves that reverberated around gardening circles, particularly in Somerset, measured ten on the horticultural Richter scale. Some felt it was a much-needed, but brave, action; others deplored the destruction of an intensely beautiful and influential garden. The gardening fraternity waited with bated breath to find out what Hobhouse proposed to do in this space. The answer was 'The Hadspen Parabola', taking its name from the curved wall of the garden; but this was a project so ambitious that it has remained unrealised since its inception in 2007. Architects and garden designers alike were asked to respond to the site, which had been laid out as a network of paths by Foreign Office Architects.

Perhaps intending to re-ignite the 1890s controversy between Robinson and Blomfield, Niall Hobhouse suggested that 'no modern garden is ever better than its gardener. As professionals, landscape designers often work within a vacuum of knowledge about plants and plant systems; in contrast, plantsmen find it hard to use their knowledge to inform a disciplined approach to overall design'. The project represented, therefore, 'a commitment to seeking out radical solutions to planting, and to exploring the links that gardening can make to other fields of creativity'.[29] With a panel of jurors, fifty strong, it is not surprising that no decision has ever been reached. Hobhouse admits that the brief may have been wrong, and the monumental task of choosing a winner from over 100 entries has ground this project into the mud. At a meeting of the Castle Cary Horticultural Society in March 2009, Hobhouse confusingly reported that none of the designs had fitted his vision for the estate, but it was agreed that the space should be used productively. To this end, plots have been marked out, whilst Penelope continues to grow her roses and propagate Iranian seeds from her travels as an overspill from her new Courtyard Garden.

Starting a new garden at the age of eighty is not for the faint-hearted, but for someone like Penelope Hobhouse making do is not an option. On a south-facing plot, enclosed on two sides by old farm buildings, she has laid out a garden with distinct elements of Italian, Mediterranean and Persian gardens. This exotic combination is not surprising given the breadth of her travels and her writing on these subjects. Axial paths, grass plats, low box hedging and strategically placed pots give structure to an otherwise unremarkable and flat terrain. Beyond the boundary, the mature trees and gently undulating Hadspen estate extend the views. Along with an extensive gardening library, which will be housed in yet another container on the grass beyond the garden confines, Hobhouse also brought many of her favourite shrubs from her previous garden at Bettiscombe in Devon, but the more tender hoheria, melianthus and escallonia will have to risk it in the harsher climate of Somerset.[30] For someone who is reported to have said they were giving up growing flowers, there is certainly a lot of colour in this garden, which is less than a year old. Sweet peas festoon an arch, way ahead of others in the area; nepeta, white stocks and poppies spill over onto the gravelled areas. Acid green *Euphorbia oblongata*, a present from Penelope Hobhouse's god-daughter Sarah Raven, sets off brilliantly the reds and purples of knautia and salvia. With a plethora of pots on the terrace, small raised beds for vegetables, and borders stuffed with contrasting textures and shades, the design is busy, but the garden still maintains a restful air. Not that Penelope Hobhouse is prone to resting; she continued pulling out the odd weed as we walked along (*colour 53*).

While Penelope Hobhouse ranks deservedly among the country's most influential garden designers and writers on gardens, Mary Anne Robb of **Cothay Manor** must surely be the most unlikely of reality TV stars.[31] Mary Anne and her husband Alastair took over the neglected gardens at Cothay in 1993. They were originally laid out in the 1920s by Colonel Reginald Cooper, a friend of Harold Nicolson's from the Diplomatic Corps.[32] Nicolson and Vita Sackville-West were regular visitors to Cothay, as was Lawrence Johnston of Hidcote, and it seems that Cooper may have advised Nicolson on the layout of the bowling green at Sissinghurst.[33] In 1993 all that remained of Cooper's design was the Oxbow, created when he moved the river Tone, and some extensive yew hedging. Within these green barriers (77) the Robbs have incorporated arches, doorways and nooks, as well as undertaking substantial replanting.

The entrance court to this most evocative of vernacular manor houses is mainly planted with simple topiary and Robb's favourite *Rosa* 'Mutabilis' and *Euphorbia amygdaloides subsp. robbiae*, named after her husband's grandmother, who introduced it in the early 1890s.[34] The meadow, which in the early spring dazzles with its swathes of the 'Queen of the Night' tulips,

77 Colonel Reginald Cooper planted the structural yews of the gardens around Cothay in the 1920s. Their enclosures have since been animated by the inspired, colour-themed planting of Mary Anne Robb

gives onto the garden rooms, which lead off the 200-yard long Yew Walk. On the terrace at the back of the Manor a red and white rose entwine. These were, allegedly, planted to mark the end of the Wars of the Roses in the fifteenth century when Richard Bluett first built Cothay.[35] The terrace itself is barely visible under a self-seeded mass of dierama, white gaultonia and blue sisyrinchium. But the most eye-catching elements here are the lavishly planted pots and the umbrella-trained wisteria. The way forward is through a maze of small gardens, each with its own controlled colour palette. The route leads from the old swimming pool, through the simple greens and whites of the Green Knight Garden and the muted shades of diagonal opposites in the herbaceous borders, to the ecclesiastically vibrant reds and purples of pittosporum, phlox, alstromeria, salvia, thalictrum and the velvety Clematis 'Black Prince' in the Bishop's Garden, which is named after Robb's uncle. The circuit ends where the old vegetable garden has been brilliantly transformed into the serene Walk of the Unicorn (*colour 54*). With its restrained planting of specially high-grafted Robinia pseudoacacia trees, White triumphator tulips

78 The grounds of Lady Farm are dramatised by a series of beautifully erotic sculptures by an artist known simply as 'Mimi'

followed by Nepeta 'Six hills giant' the Walk is one of the most beautiful spaces in the county. Christopher Hussey wrote that the nation owed a great debt to Cooper for his restoration of the manor house, and the same could be said today of the Robbs for their inspired adaptation and restoration of the gardens.[36]

Whereas the gardens at Cothay are unashamedly in the English country style, **Lady Farm**, another new Somerset garden, has taken elements from the steppe and prairie styles advocated by Piet Oudolf and Noel Kingsbury. Judy and Malcolm Pearce took over Lady Farm in the Chelwood valley on a handshake in 1972, relinquishing their smaller house to the farm owners. Work at the dairy farm continued as normal until 1990 when, with the demise of farming, the majority of the ancillary buildings were taken down. Coupled with the discovery of a spring four years later, this opened up the possibilities for an ornamental garden of 10 acres on the old fields. With the help of her friend, the horticulturist, lecturer and designer Mary Payne, Judy Pearce started to plant shelter-belts around the perimeter of the gardens. Mary Payne's influence and knowledge inspired the Prairie Garden near the end of the lake, with its combinations of helianthemums, grasses, rudbeckias and verbascums.

The entrance to the gardens is not immediately obvious. It leads around the terraces of the house, which seem rather suburban, until the descent to a sweeping lawn studded with shrubs and herbaceous planting, with the arable landscape beyond acting as a natural foil to the design. To the east is the tea room, fronted by a collection of silver birches, under-planted for the first time in 2009 with an annual wild flower mix sourced from Nigel Dunnant at the University of Sheffield. Lacking this inspired splash of planting, the curvilinear beds and randomly placed conifers on the lawns would have a 1970s feel about them.

As the mown grass path winds down towards the first lake the visitor encounters several arrestingly erotic sculptures placed at intervals: *Daedelus kissing the Maiden*, *Leda and the Swan* and *The Lovers* by an artist called Mimi (*78*). The banks of the pool are covered with the golden clumps of *Cornus alba* 'Aurea', while hidden behind a 200-year-old cedar is a wooden gorilla carved by David Johnson. Pearce's assertion that she is not particularly exercised about the plants, but just loves the landscape, is belied by her expert planting of the water marginals: zantedeschia, marsh marigold and the hooded phlomis. Combinations such as the colossal gunnera, feathery deschampsia grass or deep green umbrellas of darmera alongside the airy spires of rodgersia all add to the drama.

Eventually, the Steppe and Prairie Gardens are reached (*colour 55*), rising up the slope away from the lake. The Steppe Garden on the left has recently been replanted, incorporating more gravel and silver willows to absorb the moisture. The right-hand side is planted with an abundant mixture of *Stipa tenuissima*, the towering *Verbascum olympicum*, kniphophia, santolina, Artemisia, eryngium and hemerocallis. This is what every visitor comes to Lady Farm to see and has been much copied, notably by Simon Goodfellow at Chelford Manor in Cheshire.[37] Paths wind back up the hillside, passing Malcolm Pearce's vegetable patch, and on into the Entry Court with its two weeping silver pear trees. This leads to the gravel path, which is edged with box and yew buttresses and tightly clipped standard *Ligustrum delavayanum*. The visitor finally arrives at the highly manicured Courtyard with a space to rest under a thatched Loggia. Edged with box, the circular and quartered beds are filled with the blues, purples and pinks of salvias, verbena, echinops, lavender and penstemon.

Sadly, that touch of modernism in Mimi's erotic sculptures is not matched in other gardens of the century. These are characterised more by the perennial design response in this country of recyling past historic styles. Yet two of the pioneering examples of international modernism, both of which incorporated designed gardens, were built in the 1920s, one at Penslewood, on the far south-eastern tip of the county where it meets Dorset, and the other on the craggy hillside of Cheddar Gorge. This last launched the collaborative partnership between major landscape designers Geoffrey Jellicoe and Russell Page, and its architectural emasculation in the 1960s is one of the most grievous losses to modernist architectural and landscape design in England.

10

Modernist and traditional – a very patrician county

▼

Caveman Restaurant · Pen Pits · Clapton Court · Kilver Court
Yarlington House · Barcroft Hall · Aislaby · Babington House
Camerton Court · Dillington House · Stoberry Park · Wells Bishop's Palace
Honeywick House · Hatch Court

THE LAST CHAPTER ON INFLUENTIAL WOMEN GARDENERS DEALT WITH some of the most important twentieth-century gardens in the county, so this final chapter on the remainder will, inevitably, be short. It will, however, highlight a national trend, noticed in all the books of this series: the paucity of good modern design in this country. By its very insular and history-patterned nature, England is a country of traditionalists, none more so than gardeners. When modern designs have been attempted, they are usually in the form of clever new combinations of plants, as with Piet Oudolf's Floral Labyrinth at Trentham in Staffordshire.[1] Indeed, the final chapter in the Northamptonshire volume addressed this thorny question of what exactly determines modern design, and which recent gardens can be termed historic and likely, therefore, to stand the test of time.[2] It should be stressed that by 'modern', I do not mean 'contemporary'. 'Modernist' is perhaps a better term. Certainly the only real modernist thread apparent in Somerset's later gardens is a fondness for sculpture; often good modern sculpture, but there is precious little modernist design in the garden layouts themselves. This is understandable in such a patrician county, but it is dispiriting, given that the county was in the forefront of pioneering modernist design in the 1930s.

Cheddar Gorge is the most unlikely place in which to find a lost icon of twentieth-century modernism, but in amongst the tourist tat, where

79 Sixties tat hides the once gleaming lines of one of the country's pioneering International Modernist buildings in Cheddar Gorge

garish signs entice visitors to enjoy 'Awesome Archaeology, Geology and Ecology' in caves that have been '300 million years in the making', are the remnants of a restaurant, still clinging to a narrow shelf of the precipitous Gorge. This is now the 'Cargo Cult Shop' and 'Explorers Café-Bar' sited at the entrance to Gough's Cave (79). However, underneath the cantilevered concrete boxes of 1960s brutalism, and the rooftop terrace strewn with ugly brown tables sprouting chairs, like forlorn refugees from a deserted nature spot, lie the architectural bones of a once gleaming example of International Modernism. Tucked into the hillside like a miniature lido (80), the building was originally clean-lined with pale pink rendered walls, and dramatised by a glass-bottomed rooftop pool dappled by fountains.[3] The Caveman Restaurant, as it was first called, was designed in 1934-7 by two heavyweights of twentieth-century landscape architecture, Geoffrey Jellicoe and Russell Page.[4]

Henry Thynne, Lord Weymouth, of nearby Longleat, 'young, gay, brimming with ideas, and devoted to the property of which he was already in charge',[5] was the instigator of this extraordinary project, one

80 The Caveman Restaurant at Cheddar was the result of inspired patronage by Lord Weymouth of Longleat and brilliant design by the landscape architects, Geoffrey Jellicoe and Russell Page. John Maltby/RIBA Library Photographs Collection

which combined cutting-edge modernist design with an extremely sensitive approach to the landscape of the Gorge. It was while Page was busily re-planting and re-ordering the Capability Brown landscape at Longleat that the lease of one of two Cheddar caves lapsed, and Lord Weymouth decided to 'see what could be done to organise the running of this cave in a more efficient way'.[6] Lord Weymouth and Page drove over to Cheddar: 'Lying where the narrow road winds down between high cliffs and emerges into the plain, a hamlet of tiny colour-washed, tree-shaded cottages sells teas and Cheddar cheeses and souvenirs in a welter of rose arbours, vividly painted signs and rustic garden furniture, all executed in a sort of nineteenth-century folk-art idiom'.[7]

Their first idea was to build a corrugated-iron shelter for the bus drivers, but the project soon expanded into a ticket office, museum and restaurant. Page realised that he was completely out of his depth, as all this was to be built on 'a thirty-foot wide strip between the cliff wall and the road. If this programme was within my vision it was certainly outside my technical competence'.[8] The solution was to 'devise a building that would be long and low in order to dramatise the cave-mouth and accentuate the vertical face of the cliff. It was a landscape problem in which the controlling factor had to be the site itself'.[9] For Page, there was only one man with the expertise to pull it off:

Which architect would see it from this angle? I had, not long before, come to know Geoffrey Jellicoe as one of the founders of the then recently formed Institute of Landscape Architects and an authority on classical Italian gardens. Together we flung ourselves into the difficulties and excitements of the Cheddar project.[10]

This was Page's first collaboration with Jellicoe and it led to a long and productive partnership, which continued until the Second World War. They went hunting for the skeleton belonging to the famous Cheddar Skull, laid down a new system of floodlighting in the caves, and celebrated the completion of the new visitor centre and restaurant with a spectacular firework display. They designed all the furniture, crockery, waitresses' uniforms, knives and forks, even the ashtrays. Writing in 1962, twenty-three years afterwards, Page returned to find that 'the composition still looks fresh and unmannered'.[11] Sadly, that architectural purity was not to last. Their inland liner was soon obliterated by the 1960s rebuilding, and all of Page's landscape planting around the building and along the cliffside disappeared. Admittedly, the pool leaked; but in its prime the Caveman Restaurant was a dazzling adaptation of Erich Mendelsohn's 'articulate and modulated horizontality'.[12] Jellicoe's delicate perspective drawing of the new complex makes it seem as if the buildings had grown organically out of the Gorge.[13]

The Caveman Restaurant was a rare excursion into modernism for Somerset, 'an inspired scheme for an intelligent and ambitious client',[14] but it is not alone. Deep down in the county, at its south-eastern border with Dorset, Sir Arthur Bliss and his wife Trudy commissioned Peter Harland in 1935 to design for them a modern movement house at Penselwood. They were looking for a site to build a weekend retreat and found a neglected cottage near prehistoric earthworks, which gave the house its strange name: **Pen Pits**. Harland had made his reputation designing refined neo-Georgian houses, but Pen Pits was unashamedly modern with a covered porch for taking in the view, above which was a deck for sunbathing with an outdoor shower, accessed via a 'ship-shape' ladder.[15] The house was white-walled and brutally geometric in style, but this monochrome austerity was leavened by striking splashes of colour: chimneys painted blue, red awnings to windows also painted blue, and lemon yellow curtains. The rectangular house was sited carefully in amongst the existing trees, showing Harland's sensitivity to the terrain. The architect Oliver Hill was later to write about Harland's dexterous planning at Pen Pits: 'the rugged character of the site and the necessarily sophisticated design of the house were two factors whose contrast would be disturbing unless the layout of the grounds and gardens brought the two together'.[16] Edward Wadsworth's contemporary painting of Pen Pits shows contoured lawns below the garden front, a trellis intended to train up the wall and a cylindrical planter on the terrace, which proved to be far too tall for watering. Needless to say, this almost sculptural quality to the lawns around the house has disappeared under eighty years of growth, but the house survives, much in its first state.

To move forward from these minimalist landscape austerities to **Clapton Court** is to take a step backwards, for though the lush planting of the Woodland Garden was carried out in the 1950s, it is entirely traditional in its design and enlivens an area of Victorian shrubbery. Vestigial Victorian terracing with stone benches gives on to a meadow in which stands a majestic veteran ash (*81*), big bellied, its branches flailing out like living limbs.[17] Behind this is the entrance into the Woodland Garden, which was replanted by Louis Martineau and his cousin Guy, after Martineau bought Clapton in 1950.[18] Martineau died in 1978 and the house was purchased by Captain Simon Loder, who realised the significance of the four-acre Woodland Garden and began a restoration.

Martineau had laid out a series of formal features around the house, including a Lily Pool on the north-west side, but it is the Woodland Garden that deserves attention. It is now lusciously overgrown, a narrow stream winding through its leafy hollows and open glades. Captain Loder and his wife created a new approach via a bridge over the ha-ha, making a transitional area between the formal gardens by the house and the Woodland Garden. This was planted with fifteen different varieties of birch and smaller trees, shrubs and species roses, including amelanchier,

81 This veteran ash at Clapton Court is a startling prelude to the Woodland Garden, laid out in the 1950s by Louis Martineau and his cousin Guy

halesia, viburnum, liquidambar, alnus, sambucus and specimens of *Ulmus parvifolia* 'Frosty', also known as the lacebark elm. At this transfer point they made a pond on the stream with a waterfall, and surrounded it with moisture-loving plants. Then they turned their attention to the Woodland Garden, clearing out the overgrown areas and adding new plants. The walks close in with shrubs and trees cascading overhead, principally acers, magnolias and heavily scented azaleas. The Loders have now gone, but Susie and Mark Bullough continue to tend and restore the Woodland Garden and have added a striking new parterre garden in the walled enclosure to the rear of the house.

Such informed dedication to an important site, even one of 1950s vintage, is in direct contrast to the gardens at **Kilver Court** in Shepton Mallet. Perhaps it is unfair to criticise a garden that has been transplanted from elsewhere and expect it to perform well both visually and aesthetically. But it was surely a mistake to attempt to prettify characterful grounds that were first created by Ernest Jardine as a recreational space for factory workers. Originally known as Jardine's Park and Vegetable Gardens, they were laid out around the millpond and the boating lake in the lee of the vast arches of the Somerset and Dorset railway viaduct. As such they called for a practical and utilitarian restoration. Instead, in the 1960s the Showerings family of Babycham fame commissioned George Whitelegg to recreate his gold medal winning Chelsea Flower Show rockery garden (*colour 56*). This looks bizarrely incongruous against the backdrop of the cyclopean viaduct, as does the box-edged parterre by the factory building, more appropriate to a drawing room terrace. Apparently, due to the success of the vegetable garden at nearby Sharpham Park, Jardine's concept of model fruit and vegetable cultivation will be reinstated 'with the establishment of a sustainable bio-dynamic system for both education and to supply organic produce to the Shop and Café'.[19] It is to be hoped that this reinstatement will necessitate the destruction of both rockery and parterre and return the grounds to a more historically accurate representation of Jardine's philosophy.

Charles and Carolyn de Salis have taken an infinitely more sensitive approach to an existing site ever since they came to **Yarlington House**, near Wincanton, in the early 1960s. Inheriting few designed elements of note, they have spent the last 40 years adding features that are perfectly in accord with the house. The drive sweeps up an avenue, its grass verges studded with daffodils, primroses and aconites, to a pair of gates emblazoned with the family *rebus*, a weeping willow or *Salix* denoting de Salis. The main entrance to the house, a three-bay brick façade of diminutive Georgian proportions, faces east and its forecourt is enclosed by yew hedges. On the south side are the main far-reaching views, the windows framed by two narrow, elongated *Magnolia grandiflora*, stretching upwards rather than outwards. To the left, a stilt hedge of pleached limes encloses a Rose Garden of box-edged squares. The colours here are strictly pink and white with *Verbenia bonariensis* interplanted; Carolyn does not allow any yellow in this area. A triple-sectioned pool with bathing girl and fountain in the centre provides a focal point to the enclosure. The structure was conceived by Charles who, in the great tradition of horticultural roles, provides the architectural layouts, whilst Carolyn designs the inspired planting.

On the other side of the grounds is the Sunken Garden. Charles de Salis is a renowned expert on Napoleon, so there are several references to the Corsican here, which include a plaque on the wall above a wisteria-clad arbour. Close-cut balls of *Phyllarea angustifolia* line the path through the centre, and the beds are filled with herbaceous planting in pinks, blues, greys and whites, including peonies, alstromeria and dicentra. Pyramidal pittosporums flank the descending steps, adding evergreen structure. Behind this garden room is the private swimming pool garden, and from here crazy-paved rock paths lead to a windbreak covered with a tightly managed rubus. Yew hedging divides this from the Pool Garden

82 A Rose Arbour inspired by J C Loudon, one of several inventive additions to the grounds at Yarlington House

and a beech on the other side leads down to a Rose Arbour (*82*) inspired by J C Loudon. From here a Laburnum Walk, terminated by a statue by Peter Robinson of the de Salis' second daughter, leads towards the wider landscape. But the most exciting discovery in the grounds is The Hollow, which was found when the Pool Garden was being created. The existing bowl shape and tap at the bottom were gradually dug out and rocks were built up and planted with ferns, yews, laurels and other shade-loving plants. All it needs now is for the water to cascade gently down through the rockwork to fill the bowl. The Hollow is reminiscent of another sunken garden of the Victorian period, recently restored, at Denzell Gardens in Altrincham, Cheshire.[20]

The house and gardens at **Barcroft Hall**, South Petherton, could not be more different. Brian and Denise Herrick inherited a relatively new classical house with embryonic gardens and have completely transformed the 8-acre grounds with a chain of lakes, formal avenues of trees and a geometrically planted orchard. To connect these areas they have laid down five kilometres of footpaths, re-laid hedges and planted 2,300 trees. What is remarkable about the grounds is that they already appear well established, even though they are recent and still being developed (*colour 57*). One of the Herricks' design strategies was to provide a wildfowl release site for the RSPCA; on our visit a recovering swan patrolled the lake nearest the house.

In the Orchard to the rear of the house nine different local varieties of cider apples are grown, making the grounds productive as well as ornamental. Some of the new trees are soft fruit varieties of medlars, quince and plums, while the sweeping lawns are studded with weeping pear and silver birches; there is also a separate area of acers. A formal terraced garden to the front of the house has steps which descend to the first lake; this is flanked by another formal enclosure of pleached limes. But the most atmospheric sector of the landscape is further down the lakes, where there are living willow sculptures, a cherry avenue under-planted with veronica 'Pink Perfection', and lines of poplars which evoked, to me at least, descriptions from *Le Grand Meaulnes*. Together with the local populace, the Herricks are embarking upon a programme of 'Vegetation Education', in which the older generation will instruct the young on how to grow food on the land. Barcroft is, therefore, both well-meaning and intelligently conceived; it may prove, in time, to be one of the most significant and influential gardens in the county.

While Barcroft is firmly educational in intent and ecologically underpinned, the grounds at Aislaby are a cleverly concealed twenty-first-century sportsman's estate, combining a boating lake, swimming pool, tennis court, croquet lawn, archery butts and golf course. The landscape architect Michael Balston was responsible for the design, which was constructed between 1991 and 1992. Its most extraordinary and distinctive

83 An eighteenth-century-style rill at Aislaby, part of Michael Balston's creative design for a sportsman's estate

feature is the integration into the formal areas of the golf course, the curving lines of which blend dramatically with the terraces around the house (*colour 58*). These last provide expansive views over Blackmore Vale, while a wrought metal Summerhouse – the 'Parrot Cage' – surrounded by purple bergenias, offers seats equipped with wine-glass holders. The trellised verandah of the former rectory writhes with wisteria and a late-flowering clematis, and there are further splashes of colour in box-edged beds along the terrace, which acts as an outdoor dining room. An arch in the wall leads across a courtyard of setts to the sloping Kitchen Garden, essentially a potager combining the ornamental with the productive, which has immaculately laid herring-bone brick paths, further box-edged beds and a wooden arbour. Behind this enclosure is a lawned area through which snakes a water rill (*83*) reminiscent of Charles Bridgeman's Rill at Rousham, Oxfordshire. The gardens are meticulously maintained, and continue to be developed, by Head Gardener Jonathan Naylor.

Contemporary gardens, even if initially designed by well-known landscape architects, always rely on the skill and expertise of head gardeners

46 The homely rusticity of farm buildings at Barrington Court, enclosing a fashionable White Garden centred by a wheel-shaped arrangement of flowerbeds

47 The Long Terrace at Wayford Manor acts as a grandstand for views out towards Dorset and also as a strong architectural link between house and gardens

48 Harold Peto conceived the grounds at Wayford in two distinct moods: formal garden rooms and terraces by the house leading down to a wilder informality of exotic planting, which includes a Japanese garden

49 Thomas Mawson devised this daringly geometric 'Rosarium' at Barley Wood, Wrington, for Henry Herbert Wills in 1911. The terrace below the Garden House gives grandstand views of the Mendip ridge

50 The remains of the Grass stairway at St. Catherine's Court, now nicknamed 'the roller-coaster' and its herbaceous border planted up by Alison Jenkins

51
The planting in Margery Fish's Ditch at East Lambrook Manor was clearly inspired by William Robinson

52 Joan Loraine's horticultural eyrie at Greencombe, set high above Porlock Bay, has four national collections of plants

53 Penelope Hobhouse, weeds in hand, surveys her latest garden at the Clock House, Hadspen

54 Mary Anne Robb's Walk of the Unicorn at Cothay features *White triumphator* tulips in spring. It is an inspired replacement of the old vegetable garden

55 Prairie planting at Judy Pearce's Lady Farm, Chelwood

56 Dramatic incongruity at Kilver Court, Shepton Mallet. The Victorian viaduct of the Somerset and Dorset railway combines awkwardly with a 1960s Chelsea Flower Show rockery

57 A swan in rehab on the lake at Barcroft Hall, where a new landscape has been created, in part, as a wildfowl release site for the RSPCA

58
A sportsman's paradise at Aislaby, where the formal terraced gardens merge geometrically with the golf course

59 Camerton Court, noted for its profusion of stone sculptures, has deep herbaceous borders where tall topiary spires lift the alpine planting

60 At Stoberry Park, outside Wells, Frances Young has sited modern sculpture and ceramics amongst plants chosen with careful precision to dramatise and complement the artworks

for their continued development. None more so than the grounds at **Babington House**, near Frome, where the 1838 tithe map records the extensive pools, which survive, but little else.[21] Due to the close proximity of the Georgian parish church, there can have been little in the way of formal gardens to the entrance front of the house. All the planting appears to have been concentrated around the pools to the north-west, where there are lawns planted with Victorian specimen conifers and ornamental shrubberies. Today, the interest lies in the Kitchen Garden, which was built as part of Captain Knatchbull's late-eighteenth-century programme of improvements to the estate.[22]

This enclosure is particularly important, as it provides the produce for the hotel, which celebrated its first ten years in 2008. Head Gardener Mike Lane, who sees himself as a student of Humphry Repton, is perfecting the new Gravel Garden, designed by Urquhart and Hunt, on the approach to the walled enclosure. In addition he has planted 15,000 bulbs in the adjacent Woodland Garden. Monty Don devised the Kitchen Garden layout in 1998 with espaliered apples and compartments for vegetables, while Jekka McVicar designed the herb garden. The complex brings to mind Raymond Blanc's prolific kitchen garden at the Manoir aux Quat' Saisons in Oxfordshire, the corners of which are enlivened with sensuous modern sculptures.[23] If the Babington promotional literature is any guide – 'there is something about the whole place that is sexy' – then perhaps this Somerset hotel should follow Raymond's lead and introduce some sculptural eroticism into the Kitchen Garden.

Stone sculptures are ubiquitous in the grounds of **Camerton Court**, laid out by Ken Biggs and his wife Ivy, but they are in a completely different emotional register to those at the Manoir. Biggs is the region's most important stone and building contractor and his love affair with the material is revealed around almost every corner of the gardens at Camerton. So too is his and his wife's delight in plants. This is nowhere more apparent than in the Rock Garden Border beneath the garden front of the house (*colour 59*). It is a mass of alpines mixed with herbaceous plants in 1970s style, but lifted from the dullness of that period by brilliant vertical accents of topiary. The border is planted with dicentra, daffodils, campanula, grape hyacinths, mixed grasses and pencil yews.

The 1830s house is surrounded by lawns, which sweep down to a small lake. In amongst the specimen trees are garden incidents: a laburnum arbour by the lake, a rocky water course with miniature cascades, island beds planted with heathers in the Victorian manner, a beech-hedged Japanese Garden with gravel, pools, lanterns and bridges, a semicircular Summerhouse, a Sunken Garden (*84*) as a prelude to a swimming pool enclosure at a higher level, which is decorated with box parterres and terracotta pots, and a Walled Garden of ornamental and productive complexity. This last has eighteenth-century pastoral figures, a statue of Mercury, tunnel arbours, more box-edged beds and topiary. But the most important and original statues are closer to the house, signalled by a brooding, crouching man by the drive, like some garden guardian by Fernand Léger. Further on up the drive are the formal terraces around the house, edged by yew walls, dramatised by more sculptural topiary and their borders studded with more sculptures. Two of these are of the Revd John Skinner, Regency Rector of Camerton, and Mrs Anne Jarrett, the first owner of Camerton Court. There is more sculpture around the entrance forecourt to the house, while a consort of animal musicians (*85*) plays in the shrubbery on the other side of the drive.

All these works of art are figurative, whereas the sculptures commissioned by Wayne Bennett for **Dillington House**, near Ilminster, are entirely abstract. Dillington, which is owned by Somerset County Council, has been a residential centre for adult education and the arts since 1949 and has an enlightened policy towards the purchase of artworks. The grounds originally comprised an Arboretum, a woodland garden or Wilderness and a formal Rose Garden laid out on the terrace to the rear of the house.[24] These elements survive, though much altered, but it is the inclusion of modern sculpture that dramatises the grounds, in much the same way as the Jerwood Sculpture Park enlivens the pleasure grounds at Ragley Hall in Warwickshire. So in between the pines, cedars, holly and yews, visitors come across a shard of rust-red metal, that turns out to be Alistair Smith's *Reclining Female Figure*, or a pile of precariously balanced stones (*86*), which is labelled: Chris Booth – *Buzzard*. For aficionados of more easily recognisable sculpture, a Georgian obelisk is sited in the woodland above the house. The terrace by the house has more

84 The Sunken Garden at Camerton Court, like most of the enclosures in the grounds, is studded with pots and statuary

85 Ken Biggs has worked in the building trade all his life, and has surrounded his house at Camerton with artworks in Bath limestone by local craftsmen

86
Wayne Bennett has an eye for modern sculpture which he has sited in the grounds at Dillington House; this tower of stones represents a buzzard

87 Vase and planting in perfect accord at Stoberry Park, near Wells, conceived by Frances Young with help from local artists

artworks. One by Josep Ginestar, entitled *Two Pieces*, looks like a three-dimensional fugitive from a painting by Terry Frost, while in the heathers of a recently planted border by Nick Rigden there is a tall ceramic vase by Sandy Brown.

Easily the most important and impressive addition to Dillington is The Hyde, a frankly modern, angular building designed by Niall Phillips Architects, which overlooks the old walled garden on one side and a new sunken garden on the other. This last may prove in the near future to be one of the most interesting modernist garden enclosures in the county. It is treated as a simple Japanese-style space of raked gravel with a reflecting pool, a retaining wall of gabions and clumps of bamboo, all dramatised at night by uplighting. The gabions are planted with Persian ivy and rubus, which will eventually form a cascade of evergreen, providing a contrast to the greyness of the surroundings.

Continuing with this sculptural theme, **Stoberry Park**, perched on a hillside slope overlooking Wells Cathedral, is the most impressive garden in Somerset for the sensitive siting of artworks amongst appropriate planting.[25] Here, since 1997, Frances and Tim Young, assisted by their gardener, Lee Selley, have created a gallery garden of ceramic and stone sculptural incidents that comes close in certain areas to the effects generated by Barbara Hepworth at her Trewyn Studio in St Ives. While the walled garden itself is loosely designed with random crowded areas and open lawns, the artworks are thoughtfully placed, an architecturally linear head licked by phormium fronds (*colour 60*), or an elegantly attenuated, earthily coloured vase by Christine-Anne Richards clustered around with deep purple tulips (*87*). Blue-tinted ammonites nestle against rocks and ivy above a small pond; bulbous ceramic onions by Karen Edwards lie seemingly discarded next to railway sleeper steps, and a Giacometti-like lady gardener surveys it all. There are more metal sculptures by the lake in the open park beyond the walled garden, but it is the confines of the enclosure that hold the interest.

The enclosed gardens of the **Bishop's Palace** in Wells function in a similar way, offering a sense of private containment, but one enlivened with good modern sculpture. The entrance forecourt of the complex is bland and unexciting, but once the archway in the north screen wall of

88 David Backhouse's gaunt Pilgrim is perfectly sited against surviving fragments of the Bishop's Palace at Wells

the late-thirteenth-century Great Hall is reached the gardens open out and the surprises begin. David Backhouse's gaunt bronze figure of a Pilgrim (*88*) waiting to greet visitors is perfectly framed in the archway behind him. Shaven-headed, the Pilgrim keeps his silent vigil, his arms wrapping a cloak around himself against the cold. It is a moving interpretation of the spiritual traveller, more Buddhist than Christian in its visual impact. Then, past a box-edged formal garden given in July 2005 by the Phelps Family of Palace Farm, set in an angle between buildings, there is a striking trio entitled: *The Expulsion Group*. These were carved from a yew tree that once grew in St Paul's churchyard, Tiverton. The yew was felled in 1946 and carved by E J Clack. The sculpture was exhibited at the Royal Academy in 1948; thereafter, it was installed in the gardens at Limnerslease, Surrey, and eventually came to the Bishop's Palace in 1963. It depicts the moment of Adam and Eve's banishment from the Garden of Eden (*89*), presenting them as elongated figures looking more sorrowful and thoughtful than agonised. The third element represents the winged creatures and the fiery flashing sword, which guarded the way to the Tree of Life; the snake is entwined in this figure.

89
The moment of Adam and Eve's expulsion from the Garden of Eden, carved from a yew felled in 1946, enlivens a corner of the grounds within the moated Bishop's Palace

These modern sculptural excursions are rare in a county more inclined to look for inspiration back to the past. The recently planted garden at **Honeywick House**, near Castle Cary, is a case in point. Within a small valley where some features survived from the 1920s, Camilla Carter has devised, with advice from Julian Bannerman, a contemporary garden perfectly attuned to a minor country house. There is a small formal terrace of rectangular beds, planted up with tulips on our spring visit, terminating at one end in a glasshouse and the other in a Doric-columned Pergola. Steps lead up into the combe towards an octagonal Summerhouse set high on a slope to the left offering views back down to the house. The hillside slopes were adrift with spring bulbs, while camellias, azaleas and rhododendrons were waiting to flower. Nothing could be more closely associated with past garden styles, nothing more synonymous with this intensely traditional county.

It is this inherent, almost instinctive, nostalgia for the past that has produced one of the latest garden buildings in Somerset. As a twenty-first-century reminder of the friendly rivals who created templed circuits in the mid-eighteenth century, a Gothick folly of decidedly Batty

90
A Gothic Folly for the twenty-first century under construction in the summer of 2009 at Hatch Court

Langleyesque character has just been constructed at **Hatch Court**. Where John Collins once laid out a linear park of follies and grottoes – the Line Wood Walk – above West Sedge Moor, Philip Gibbs has added his own Folly (*90*) to the west of the house. It is as if that 'Great Master of Gothick', Sanderson Miller, had come down to Hatch Beauchamp to see his friend Thomas Prowse, who was engaged upon the construction of the Court, and left as a courtesy a sketch for a garden building. Beautifully constructed of golden limestone and with an interior of delicate Gothick plasterwork, it will prove to be longer lasting than the lath-and-plaster follies of the past, as it richly deserves. It epitomises perfectly a county whose reverence for the cultural history of England has spanned centuries.

Chapter Notes

Introduction, pages 9-16: Alfred, Arthur and the Holy Thorn – a county of Dark Age legends

1. The site of his fortress is marked by an obelisk, which was set up in 1801.
2. William Wordsworth & Samuel Taylor Coleridge, *Lyrical Ballads* (Bristol, 1798), Advertisement.
3. English Heritage Register entry. See also H Avray Tipping, 'Poundisford Park, Somerset' and 'Poundisford Lodge, Somerset', *Country Life*, 17 & 24 June 1916, and Christopher Hussey, 'Poundisford Park, Somerset I-II', 4 & 11 August 1934. James Bond, *Somerset Parks and Gardens: A Landscape History* (Somerset Books, Tiverton, 1998), pp.25-31 mentions Poundisford in passing. Bond's book is particularly sound on medieval and later deer parks in the county, so this present survey will not cover them in any detail unless they have later designed elements.
4. *Country Life*, 4 August 1934.
5. Ibid.
6. See *Country Life*, 24 November 1906 for this and other examples of lead cisterns.
7. Illustrated in *Country Life*, 24 June 1916.
8. Revd Edmund Butcher, *An Excursion from Sidmouth to Chester in the summer of 1803*, 2 vols., 1805, 2, p.440.
9. Jay-Z headlined the Glastonbury Festival on the Pyramid Stage in the summer of 2008.
10. For the legend and Glastonbury as the capital of the New Age, see Ronald Hutton, *Witches, Druids and King Arthur*, 2003, Chapter 3: 'Glastonbury: Alternative Histories'.
11. F Hardcastle, *Chalice Well, Glastonbury: A Short History* (Glastonbury, 1959), p. 3
12. Oliver G Villiers, *Wellesley Tudor Pole: Appreciation & Valuation* (booklet, Hythe, 1977), p.20.
13. Hardcastle, *Chalice Well*, p.2.
14. Ibid., p.8.
15. Villiers, *Wellesley Tudor Pole*, title page.
16. *The Swan Circle* (undated booklet), p.1. We are most grateful to Michael Eavis for allowing us access to the Circle just prior to the 2009 Festival.

Chapter 1, pages 17-35: Water closets, banqueting houses and a lost botanical garden

1. Robert Laneham's 'Account of the Queen's Entertainment at Killingworth Castle, 1575', in John Nicholls, *The Progresses and Public Processions of Queen Elizabeth*, 3 vols., 1778, 1, p.46.
2. Quoted in Elizabeth Story Donno, *Sir John Harington's A New Discourse of a Stale Subject, Called the Metamorphosis of Ajax*, 1962, p.7: Letter of April 1603 to Thomas Howard in the Salisbury MSS.
3. Sir John's parents had also owned St. Catherine's Court.; see *Country Life*, 24 December 1898.
4. John Collinson, *The History and Antiquities of the County of Somerset*, 3 vols., 1791, p.128.
5. Ibid.
6. *Oxford Dictionary of National Biography*.
7. Donno, *A New Discourse*, p.56.
8. Ibid., pp.55-6.
9. opposite p.41.
10. Revd Richard Warner, *The History of Bath*, 1801, p.187.
11. Norman E McClure (ed.), *The Letters and Epigrams of Sir John Harington* (Pennsylvania, 1930), p.122, quoted in Stephen Greenblatt, *Renaissance Self-Fashioning: From More to Shakespeare* (Chicago, 1980), p.168. I owe this reference to Adam Mowl.
12. Ibid.
13. Guido Waldman (trans.), Ludovico Ariosto, *Orlando Furioso* (Oxford, 1974), Canto 42, 78-87, p.506.
14. Ibid., p.508.
15. James Edgar & Rob Iles, 'Kelston village, manor house and garden remains', *Bristol Archaeological Research Group Review*, vol.2 (1981), pp.66-72. We are also indebted to two reports on the site carried out for the MA in Garden History at the University of Bristol by Charlotte Gale and Joy Brown.

Chapter Notes

16 Revd Francis Poynton, *Memoranda, Historical and genealogical related to the Parish of Kelston in the county of Somerset in four parts*, 1877-1885.

17 Bath Reference Library.

18 Joy Brown Report, p.11.

19 A similar table fountain is included in the Lumley Castle Inventory of 1590; see Paula Henderson, *The Tudor House and Garden: Architecture and Landscape in the Sixteenth and Early Seventeenth Centuries*, 2005, p.189.

20 We are grateful to Magdalene Cordel for allowing us access to the garden.

21 A copy of this sketch with the inscription from Harington's papers was shown to us by Magdalene Cordel.

22 Donno, *A New Discourse*, p.187.

23 Ibid., p.196.

24 Ibid., p.57.

25 See Michael Aston, 'Gardens and Earthworks at Hardington and Low Ham', *Somerset Archaeology and Natural History*, vol.122 (1978), pp.11-28.

26 Ibid., p.24. Aston believes it was on the ridge, whereas later fieldwork, carried out by Robert Wilson-North, contends that it was down by the church; see Chapter Two of this study.

27 Malcolm Rogers, *Montacute House* (National Trust, 2000), p.58.

28 Dates vary for this survey. Rogers gives *c*.1782; the 2003 Historic Landscape Assessment of Montacute by Peter Bellamy dates it to 1774.

29 In addition to the National Trust guidebook, which gives an account of the family, see *Country Life*, 16 & 23 April 1898.

30 Ibid., p.59.

31 It is not mentioned in the 23 April 1898 article in *Country Life*. The decoration on the arches is identical to that on the Summerhouse at Cothelstone.

32 It was made into a garden when the orientation of the house was reversed by Edward Phelips in 1786 with the construction of the Clifton Maybank façade, which formed a new west entrance.

33 It is not shown on the Donne survey.

34 We are indebted to Raymond Asquith for allowing us access to these important archives.

35 Rogers, *Montacute House*, p.58.

36 For architectural devices see Mark Girouard, *Robert Smythson & the Elizabethan Country House*, 1983, pp.21-8. For the banquet course and banquet pavilions see Mark Girouard, *Life in the English Country House*, 1978, pp.105-8.

37 They were subsequently used as game larders, hence the removal of the staircases and floors so that game could be hung freely.

38 Rogers, *Montactute House*, p.59.

39 Ibid., p.59.

40 We are grateful to Nicki Faircloth for guiding us around Cothelstone and for Jane Warmington's hospitality at Terhill.

41 It was demolished in 1968; see Roy Strong, Marcus Binney, John Harris (eds.), *The Destruction of the Country House*, 1974, 124.

42 Moved here from Tetton House in the late nineteenth century (EH Register entry).

43 Hazel Riley, *The Historic Landscape of the Quantock Hills*, 2006, p.117.

44 SRO DD\ES/C/2217.

45 Riley, *Quantock Hills*, p.117.

46 Frustratingly, it is not either illustrated or mentioned in *Country Life*, 11 January 1908.

47 See Christopher Hussey, 'Lytes Cary, Somerset-I & II', *Country Life*, 18 & 25 July 1947.

48 Oliver Garnett, *Lytes Cary* (National Trust, 2001), p.4.

49 Edmund Spenser, *A Ditty*, quoted in Miles Hadfield, *A History of British Gardening*, 1985, p.47.

50 Hadfield, *British Gardening*, p.47.
51 Garnett, *Lytes Cary*, p.5.
52 Quoted in *Country Life*, 17 November 1917.
53 John Harvey, *Medieval Gardens*, 1981, p.139.
54 John Harvey, *Restoring Period Gardens*, 1988, p.30.
55 Christopher Hussey, 'Mells, Somerset-I', *Country Life*, 23 April 1943, fig.6.
56 For Clevedon see *Country Life*, 2 December 1899, 30 June & 7 July 1955 and Julia Elton & Anne Yarrow, *Clevedon Court* (National Trust, 2003); for the Eltons see Margaret Elton, *Annals of the Elton Family* (Alan Sutton, Stroud, 1994).
57 Elton & Yarrow, *Clevedon Court*, p.20.
58 Ibid., p.20.
22 R C Turner, *Gawsworth Hall Gardens: A History and Guide to the Great Elizabethan Garden at Gawsworth, Cheshire* (Macclesfield & Vale Royal Groundwork Trust, 1990), p.10.
23 Ibid.
24 Ibid.
25 Ibid., p. 21.
26 Richards, *Gawsworth Hall*, p.32. The tradition of entertaining is continued today by the Richards family who host summer seasons of open-air theatre and music.
27 Quoted by Turner, *Gawsworth Hall Gardens*, p.4.
28 Ibid., p.5.
29 Ibid.
30 Ibid.
31 This has a font, the first of several architectural fragments dotted around the skirts of the house collected by Raymond Richards, who was Chairman of the Ancient Monuments Society.
32 Oliver Heywood by J W Swynnerton.
33 Turner, *Gawsworth Hall Gardens*, p.7.

Chapter 2, pages 36-58: Earthworks, an episcopal canal and wildernesses – formality subverted

1 Illustrated in Bond, *Parks and Gardens*, fig.6.1; the original map is owned by Lady Gass of Fairfield. Another Thomas England survey of about 1775 (SRO, DD\SAS/C 1207/1B) shows the Castle mound crowned with a celestial classical city of domes and turrets. Can this ever have been a serious proposal?
2 There is another classical gazebo, now decayed, in the grounds of The Sales at Shepton Mallet. It is octagonal, of two storeys, with round-arched openings on both floors.
3 There is an oil-on-panel painting of the layout in the Victoria Art Gallery, Bath.
4 Robert Wilson-North & Phil Newman, 'Low Ham, Somerset', *RCHM*, 1996.
5 John Collinson, *The History and Antiquities of the County of Somerset*, 3 vols., 1791, 3, p.445.
6 SRO, DD\MKG Box 4.
7 Collinson, *Somerset*, 3, p.445.
8 Wilson-North & Newman, 'Low Ham', p.10.
9 Ibid., Appendix 2.
10 SRO, DD\MKG 22; quoted in Wilson-North & Newman, 'Low Ham', p.12.
11 Robert Wilson-North, 'From Carthusian monastery to Country House', *Current Archaeology*, vol.13, no.4 (1996), pp.151-6.
12 James Cartwright (ed.), 'The Travels through England of Dr Richard Pococke', *Camden Society*, 2 vols., 1888-89, 2, p.42.
13 Ibid.
14 Wilson-North, 'Carthusian monastery', p.155.

Chapter Notes

15 Ibid.

16 There is a similar complexity of layering about the grounds that were laid out around Shapwick House, now Shapwick Hotel on the Polden Hills. The 1515 moated site was remodelled in the eighteenth century when many of its original feaures were lost. But it is known that there was a great and a little garden at Shapwick in the later thirteenth century, and that in 1620 the north side of the moat was filled in, when a terraced garden was created. This comprised raised walks with bastions, two canals, a banqueting house, flowerbeds and wilderness walks. See Michael Aston & Christopher Gerrard, '"Unique, Traditional and Charming", The Shapwick Project, Somerset', *The Antiquaries Journal*, vol.79 (1999), pp.1-58; see also Bond, *Parks and Gardens*, p.39.

17 Anna Maria Crino (ed.), *Un Principe di Toscana in Inghilterra e in Irlanda nel 1669* (Rome, 1968), p.38; quoted by John Harvey, 'Parks, Gardens and Landscaping', in Michael Aston (ed.), *Aspects of the Mediaeval Landscape of Somerset* (Somerset County Council, 1988), pp.99-108; Appendix on p.106.

18 Ibid.

19 Leonard Knyff & John Kip, *Britannia Illustrata*, 1707 (1984 facsimile edition by John Harris & Gervase Jackson-Stops, Bungay, 1984).

20 See *Country Life*, 26 November 1898, 30 November 1907, 7 & 14 May 1927.

21 Bodleian Library, Gough Maps, vol.29, f.20B.

22 Bond, *Parks and Gardens*, p.64. Hinton also had a Banqueting House by the Bowling Green

(EH Register entry). Avenues were laid out there by the 1st Earl Poullet who in 1704 erected a statue of Diana at Diana Pond, one mile west of the house. She was moved before 1800 to a circular grove of limes in the park shown on an estate map (SRO, M/5201 1). The statue has now been re-sited on a stone plinth at the entrance to the grounds.

23 The narrow canal is still shown on the 1838 tithe map (SRO, DD\Rt/M 70), and on the first edition OS map of 1886.

24 Howard M Colvin, *A Biographical Dictionary of British Architects 1600-1840*, 2008, p.1030.

25 We are most grateful to Lady Gass for allowing us to reproduce these paintings and for her hospitality at Fairfield.

26 SRO, D/P/Stogs 23/4.

27 We are indebted to Mark Horton's recent researches at Wells, compiled during an excavation between 2003 and 2004. The results of this have been conveyed to us in manuscript form.

28 Christopher Morris (ed.), *The Illustrated Journeys of Celia Fiennes c.1682-c.1712* (Exeter, 1982), p.195; p.199.

29 These were part of Carter's 'Cathedrals Series', which were intended to be published by the Society of Antiquaries as an attempt to match the classical publications of the Society of Dilettanti; see J Mordaunt Crook, *John Carter and the Mind of the Gothic Revival*, The Society of Antiquaries of London, Occasional Papers, vol.17 (1995).

30 Timothy Mowl, 'Rococo and later landscaping at Longleat', *Garden History*, vol.23, no.1 (Summer, 1995), pp.56-66.

31 Michael McGarvie & John Harvey, 'Revd George Harbin and his memoirs of gardening 1716-1723', *Garden History*, vol.11, no.1 (Spring, 1983), pp.6-36.

32 Pat Robinson, *The Bishop's Palace Wells* (Wells, 2002), pp.10-11.

33 *Country Life*, 24 June 1911.

34 A monochrome print of this painting is held by the National Monuments Record (hereafter NMR), and it is redrawn and discussed in *Country Life*, 24 June 1911.

35 *Country Life*, 24 June 1911.

36 For Hackwood see Peter Willis, *Charles Bridgeman and the English Landscape Garden* (Newcastle-upon-Tyne, 2002), s 200, 200a & 200b.

37 Philip Miller, *The Gardener's Dictionary*, 1731, entry on Wildernesses, no pagination; I owe this quotation to Jim Bartos.

38 *Country Life*, 29 October 1898.

39 There are prints of Burton's drawings in the NMR. For the proposed garden front see Negative Number: BB 83/4885.

40 SRO, A/ARW/3/1: Account Book of John Periam for the construction of Hill House.
41 Illustrated in 'Sandhill Park, Bishop's Lydeard, Somerset: Historic Landscape Appraisal', Parklands Consortium Limited, 2007. The report was commissioned by Gladeclear Ltd. We are grateful to Colin Wilkins for supplying us with a copy of this report.
42 We are most grateful to Merriel Laverack for help with the archives, and to Chris Silverwood and Pep Hill for guiding us through Blackdown Wood.
43 SRO, A/ASM 5/22: Somerset Gardens Trust file on Orchard Wyndham.
44 Katherine Wyndham & Richard Haslam, 'Orchard Wyndham, Somerset-II', *Country Life*, 28 March 1985.
45 SRO, DD\WY Box 8, Zn1.
46 See John Harris, *The Artist and the Country House: A history of country house and garden view painting in Britain 1540-1870*, 1979, p.96; pp.161-2.
47 It is also shown in a companion painting by Griffier at the house. An earlier painting of about 1730 shows the mirror pool in front of the house within a walled forecourt and tree avenues across the parkscape.
48 We are most grateful to Michael McGarvie for sharing with us his extensive knowledge of the landscape at Marston and for alerting us to the archival sources. His two published works on the estate have been extremely valuable: *The Book of Marston Bigot* (Buckingham, 1987), and 'Notes towards a History of Gardening at Marston House, Frome 1660-1905', Frome Historical Research Group, Occasional papers, no.4 (1987).
49 Stephen Switzer, *An Introduction to a General System of Hydrostaticks and Hydraulicks*, 2 vols., 1739, 1, Preface, p.xxxi.
50 McGarvie, 'Gardening at Marston House', p.4.
51 Ibid., p.8.
52 Ibid., p.9.
53 Ibid., p.10.
54 Ibid.
55 For Heythrop see Timothy Mowl, *The Historic Gardens of England: Oxfordshire* (Stroud, 2007), pp.54-62.
56 McGarvie, 'Gardening at Marston House', p.14.
57 Ibid.
58 There was also another Grotto by the church, dedicated to the Orrerys' friend Dr William King, and a hermitage and rustic cottage in an extension of the gardens to the north-west.
59 James Cartwright (ed.), 'The Travels through England of Dr Richard Pococke', *Camden Society*, 2 vols., 1888-89, 2, p.401.
60 McGarvie, 'Gardening at Marston', p.20.

Chapter 3, pages 59-92: Rivals in Arcady

1 James Cartwright (ed.), 'The Travels through England of Dr Richard Pococke', *Camden Society*, 2 vols., 1888-89, 2, p.41.
2 James Howley, *The Follies and Garden Buildings of Ireland*, 1993, p.204.
3 Orrery Papers for 24 June 1747, quoted in Barbara Jones, *Follies & Gottoes*, 1974, p.438.
4 The term 'Rococo', used to describe these eclectic gardens, was first coined by John Harris in the 1970s in relation to Thomas Robins' paintings of the layouts; for a full account of the period see Timothy Mowl, *Gentlemen & Players: Gardeners of the English Landscape* (Stroud, 2002), Chapter 11: 'Gentlemen in Control – The 'Rococo' Garden', pp.136-48.
5 Lady Llanover (ed.), *The Autobiography and Correspondence of Mary Granville, Mrs Delany*, second series, 3 vols., 1861, 2, pp.492-3.
6 Ibid., p.492.
7 See Timothy Mowl & Brian Earnshaw, *An Insular Rococo: Architecture, Politics and Society in Ireland and England, 1710-1770*, 1999, Chapter 4: 'A Wandering Bishop', pp.73-87.

Chapter Notes

8   SRO, DD\L 1/22/7A.

9   James Savage, *History of the Hundred of Carhampton* (Bristol, 1830), p.145.

10 A report on the Summerhouse was carried out by Dr Kate Felus: 'The Octagon Summerhouse, Hestercombe Somerset: History, Design, Context and Outline Proposals for Restoration' (November 2005). We are grateful to Dr Felus for first alerting us to the Phelps sketches.

11 Illustrated in Gervase Jackson-Stops, 'Arcadia under the Plough: The Garden at Halswell, Somerset', *Country Life*, 9 February 1989, fig.2.

12 SRO, DD\S/WH/269: Escott Journal.

13 We are grateful to Graeme Bond and Mark Cranfield for allowing us access to the park and for sharing with us their researches on Halswell.

14 We are grateful to Sue Shephard and to Judy Preston for their researches into Wright's patronage network; thanks also to Eileen Harris whose seminal articles on Wright published in *Country Life*, 26 August, 2 & 9 September 1971 first alerted garden historians to this extraordinary character. For Wright's work at Badminton and Stoke Park see Timothy Mowl, *Historic Gardens of Gloucestershire* (Stroud, 2002), pp.89-90.

15 Illustrated in *Country Life*, 9 February 1989, fig.11.

16 Ibid.

17 Ibid.

18 For Moses and the Tabernacle see Timothy Mowl & Brian Earnshaw, *John Wood: Architect of Obsession* (Bath, 1988), pp.125-31; for Freemasonry in general see James Stevens Curl, *The Art & Architecture of Freemasonry*, 1991.

19 Arthur Young, *The Farmer's Tour through the East of England*, 4 vols., 1771, 4, p.14.

20 Judy Preston, 'A Polymath in Arcadia: Thomas Wright (1711-1786)', unpublished manuscript to appear in 2010 in *Garden History*. We are most grateful to Judy Preston for making this available for study prior to publication.

21 Thomas Wright Manuscripts, University of Durham, Special Collections. We owe this reference to Judy Preston.

22 Magnus Olausson, 'Freemasonry, Occultism and the Picturesque garden towards the end of the Eighteenth Century', *Journal of Garden History*, vol.20, no.1 (1981), pp.413-34; p.423. We owe this reference to Judy Preston.

23 See Rosemary Sweet, *Antiquaries: The Discovery of the Past in Eighteenth-Century Britain*, 2004, and Ronald Hutton, *Blood & Mistletoe: The History of the Druids in Britain*, 2009.

24 Information from Derek Gibson of the Halswell Park Trust.

25 SRO, DD\S/WH/320: Sir Charles Kemeys-Tynte's Diary.

26 Preston, 'A Polymath in Arcadia'; quoted from the Wright MSS.

27 Ibid.

28 Young, *Tour*, 4, p.14.

29 Ibid.

30 SRO, DD\S/WH/320.

31 *Country Life*, 9 February 1989.

32 Mark Girouard, 'Hatch Court, Somerset-I & II', *Country Life*, 22 October 1964.

33 Taken from E H Register entry composed by Jonathan Lovie.

34 SRO, DD\CC.

35 SRO, DD\TN9.

36 Collinson, *History*, 1, p.43.

37 The Grotto was excavated in 1998; the Chapel and Bastion in 2006.

38 There is another detached bowling green in the woods at Brockley Hall; information from Bryan Smith.

39 SRO, DD\S/WH/320.

40 Young, *Tour*, 4, p.2.

41 Ibid.

42 Ibid.

43 Ibid.

44 Ibid.

45 Information from Kate Felus, citing a letter in the archives.

46 Philip White, his architect Robert Battersby and Kate Felus have looked at all these drawings and concluded that those by Phelps are coarser in their treatment and the buildings depicted have a slight leftward lean.

47 Edward Knight Junior's pocketbook: 'Account of journey and pocket books, 1749-1778', Worcestershire Record Office, 899:310 BA10470, parcel 2.

48 See Richard Haslam, 'Dunster Castle, Somerset-II', *Country Life*, 16 July 1987.

49 For example, SRO, DD\L 2/43/8 and DD\L 2/45/19 of 1758 and 1779 respectively.

50 Edward Phelps was to do much the same at Montacute in 1760 when he built a folly tower on St Michael's Hill as an eye-catcher to be viewed from the grounds. This is shown on a view of the east front of the house in Collinson's *History*. Bonnor's view also shows a grotto with a statue of a female nude at the south end of the pool, but it is not clear if this was ever executed. The view is illustrated in Rogers, *Montacute*, p.60.

51 Oliver Garnett, *Dunster Castle* (National Trust, 2003), pp.42-3.

52 Savage, *Hundred of Carhampton*, p.442.

53 See Hazel Riley, *The Historic Landscape of the Quantock Hills* (Swindon, 2006), pp.119-20. We are also indebted to Vivienne Lewis' unpublished report on Crowcombe, carried out for the MA in Garden History at the University of Bristol (February, 2005).

54 Illustrated in *Country Life*, 22 April 1933, fig.4.

55 SRO, DD\TB/ 51/2.

56 We are most grateful to Dr Patricia and Richard Smith for allowing us access to the grounds and for information on the house and gardens.

57 SRO, DD\TB 27/4/1-63.

58 We are most grateful to Anthony Trollope-Bellew for allowing us access to the combe.

59 *Country Life*, 22 April 1933, fig.5.

60 SRO, DD\TB 51/2.

61 Phelps is also likely to have designed the Gothick Willett Tower, just south of Elworthy, which was built in 1774 by subscription, but with Bernard as the chief organiser; see Enid Byford, *Somerset Curiosities* (Wimborne, Dorset, 1987), pp.96-7. Phelps may also have designed the Beacon Tower on Cothelstone Hill, now destroyed, at some point between 1768 and 1780. It is illustrated in Riley, *Quantock Hills*, fig.5.16 on p.126.

62 SRO, DD\ES/18/26.

63 Riley, *Quantock Hills*, p.122, citing SRO, Esdaile Manuscripts.

Chapter 4, pages 93-111: Poetry, Politics and Moses' Holy Tabernacle in the Bath hinterland

1 Cartwright, *Camden Society*, 2, p.153.

2 See Mowl, *Gentlemen & Players*, p.140, and Mowl & Earnshaw, *Insular Rococo*, p.84.

3 The best illustrated account of the landscape is Gillian Clarke, *Prior Park: A Compleat Landscape* (Bath, 1987).

4 See Philip Sales, 'Ordered Naturalness at Bath', *Country Life*, 22 March 1979 for early pictures of the landscape, and Anthony Woodward, 'Prior Park, Bath', *Country Life*, 19 September 1996, for the recent restoration.

5 In addition to the Gothic Temple there was a Gothick Lodge, which is marked on Thorp's 1742 map. Thomas Robins sketched the Lodge in about 1760; it was partially rebuilt as a memorial to Allen by Bishop Warburton, who married Allen's niece and succeeded Allen at Prior Park after the latter's death in 1764. It was demolished in 1953.

6 Marjorie Williams, *Lady Luxborough goes to Bath*, (Oxford, 1945), p.58.

Chapter Notes

7 John Dixon Hunt & Peter Willis (eds.), *The Genius of the Place*, 2000, p.250.

8 Marion Mako, *Cascades of the seventeenth and eighteenth centuries* (Unpublished report for the National Trust, 2005), p.28.

9 Daniel Defoe, *A Tour thro' the Whole Island of Britain*, 1742 (New York, Garland facsimile ed., 1975), pp.265-6.

10 Timothy Mowl & Brian Earnshaw, *John Wood: Architect of Obsession* (Bath, 1988), Chapter 7, pp.99-118; p.112.

11 Ibid., pp.99-100; pp.125-31.

12 Tim Mowl, *Palladian Bridges: Prior Park and the Whig Connection* (Bath, 1993), pp.31-6. See also *New Arcadian Journal*, vol.43/44 (1997): 'The Political Temples of Stowe'.

13 Ibid., p.33.

14 Ibid., p.34. The original document is in Bath Reference Library.

15 This was moved to the east pediment of the Temple of Concord and Victory overlooking the Grecian Valley in 1761.

16 Matthew Ward, *Prior Park Landscape Garden* (National Trust, 2009), p.5.

17 Cathryn Spence & Daniel Brown, *Thomas Robins the Elder (1716-1770): An Introduction to his Life and Work* (Bath, 2006), p.5. See also John Harris, *Gardens of Delight: The Rococo English Landscape of Thomas Robins the Elder*, 2 vols., 1978. For Robins watercolours of Bath houses and gardens see: www.bathintime.co.uk

18 The suggestion that Robins might also have been a designer was first put forward in Timothy Mowl & Roger White, 'Thomas Robins at Painswick', *Journal of Garden History*, vol.4, no.2 (1984), pp.163-78.

19 Arthur Oswald, 'Widcombe Manor, Somerset', *Country Life*, 28 August 1937; it had been brought to Widcombe by the prevous owner, Sir John Roper Wright.

20 Illustrated in *Country Life*, 28 August 1937, fig.4.

21 Jonathan Holt, 'Widcombe Manor: A Tour round "The Golden House"', *The Follies Journal*, no.2 (Winter, 2002), pp.53-63; p.58.

22 Ibid., fig.5. John Harris believes that this was in the Lyncombe Pleasure Gardens rather than at Widcombe.

23 John Wood, *An Essay towards a Description of Bath*, 3rd edition, 1765 (Kingsmead Reprints, Bath, 1969), of the 'Spaw' opposite p.80.

24 Ibid., p.423.

25 John Wood, *The Origin of Building, or the Plagiarism of the Heathens Detected*, 1744 edition, p.93.

26 Wood, *Origin*, p.94.

27 Wood, *Essay*, p.235.

28 Ruth Aveline Hesselgrave, *Lady Miller and the Batheaston Literary Circle* (New Haven & London, 1927). We owe this reference to Jane Dunn.

29 The bow and verandah do not feature in an 1825 Buckler watercolour of the house, but they do in images thereafter.

30 Cartwright, *Camden Society*, 2, p.33.

31 W S Lewis (ed.), *The Yale Edition of Horace Walpole's Correspondence*, 48 vols (New Haven & London, 1937-83), 10, p.233: Walpole to Montagu, 22 October 1766.

32 Ibid., 10, p.234: Montagu to Walpole, 27 October 1766.

33 We are most grateful to Jane Dunn for allowing us access to the grounds and for sharing with us her knowledge of Lady Miller.

34 Collinson, *History*, 1, opposite p.65: 'She departed this life at the Hot-Wells of Bristol the 24th June 1781, in the 41st year of her age'.

35 Lewis, *Walpole's Correspondence*, 32, pp.221-2: Walpole to Lady Ossory, 12 January 1775.

36 Ibid., 32, p.224: Walpole to Lady Ossory, 19 January 1775.

37 Ibid., 39, pp.240-1.

38 We owe this observation to Wendy Smayle, who has written an anlysis of the grounds for her MA Garden History coursework at the University of Bristol. For more information on satirical prints see Philippa Bishop, 'The Sentence of Momus: Satirical Verse and Prints in Eighteenth-Century Bath', *Bath*

History, vol.4 (1994), pp.51-79. I am grateful to Gillian Sladen for informing me of this article.

39 Nick Owen, 'Burton Pynsent, Somerset: Brown's Column and the Landscape of William Pitt and Hester Pitt', *The Follies Journal*, Number 7 (winter, 2007), pp.41-54.

40 Ibid., p.45.

41 PRO, Chatham Papers, 30/8/62: Lord Temple to Lady Chatham, Stowe, 4 August 1765.

42 Ibid., 30/8/61: Letters from Lord Temple to Wm. Pitt, 5 August 1755.

43 Ibid., 30/8/61: 25 June 1749.

44 Ibid., 30/8/61: 5 November 1765, from Stowe.

45 Michael Symes, 'William Pitt the Elder: The Gran Mago of Landscape Gardening', *Garden History*, vol. 24, no. 1 (Summer, 1996), pp.126-36; p.129.

46 Owen, 'Burton Pynsent', p.45, quoting from the Chatham Papers in the Public Record Office.

Chapter 5, pages 112-146: Somerset gentry spurn Lady Nature's second husband

1 Information from Richard Combe, which conflicts with Christopher Hussey's article on the house in *Country Life*, 13 & 20 October 1960, in which Hussey, citing documents in the SRO, argues that the house was completed in 1731 for Henry Combe at the cost of £10,000 'after the Italian manner', possibly by a Bristol architect. We are most grateful to Richard for clarifying the early history of the house, guiding us around the estate and allowing reproduction of the estate plan.

2 Horace Walpole's description of Brown on his death in a letter to Lady Ossory of 8 February 1783; Lewis, *Correspondence*, 33, p.385.

3 Bodleian Library, Oxford, Gough Maps, vol.29, f.21.

4 Joanna Martin, *Wives and Daughters, Women and Children in the Georgian Country House*, 2004, p.266.

5 *The Victoria County History: Somerset* (hereafter *VCH*), vol.7, p.28.

6 The survey is in the Dorset Record Office, but uncatalogued; an illustration based on the survey is given in *VCH*, 7, p.27; it is also illustrated in Mark Laird, *The Flowering of the Landscape Garden: English Pleasure Grounds 1720-1800* (University of Pennsylvania Press, Philadelphia, 1999), fig 141.

7 Martin, *Wives and Daughters*, p.267.

8 Ibid., p.271. See also Timothy Mowl, *Historic Gardens of Dorset* (Stroud, 2003), pp.151-2.

9 Ibid., p.267.

10 Laird, *Flowering of the Landscape Garden*, pp.233-7.

11 Ibid., p.236.

12 Ibid., p.237.

13 R Richardson, 'A Map of the West Part of Redlynch Estate in the County of Somerset', 1800, Dorset Record Office, D/FSI A/11 D124.

14 We are most grateful to Raymond, Viscount Asquith, for his kind hospitality at Mells Manor, for allowing us access to the archives and for permission to reproduce some of the drawings here.

15 There is a drawing for a Chinese gate and a Chinese pavilion with a pyramidal roof in the archives, which may be related to this bridge.

16 There is also a drawing in the archives for a set of Gothick gates with attached railings.

17 EH Register entry.

18 Michael McGarvie, 'Notes towards a History of Mells Park', *Frome Society Year Book*, vol.4 (1990-1992), pp.31-40; p.38.

19 Frances Horner, *Time Remembered*, 1933, p.181.

20 McGarvie, 'Notes towards a History of Mells Park', p.45.

21 Ibid., p.44.

22 Ibid., p.46.

23 Ibid., pp.45-6.

Chapter Notes

24 Information from Viscount Asquith.

25 E H Register entry; McGarvie, 'Notes towards a History of Mells Park', p.46.

26 Soane's drawings are preserved in a scrapbook confusingly entitled: 'Mells Park Drawings by Sir Hans Sloane 1810'.

27 Soane Museum Archives, Mells Park 4, Letters 17 August 1810-12 July 1828 from Colonel Horner, Sir John Soane's Journals/Account books and Ledger E, Bankers Acct. 1817-35.

28 McGarvie, 'Notes towards a History of Mells Park', p.47.

29 This two-storey building has a Gibbs surround to the doorway and a pyramidal roof; there are later, lower two-storey wings either side. The lawns surrounding the Summerhouse are alive with statuary, and there is a fine enclosure of garden gnomes.

30 John Horsey, Barwick Park Report for MA Garden History coursework, University of Bristol (2009). We are most grateful to John for guiding us around the park at Barwick.

31 Barbara Jones, *Follies & Grottoes*, 1974, p.227.

32 Ibid., p.229.

33 Ibid., p.230.

34 The date is included in his Red Book, but a payment to him of £47 on 4 February 1791 suggests that surveying may have begun earlier; see Anthony Woodward, 'Ston Easton Park, Somerset', *Country Life*, 13 November 1997.

35 Alfred Tennyson, *The Lady of Shalott*, Part 1, line 15.

36 The Lodge is included as a vignette on a plan of the estate by Robert Burton, who surveyed Orchardleigh in 1818-19; this is illustrated in Bond, *Somerset Parks and Gardens*, fig.8.25.

37 These watercolours are both owned by Michael McGarvie, to whom we are most grateful for allowing reproduction of the twin pair.

38 Christopher Hussey, 'Ammerdown House', Somerset I & II, *Country Life*, 16 February & 2 March 1929.

39 Illustrated in Timothy Mowl & Brian Earnshaw, *Trumpet at a Distant Gate: The Lodge as Prelude to the Country House*, 1985, colour 16.

40 The Hon Andrew Jolliffe has taken over from Lord Hylton and hopes one day to restore them.

41 Illustration from the Charles Tite Collection, Somerset Studies Library, vol.1.

42 Timothy Mowl, '"Against the time in which the fabric and use of gunpowder shall be forgotten": Enmore Castle, its origins and its architect', *Architectural History*, vol.33 (1990), pp.102-19.

43 We are grateful to Simon and Anne Stoye for allowing us access to the grounds.

44 J Mordaunt Crook, *John Carter and the Mind of the Gothic Revival*, Society of Antiquaries Occasional Papers, vol. 17 (1995), pp.50-1.

45 See Jones, *Follies & Grottoes*, pp.285; also Christopher Hussey, 'Midford Castle, Somerset-I', *Country Life*, 3 March 1944, which illustrates the ruined Chapel, or 'Priory', at figs.5, 7 & 8.

46 Collinson, *History*, 1, p.136.

47 Stewart Harding & David Lambert, *Parks and Gardens of Avon* (Bristol, 1994), p.43.

48 E H Register entry.

49 We are grateful to Mary Hill and Charles and Linda Hill for allowing us access to the house and grounds and giving permission to reproduce the plan.

50 SRO, DD\X TH/1. This also has an illustration of the house with its loggia.

51 Ibid.

52 Humphry Repton, *Observations on the Theory and Practice of Landscape Gardening*, 1805, p.200.

53 Ibid., List of s.

54 Ibid., p.200.

55 Ibid., p.201.

56 SRO, DD\HI\A/265.

57 See Bryan Little, 'Ston Easton Park, Somerset I, II & III', *Country Life*, 23 & 30 March, 6 April 1945.

58 Ston Easton Red Book, private collection. We are grateful to the Head Gardener, Dorian Poole, for

making a copy of the Red Book available for research. We are grateful to Mrs Kathleen Hippisley for allowing reproduction of the Red Book watercolours.

59 E H Register entry.

60 Much of the biographical information presented here is taken from Nicholas Pearson Associates, 'Newton Park: Historic Survey and Restoration Plan' (Report to the Duchy of Cornwall, 1993); also from Graham Davis, *The Langtons of Newton Park, Bath* (Bath, no date). We are grateful to the late Tony Dewberry and Professor David Timms for supplying us with a copy of the Pearson Associates Plan and for allowing access to the grounds. Thanks are also due to Head Gardener Jacqueline McKenna for sharing with us her thoughts about the development of the landscape.

61 Pearson Associates Plan, p.18.

62 Illustrated in Bond, *Parks and Gardens*, fig.6.12.

63 We are grateful to Jacqueline McKenna for supplying us with a typescript of the Red Book text.

64 Susi Batty, ' Conservation Statement for Leigh Court' (MA Garden History coursework report, University of Bristol, 2001).

65 'Report concerning Abbots Leigh near Bristol The Property of Philip John Miles Esq by H Repton 1814', University of Bristol, Special Collections.

66 Stewart Harding, *Repton in Avon* (Avon Gardens Trust, Bristol, 1989), no pagination.

Chapter 6, pages 147-172: Science, technology, biblical exegesis and the true source of *Frankenstein*

1 This account is a reduced version of one already published: Stuart Prior & Timothy Mowl, 'Garden of a Modern Prometheus – Fyne Court, Somerset', *Garden History*, vol.37, no.1 (Summer, 2009), pp.111-24.

2 See Iwan Rhys Morus, *Frankenstein's Children: Electricity, Exhibition, and Experiment in Early-Nineteenth-Century London* (New Jersey: Princeton University Press, 1998), pp.102-3.

3 Biographical information on Crosse is taken from Peter Haining, *The Man who was Frankenstein* (London: Frederick Muller, 1979).

4 Crosse's experiments are described in Cornelia A. H. Crosse, *Memorials Scientific and Literary, of Andrew Crosse, The Electrician*, 1857.

5 Cited and quoted in Rhys Morus, *Frankenstein's Children*, p.111.

6 Richard Phillips, 'A Brief Account of a Visit to Andrew Crosse, Esq.', *Annals of Electricity* 1 (1836-7), pp.135-45; quoted in Cultural Heritage, 'Archaeological and Historic Landscape Survey: Fyne Court, Broomfield, Somerset, Taunton' (2005), p.71.

7 Quoted in Cultural Heritage Survey, p.71.

8 Included in Nick Berry, 'Fyne Court – Survey Report on the Historical Development of the Park and Garden', prepared for the National Trust, Holnicote Estate Office (1997).

9 I & H Clayton, *Survey of the Parish of Broomfield* (1812): SRO, DD\NA/21.

10 Robert Turner, 'Fyne Court, Somerset', Coursework for MA in Garden History, University of Bristol, 2010.

11 Elaine Jamieson, 'Fyne Court, Broomfield, Somerset. An 18th Century Landscape Park', Survey Report for English Heritage (2003), p.4.

12 For a telling account of Crosse's mild nature and gentle self-projection see E. Littell, *Littell's Living Age* (Boston MA, second series, vol. xix, October-December, 1857), pp.220-22.

13 Mary Shelley's Journal for 28 December 1814. See Paula R Feldman & Diana Scott-Kilvert (eds.), *The Journals of Mary Shelley 1814-44*, 2 vols (Oxford: 1987), 1, p.56.

14 Haining, *The Man who was Frankenstein*, p.65.

15 Peter Fairclough (ed.), *Three Gothic Novels: Walpole/The Castle of Otranto, Beckford/Vathek, Mary Shelley /Frankenstein* (Penguin, 1968), p.300.

16 For the development of the estate and house see *VCH*, 5, pp.131-3.

17 SRO, DD\AH 64/5: 'A Beautiful Grotto formed with Shells, Fossils, &c., with Stained Glass Door and Windows, Commanding Delightful Views of the Channel'.

Chapter Notes

18 Ibid.

19 Hazelle Jackson, 'Jordans Grotto, Ashill, Somerset', *Somerset Gardens Trust Report*, 2003, p.3.

20 1950s photographs show these rockeries in more detail: SRO, DD\X CND/2 2-30.

21 We are grateful to Peter Speke for allowing us access to the Grotto.

22 Jackson, 'Jordans Grotto', p.19.

23 Collinson, *History*, 2, p.449.

24 Ibid.

25 SRO, A/AW1 188/4: Survey by White Young Green, undated.

26 Robin Atthill, 'A Dynasty of Ironmasters', *Country Life*, 24 May 1962.

27 Richard Rosenfeld, 'Water Music', *The English Garden*, July 1998.

28 Mark Girouard, 'A house built by an ironmaster', *Country Life*, 1 June 1961. For the ownership of the house by the novelist Anthony Powell see Harry Mount, 'The Chantry, Somerset', *Country Life*, 27 October 2005. The attribution to Pinch is made by Girouard and also by David Rawlings, *Chantry: Village and Church* (Frome, 2003), p.3.

29 See David Lambert, 'The Prospect of Trade: The Merchant Gardeners of Bristol in the second half of the eighteenth century', in Michel Conan (ed.), *Bourgeois and Aristocratic Cultural Encounters in Garden Art 1550-1850*, Dumbarton Oaks colloquium, 2002, pp.123-145.

30 We are grateful to Raj Russell for showing us his copy of these particulars.

31 Raj Russell has also restored the canal sides and introduced a new footbridge, which gives access to the Grotto.

32 The Ride has been covered by several writers so will not be analysed in detail here. See James Lees-Milne, *William Beckford* (Tisbury, 1976), pp.87-93; Timothy Mowl, *William Beckford: Composing for Mozart*, 1998, pp.288-92; Derek E Ostergard (ed.), *William Beckford 1760-1844: An Eye for the Magnificent* (Bard Graduate Center, New York, 2001), pp.279-93. This last has an illustration of the map of the Ride Hugh Crallan prepared for an exhibition on Beckford held at the Holburne Museum in 1966 (Fig.16-3).

33 John Britton, *Autobiography of John Britton*, 3 parts, 1849-50, part 1 (1850), pp.180-1.

34 Edmund English, *Views of Lansdown Tower*, 1844, p.4. The Latin plant names are contemporary and do not necessarily relate to today's nomenclature.

35 Jane Austen, *Northanger Abbey*, 1818 (Oxford University Press edition, 1975), p.100.

36 The best source of information on the artist Benjamin Barker is: *The Barkers of Bath* (Bath Museums Service, 1986). A previous owner, Michael Forsyth, has covered the architectural development of the house in a scholarly article entitled: 'Edward Davis, Nineteenth Century Bath Architect and Pupil of Sir John Soane', *Bath History*, 1998. Tim Mowl's two articles: 'The Williamane, Architecture for the Sailor King', in *Late Georgian Classicism* (1987 Georgian Group Symposium), and 'A Taste for Towers', *Country Life*, 1 October 1987, deal with the aesthetic context of the period as regards architecture and gardens, but with specific reference to Bath, and Michael Forsyth has published a digest of his Edward Davis article in *Pevsner Architectural Guides: Bath* (2003). See also Neil Jackson, *Nineteenth Century Bath: Architects and Architecture* (Bath, 1991), Chapter 4: 'Picturesque Architecture and the Landscape'. For the garden at Oakwood see *'Oakwood: A Villa Garden'* (Bath Preservation Trust pamphlet, no date).

37 John Britton, *Autobiography of John Britton*, 3 parts, 1849-50, part 1 (1850), p.178.

38 Image in the Somerset Studies Library, Charles Tite Collection, volume 6.

39 See Mowl, 'The Williamane', fig.16.

40 See Dennis Comer, *The Book of Porlock* (Tiverton, 1999), p.17.

41 James Savage, *History of the Hundred of Carhampton* (Bristol, 1830), p.76.

42 SRO, DD\CCH 3/3.

43 B H Neumann, 'Byron's Daughter', *The Mathematical Gazette*, vol.7, no.400 (June, 1973), pp.94-7.

44 Ibid., p.95.

45 Ibid.

46 www.thephilosophersgarden.com/page3/index.php; accessed 22 December 2009.

47 Ibid.

48 Ibid. See also www.minehead-online.co.uk/ashley.htm; accessed 22 December 2009.
49 www.thephilosophersgarden.com/page3/index.php; accessed 22 December 2009.
50 John Rutter, *Delineations of Somerset* (Shaftesbury, 1829), p.148.
51 Ibid., p.147.
52 John Chapman, *A Short History of Banwell Caves* (Banwell Caves Heritage Group, Cheddar, 2007), p.10. See also Mike Chapman, 'The Banwell Caves Historic Garden Grounds', *Avon Gardens Trust Newsletter*, no.22 (Summer, 2000), pp. 26-34; we are grateful to Peggy Stembridge for this reference.
53 Chapman, *Short History*, p.8.
54 Rutter, *Delineations*, p.149.
55 Ibid., p.150.
56 Ibid., p.153.

Chapter 7, pages 173-187: Garish bedding, terraces and a confusion of style – the Victorians

1 SRO, A/BEN/13/2.
2 We are grateful to Nick Rigden for guiding us around the grounds at Nynehead and for sharing with us his researches on the site.
3 Marion Mako, 'Parish's House, Timsbury', Historic Landscape Report, 2008; the attribution to Baldwin is made by Christopher Hussey, *Country Life*, 7 July 1944. There are sketches by G S Repton for Camerton in the Royal Institute of British Architects Drawings Collection.
4 John Skinner, *Journal of a Somerset Rector 1803-1843* (Bath, 1930), p.423.
5 We are most grateful to Bryan Smith for sharing with us his knowledge of the landscape at Brockley. For information on the Smyth-Pigotts and Brockley see Frances Smith, *Just Passing Through: The Story of Brockley Hall* (Nailsea, 2003).
6 Rutter, *Delineations*, pp.30-1.
7 Ibid.
8 Ibid.
9 Ibid.
10 We are grateful to Kate Hughes for her translation of this tablet.
11 Ibid.
12 Smith, *Just Passing Through*, p.22.
13 Information from Bryan Smith.
14 Lanning Roper, 'The Making of an Anglo-American Garden', *Country Life*, 19 March 1970.
15 Illustrated in Helene Gammack, 'An Italianate Garden at Claverton Manor', *America in Britain*, vol.45 (2007), p.19.
16 James Ayres, 'Claverton and its Manors', *America in Britain*, vol.39 (2001), p.9.
17 For Roos see Richard Garnier, 'Alexander Roos (c.1810-1881)', *Georgian Group Journal*, vol.25 (1996), pp.11-68.
18 Gammack, 'An Italianate Garden', p.19.
19 Ibid., p.20.
20 Francis Greenacre, *Tyntesfield* (National Trust, 2003), p.34.
21 Illustrated in *Country Life*, 17 May 1902.
22 Shown in a watercolour of about 1845, illustrated in James Miller, *Fertile Fortune: The Story of Tyntesfield*, 2003, p.16.
23 We are grateful to Kevin and Michelle Adeson for their hospitality at Maperton.
24 National Monuments Record (hereafter NMR).
25 Illustrated in *Country Life*, 17 June 1899.
26 Ibid.

Chapter Notes

27 Julia Elton & Anne Yarrow, *Clevedon Court* (National Trust, 2003), p.21. Photographs on pages 20 and 21 show the bedding schemes. There is a more extensive photographic survey in *Country Life*, 2 December 1899.

28 Bond, *Somerset Parks and Gardens*, p.115.

29 Ibid.

30 Reginald Blomfield, *The Formal Garden in England*, 1892, p.184.

31 See Robert Ladd, 'Orchardleigh Park: A Case Study', in Bond, *Somerset Parks and Gardens*, pp.160-3.

32 Ibid., p.161.

33 Bond, *Somerset Parks and Gardens*, p.117. There are two later Pulhamite rock gardens at Bracken Hill House and Rayne Thatch in the residential sector of Leigh Woods, just across the Avon Gorge from Clifton; see Harding & Lambert, *Parks and Gardens of Avon*, pp.90-1, and Bond, *Somerset Parks and Gardens*, p.117.

34 *Country Life*, 21 December 1901.

35 The same might be said for the garden at Bindon House Hotel, Langford Budville, on the border with Devon. The eccentric eighteenth-century house, its tall semicircular bays topped by shaped gables like bishops' mitres, has been beautifully restored, but the formal walled garden below remains neglected. This is laid out in quadrants with a decayed summerhouse or bothy at one corner. Its date is uncertain, but the enclosure appears on the 1887 Ordnance Survey map.

36 In December 2003 Colin and Vaun received a Historic Landscape Restoration Commendation from Taunton Deane Borough Council.

37 SRO, DD\FS Box 7, vol.2 (1736-1789).

38 Sale details of 27 June 1925 mention a fernery with heating apparatus; we owe this reference to Vaun Wilkins.

39 *Crowe Hall, Bath* (pamphlet, 1997), no pagination. We are grateful to David Carrington, Head Gardener, for guiding us around the grounds.

40 We are most grateful to the Barratt estate for allowing us to reproduce one of the photographs here.

41 *Country Life*, 27 July 1901.

Chapter 8, pages 188-228: Where stone flowers at least as vigorously as the plants – the Edwardian gardens

1 The gardens are shown, newly constructed, in *Country Life*, 18 January 1902.

2 David Ottewill, *The Edwardian Garden*, 1989, pp.13-21.

3 For Athelhampton see Timothy Mowl, *Historic Gardens of Dorset* (Stroud, 2003), pp.124-9; also Ottewill, *Edwardian Garden*, pp.14-16.

4 See Jane Abdy & Charlotte Gere, *The Souls*, 1984.

5 Information from Ian Barron.

6 This is illustrated in *Country Life* as the Sundial Court, though no such dial survives today in this courtyard. The sundial on the Terrace may have originally been in this position.

7 Illustrated in Jane Brown, *The Art and Architecture of English Gardens*, 1989, pp.124-5.

8 Ibid., pp.128-9.

9 *Country Life*, 16 & 23 April 1898.

10 *Country Life*, 16 April 1898.

11 Manuscript by Judith Patrick, containing her own research on Cave, and with some references to a 2008 paper written for the National Trust, 'Walter Cave and The Orangery at Tyntesfield, A Study in Arts and Crafts Neo-classicism', by Thomas Rinaldi.

12 Parsons may also have provided designs for Sharcombe Park, but this is not proven.

13 Letter from Alfred Parsons to Charles Tudway, inviting him to lunch with him and Partridge at the Arts Club to 'talk over our possible scheme'; 24 January 1899. For more detailed information about the partnership see Marion Mako, 'Painting in three dimensions: Alfred Parsons in Broadway', MA Garden History Dissertation, University of Bristol, 2004; see also Nicole Milette, 'Landscape painter as landscape gardener, the case of Alfred Parsons, RA', PhD thesis, University of York, 1997.

14 EH Garden Register.

15 SRO DD\TD/48.

16 D C Tudway Quilter, *Milton Lodge Gardens* (Guidebook, no date), unpaginated.

17 *Country Life*, 27 March 1926.

18 Letter from Parsons to Tudway, 24 January 1899: SRO, DD\TD/48.

19 Letter from Capt W Partridge to Tudway, 27 February 1913: SRO, DD\TD/47. The sketch that accompanies the letter is missing.

20 For a good description of the planting in the 1970s see Lanning Roper, 'A Panoramic Mendip Garden: Milton Lodge, Somerset', *Country Life*, 12 May 1977; see also George Plumptree, 'All Points of View', *Country Life*, 28 June 1990.

21 Information from Helena Gerrish.

22 Byford, *Somerset Curiosities*, p.67; it commemorates Vice Admiral Sir Samuel Hood (1762-1814).

23 For Mathern see H Avray Tipping, *English Gardens*, (Country Life, 1925), pp.217-24.

24 Lytes Cary has been the subject of several articles. They include: Christopher Hussey, 'Lytes Cary, Somerset – I, II & III', *Country Life*, 18 & 25 July, 1 August 1947; Arthur Hellyer, 'Epitome of Englishness: Garden of Lytes Cary, Ilchester, Somerset', *Country Life*, 2 September 1982, and Patrick Taylor, 'Hand in Glove', *Country Life*, 1 June 2006.

25 Recorded on an inscribed stone set into one of the walls.

26 21 December 1912.

27 Sylvia Hope Evans, *The Book of Nailsea Court*, 1923, p.124.

28 A sketch plan of the layout is given in Jane Brown, *Gardens of a Golden Afternoon – The Story of a Partnership: Edwin Lutyens & Gertrude Jekyll*, 1985, p.79.

29 We are most grateful to the Hon Andrew Jolliffe for his hospitality at Ammerdown, and for allowing us to reproduce one of the pastel paintings on the back cover of this book.

30 Christopher Hussey, 'Ammerdown House, Somerset–II', *Country Life*, 2 March 1929.

31 Ibid. They originally stood at the foot of the Ammerdown column until moved to their present site in 1925 by George, Lord Hylton.

32 Ibid.

33 Ibid.

34 There is some confusion here, as the E H Register entry dates this comission to 1901, but then maintains that Lutyens developed the gardens in 1913, when the 6th Earl had already sold it.

35 Miss Jekyll's brother Herbert was married to Agnes, Frances Horner's sister.

36 Allyson Hayward, *Norah Lindsay, the Life and Art of a Garden Designer*, 2007, p.105.

37 Horner, *Time Remembered*, p.196.

38 Hayward, *Norah Lindsay*, p.78.

39 Undated plan, Mells Estate archives.

40 Email correspondence, Raymond Asquith to Marion Mako, 30 June 2009. We are most grateful to Viscount and Viscountess Asquith for sharing with us their knowledge of the Horners and allowing access to the Mells Estate archives.

41 Hayward, *Norah Lindsay*, p.108.

42 There were two *Country Life* articles in 1908 and 1927; see also Lawrence Weaver, *Houses and Gardens by E L Lutyens*, 1913, pp.140-57, and Tipping, *English Gardens*, pp.189-98.

43 Philip White, *Hestercombe Gardens: An Illustrated History and Guide* (Hestercombe Gardens Project Limited, 1999), p.23. One of Jekyll's plans for the Dutch Garden, dated February 1907, is illustrated in this Guide (p.22).

44 Brown, *Gardens of a Golden Afternoon*, p.83.

45 Information from Philip White.

46 Tipping, *English Gardens*, p.198.

47 Forbes' plan for the gardens is illustrated in *Barrington Court* (National Trust Guidebook, 1997), p.7.

Chapter Notes

48 For white gardens see Fenja Gunn, 'Where White is Right', *Country Life*, 8 December 1994.

49 Ibid., p.10.

50 Robin Whalley, *The Great Edwardian Gardens of Harold Peto*, 2007, p.9.

51 Ibid., p.21.

52 The Glencot House Hotel is run by Martin Miller; see *Somerset Life*, February 2009, pp.22-5.

53 All this biographical information on the family is taken directly from Whalley's most informed book on Peto.

54 We are grateful to Robin and Wendy Goffee for their hospitality at Wayford. The gardens are open for charity, as part of the NGS, on certain Sundays between April and June most years.

55 Peto certainly designed this, but it was probably constructed by Ernest George and his new partner, Alfred Yeates, when they were remodelling the house between 1901 and 1902.

56 Blomfield, *Formal Garden*, p.210.

57 Whalley, *Peto*, p.117.

58 Ibid., p.119.

59 Arthur Oswald, 'Wayford Manor, Somerset', 29 September 1934.

60 Christopher Hussey, 'Burton Pynsent, Somerset', *Country Life*, 6 October 1934.

61 Information from Robin Walley.

62 Jonathan Holt, 'Widcombe Manor: A Tour Round "The Golden House"', *The Follies Journal*, no.2 (winter, 2002), pp.53-63; p.60.

63 Arthur Oswald, 'Widcombe Manor, Somerset', 28 August 1937, fig.4.

64 Ibid.

65 The following entry is informed in part by Kate Hughes' coursework for the MA in Garden History, University of Bristol (2004).

66 Mary Alden Hopkins, *Hannah More and her Circle* (New York & Toronto, 1947), pp.114-5.

67 Ibid., p.115.

68 There is a photograph of the Temple taken from an Edwardian postcard in the Walled Garden shop.

69 Thomas Mawson, *The Life and Work of an English Landscape Architect*, 1927, p.185.

70 Ibid.

71 Ibid., p.208.

72 Gertrude Jekyll, 'St Catherine's Court, Somersetshire – II', *Country Life*, 1 December 1906.

73 Helene Morling, 'St Catherine's Court: Conservation Statement', coursework for MA in Garden History, University of Bristol (2005).

74 *The Studio* (Winter, 1926-7), p.55.

75 Morling, 'St Catherine's Court'.

Chapter 9 pages 229-246: Twentieth-century plantswomen take centre stage

1 Catherine Horwood, *Oxford Dictionary of National Biography*, pp.2004-9.

2 Margery Fish, *We made a garden* (New York, 2002), p.21; first published in 1956.

3 Carrie McArdle, 'The Legacy of Lambrook', *The Garden*, January 2002, pp.18-23.

4 Fish, *We made a garden*, p. 81.

5 John Sales, *West Country Gardens* (Gloucester, 1980), p.150. Margery Fish wrote eight books and contributed to several others, as well as lecturing, writing gardening columns and broadcasting on radio.

6 E H Register entry.

7 Bond, *Parks and Gardens of Somerset*, p.140.

8 Sara Glossop, Brympton blog, 19 March 2009. She states that the cottage garden adjacent to the lodge was full of old roses that had to be dug out, and that it would shortly be replanted with new roses according to plans Jekyll left behind.

9 Bond, *Parks and Gardens of Somerset*, p.140.
10 Ibid., p.140.
11 Ibid., p.142.
12 E H Register entry.
13 Lanning Roper, 'The Smaller Garden IV, Tintinhull House', *Journal of the Royal Horticultural Society*, January 1955, pp.24-32.
14 Penelope Hobhouse, 'Phyllis Reiss at Tintinhull', *Hortus*, i/1 (Spring, 1987), pp.21-6.
15 E H Register entry.
16 Floyd Summerhayes & Oliver Garnet, *Tintinhull House and Garden* (National Trust, 1999), p.5.
17 Graham S. Thomas, 'Phyllis Reiss and her Garden', *Gardener's Chronicle Gardening Illustrated*, 17 February 1962, pp.118-9; p.125.
18 Hobhouse, 'Phyllis Reiss at Tintinhull', *Hortus*, i/1 (spring 1987), p. 26.
19 Conversation with Penelope Hobhouse, Hadspen, 25 June 2009.
20 For an in-depth description of the plants at Tintinhull see Penelope Hobhouse, *On Gardening*, 1994.
21 Hobhouse, 'Phyllis Reiss at Tintinhull', p.22.
22 We are grateful to Joan Loraine for her hospitality and kindness in allowing us full access to the gardens at Greencombe and sharing with us her extensive knowledge.
23 Arthur Hellyer, 'Sizzling Colour in a Green Combe', *Country Life*, 13 February 1986.
24 Taken from an information board in the Chapel.
25 See Geoffrey Collens & Wendy Powell, *Sylvia Crowe* (Landscape Design Trust Monographs, no.2, Reigate, 1995), pp.21-46.
26 Conversation with Michael Stancombe at Barford Park, 13 February 2009.
27 Alvilde Lees-Milne & Rosemary Verey (eds.), *The Englishwoman's Garden*, 1983, pp.63-66.
28 Tim Richardson & Noel Kingsbury (eds.), Vista podcast from The Garden Museum, London, 8 March 2009.
29 www.thehadspenparabola.com, accessed 27 March 2009.
30 Penelope Hobhouse, 'Starting all over again', *The Garden,* April 2009, p.233.
31 'Country House Rescue', Channel 4, 2008; repeated 11 November 2009.
32 See *Country Life*, 22 October 1927.
33 www.garden-guide.co.uk 22 December 2009.
34 J Hillier & A Coombes, *The Hillier Manual of Trees and Shrubs* (Devon, 2002), p.116.
35 Mary Anne Robb, *Cothay Manor and Gardens* (Derby, 2003), p.31.
36 This description of Cothay is based on an original article by Marion Mako, published in the *Avon Gardens Trust Bulletin*, 2005.
37 Mowl & Mako, *Historic Gardens of Cheshire*, p.250.

Chapter 10 pages 247-272: Modernist and traditional – a very patrician county

1 See Timothy Mowl & Dianne Barre, *The Historic Gardens of England: Staffordshire* (Bristol, 2009), pp.297-8.
2 Timothy Mowl & Clare Hickman, *The Historic Gardens of England: Northamptonshire* (Stroud, 2007), pp.180-1.
3 The original colour is recorded in Marchioness of Bath, *Cheddar Caves* (Longleat Estate, 1953), p.7; the booklet also contains a contemporary photograph of the complex (p.7).
4 We are grateful to Kate Harris, Longleat Archivist, for allowing access to those archives concerning the commission.
5 Russell Page, *The Education of a Gardener*, 1962, p.25.
6 Ibid., p.29.
7 Ibid.
8 Ibid.

Chapter Notes

9 Ibid.

10 Ibid.

11 Ibid., p.30.

12 Michael Spens, *Gardens of the Mind: The Genius of Geoffrey Jellicoe* (Woodbridge, Suffolk, 1992), p.54.

13 Ibid., p.53. Spens also illustrates contemporary photographs of the project (pp.54-5).

14 Ibid., p.52.

15 Alan Powers, 'Harmonious Mansions: Two Composers' Houses of the 1930s', *Country Life*, 29 August 1985.

16 Ibid.

17 The ash is featured in Thomas Pakenham, *Meetings with Remarkable Trees*, 1996, p.21.

18 Arthur Hellyer, 'Contrasts all Seasons: The Gardens of Clapton Court, Somerset', *Country Life*, 26 March 1987.

19 www.kilvercourt.com/kilvercourtgardens.htm; accessed 14 April 2009.

20 Timothy Mowl & Marion Mako, *The Historic Gardens of England: Cheshire* (Bristol, 2008), p.193.

21 SRO, D/D/Rt/M/48.

22 Christopher Hussey, 'Babington, Somerset', *Country Life*, 16 April 1943.

23 See Timothy Mowl, *The Historic Gardens of England: Oxfordshire* (Stroud, 2007), pp.167-9.

24 'Dillington House – Gardens and Grounds, Historic Landscape Survey and Restoration Plan', Nicholas Pearson Associates (October, 2005). We are most grateful to Wayne Bennett for providing a copy of this report for our research.

25 Jean Vernon, 'A Beguiling Garden', *Somerset Life*, May 2009.

Gazetteer

The following is a list of the gardens of significant historic importance which are covered in this book and are open to the public.

Abbreviations

NT	National Trust
P	Privately owned but open occasionally or regularly
NGS	Privately owned but open occasionally as part of the National Gardens Scheme
C	Conference Centre
E	Educational Establishment
G	Golf Course
H	Hotel
M	Museum
PP	Public Park
U	University
W	Wedding Venue

Ashton Court	PP	ashtoncourtestate.co.uk
Ammerdown	P/C	ammerdown.org/ammerdownopengardens.htm
Babington House	H	babingtonhouse.co.uk
Banwell Caves	P	banwellcaves.org
Barcroft Hall	P	barcrofthall.co.uk
Barford Park	P	
Barrington Court	NT	nationaltrust.org.uk/main/w-barringtoncourt
Bindon House	H	bindon.com
Bishop's Palace, Wells	P	bishopspalacewells.co.uk
Camerton Court	P/NGS	
Cavememan Restaurant	P	
Chalice Well Garden	P	chalicewell.org.uk
Claverton Manor	M	americanmuseum.org
Clevedon Court	NT	nationaltrust.org.uk/main/w-clevedoncourt
Cothay	P/W/NGS	cothaymanor.co.uk
Cricket House	H/TP/NGS	warnerleisurehotels.co.uk
Crowcombe Court	W	crowcombecourt.co.uk
Dillington House	C/E	dillington.co.uk
Dunster Castle	NT	nationaltrust.org.uk/main/w-dunstercastle
East Lambrook Manor	P/NGS	eastlambrook.co.uk
Fairfield	P/NGS	

Fyne Court	NT	nationaltrust.org.uk/main/w-fynecourt
Glencot	H	glencothouse.co.uk
Greencombe	P	greencombe.org.uk
Halswell	C/W	halswellweddings.co.uk
Harptree Court	NGS	harptreecourt.co.uk
Hestercombe	P/C/NGS	hestercombe.com
Kilver Court	P/NGS	kilvercourt.com
Lady Farm	P/NGS	ladyfarm.com
Leigh Court	C/W	leighcourt.co.uk
Line Wood	P	tauntondeane.gov.uk
Lytes Cary	NT	nationaltrust.org.uk/main/w-lytescarymanor
Milton Lodge	P/NGS	miltonlodgegardens.co.uk
Montacute	NT	nationaltrust.org.uk/main/w-montacute
Nailsea Court	P	rnli.org.uk
Nettlecombe Court	E	field-studies-council.org/nettlecombecourt
Newton Park	U	bathspa.ac.uk
Orchard Wyndham	P/NGS	
Orchardleigh	G/W	orchardleigh.net
Prior Park	NT	nationaltrust.org.uk/main/w-priorpark
St. Audries	W	countryhouseweddings.co.uk
Stoberry Park	P/NGS	stoberry-park.co.uk
Ston Easton	H/NGS	stoneaston.co.uk
Tintinhull House	NT	nationaltrust.org.uk/main/w-tintinhull
Tyntesfield	NT	nationaltrust.org.uk/main/w-tyntesfield
Wayford Manor	P/NGS	
Yarlington House	P/NGS/W	yarlingtonhouse.com

The Gardens

Not all gardens shown are open to the public

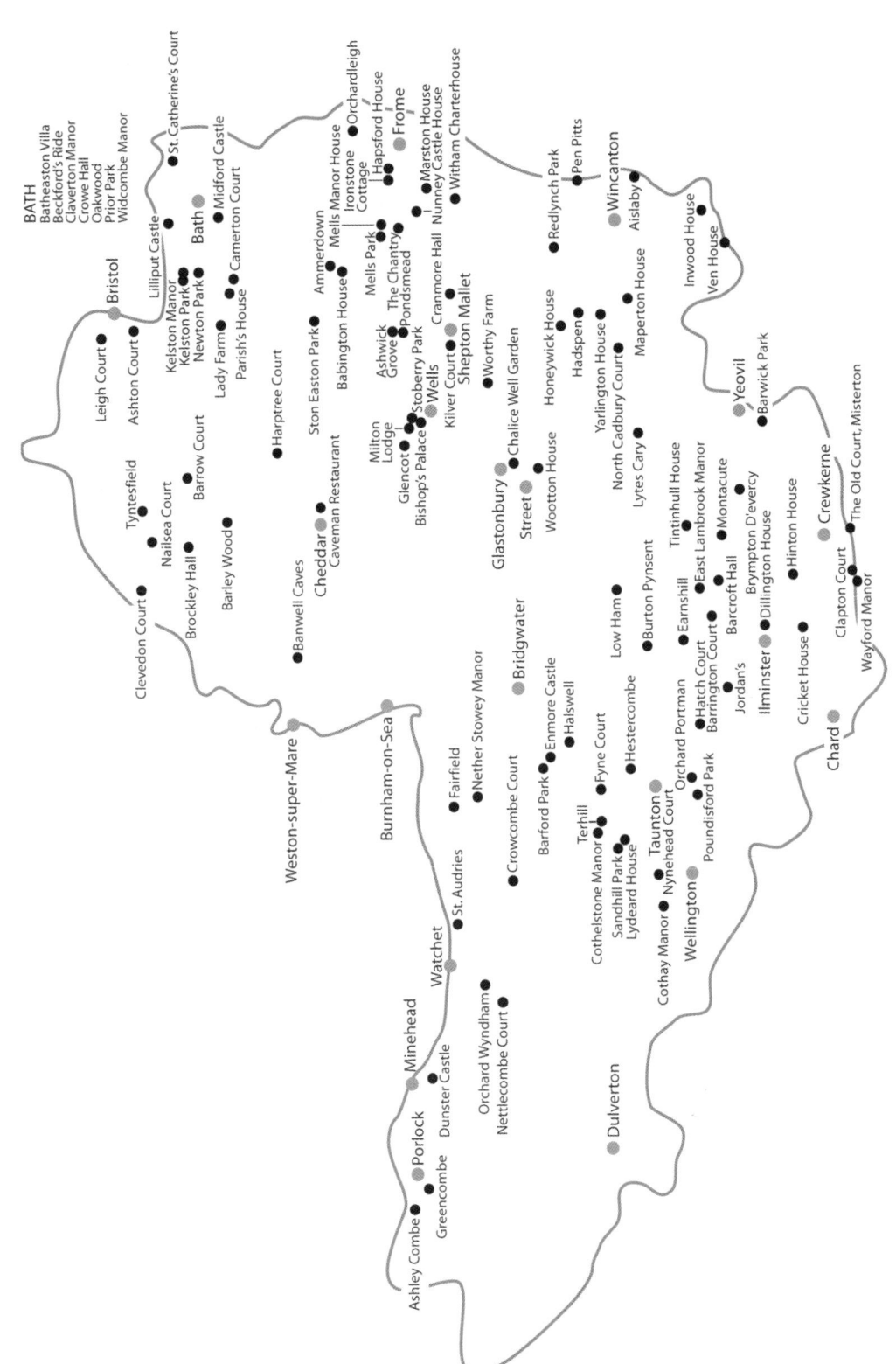

BATH
Batheaston Villa
Beckford's Ride
Claverton Manor
Crowe Hall
Oakwood
Prior Park
Widcombe Manor

St. Catherine's Court
Lilliput Castle
Midford Castle
Bath
Cameron Court
Orchardleigh
Hapsford House
Frome
Marston House
Ironstone Cottage
Nunney Castle House
Witham Charterhouse
Redlynch Park
Pen Pitts
Wincanton
Aislaby
Bristol
Leigh Court
Ashton Court
Kelston Manor
Kelston Park
Newton Park
Lady Farm
Parish's House
Harptree Court
Ston Easton Park
Ammerdown
Mells Manor House
Mells Park
Ashwick Grove
The Chantry
Babington House
Pondsmead
Stoberry Park
Wells
Cranmore Hall
Kilver Court
Shepton Mallet
Worthy Farm
Chalice Well Garden
Honeywick House
Hadspen
Yarlington House
Maperton House
Inwood House
Ven House
Tyntesfield
Nailsea Court
Barrow Court
Clevedon Court
Brockley Hall
Barley Wood
Banwell Caves
Cheddar
Caveman Restaurant
Milton Lodge
Glencot
Bishop's Palace
Glastonbury
Street
Wootton House
North Cadbury Court
Lytes Cary
Tintinhull House
East Lambrook Manor
Montacute
Brympton D'evercy
Dillington House
Yeovil
Barwick Park
Hinton House
Clapton Court
Crewkerne
The Old Court, Misterton
Weston-super-Mare
Burnham-on-Sea
Fairfield
Nether Stowey Manor
Bridgwater
Barford Park
Enmore Castle
Halswell
Low Ham
Burton Pynsent
Earnshill
Hatch Court
Barrington Court
Jordan's
Ilminster
Barcroft Hall
Cricket House
Wayford Manor
Chard
St. Audries
Crowcombe Court
Terhill
Fyne Court
Hestercombe
Cothelstone Manor
Sandhill Park
Lydeard House
Taunton
Nynehead Court
Wellington
Orchard Portman
Poundisford Park
Cothay Manor
Watchet
Minehead
Porlock
Dunster Castle
Orchard Wyndham
Nettlecombe Court
Dulverton
Ashley Combe
Greencombe

293

Index Page numbers in **bold** refer to illustrations and captions

Abbotsbury, Dorset, 116
Acland family, 86
Acland, Lady Harriet, 121
Acland Hood family, 205
Acland-Hood, Sir Alexander, 153
Adam, Robert, 40
Ailesbury, Caroline, Countess of, 107
Aislaby, 255-6, **256**, **colour 58**
Alfoxton House, 11
Alfred the Great, King, 9
Alfred Jewel (Saxon), 46
Allen, Ralph, 93, 96-100, 178
Allingham, Helen, 208
American Museum, 177
Ammerdown, 125-6, **127**, 208-10, **209**, **210**
Ancient Monuments Society, 228
Arcadian style, **63**, 94
Ariosto, Ludovico: *Orlando Furioso*, 18, 20
Arno's Vale, 158
Art Deco, 222
Art Nouveau, 14, **15**
Arts and Crafts movement, 31, 182-3, 205-6, 216, 220
Arundel, Thomas, 19
Ashley Combe, 163-7, **164**
Ashton Court, 138
Ashwick Grove, 156
Aston, Michael, 37, 40
Athelhampton, Dorset, 188-9
Athelney Hill, 9
Athelney, Isle of, 9
Aubrey, John, 32
Austen, Jane: *Northanger Abbey*, 161
aviaries, 115, 178
Avon, river, 18
Axe, river, 220

Babbage, Charles, 163, 166
Babington House, 265
Backhouse, David, 270, **270**
Badminton, Gloucestershire, 64, 83
Baker, Helen (*née* Peto), 219
Baker, Humphrey, 221
Baker, Ingham, 219
Balch, Christina, 153, **colour 29**
Baldwin, Thomas, 174
Balfour, Arthur James, 1st Earl, 189
Balfour, R. Shackleton, 201
Balfour, R.S., 28
Balston, Michael, 255, **256**
Bampfylde family, 86
Bampfylde, Coplestone Warre, 62, 76, 78, 80-4, **colour 10**
Banksy (artist), 14
Bannerman, Julian, 271

banqueting pavilions, **27**, 28-30
Banwell Bone Caves, near Weston-super-Mare, 60, 153, 167-9, **170**, 171-2, **colour 33**
Barcroft Hall, 255, **colour 57**
Barford Park, 229, 239
Barker, Benjamin, 162, **colour 31**
Barley Wood, Wrington, 222-5, **224**, **colour 49**
baroque, 49
Barratt, John, 184
Barratt, Sir Sydney and Isabel Vaughan, Lady, 184-5
Barrington Court, 216-17, **colour 46**
Barrow Court, 188-90, **191**, 192, **192**, 208, **colour 40**
Barrow Mump, 9
Barry, Sir Charles, 178
Barton Grange, 11
Barwick Park, 121-4, **122**, **colour 19**
Bassett House, 163
Batheaston Villa, 104-5, **106**, 107-8
bathing pools *see* cold baths
Battlefields House, 103
Beadford, John, 53
Beales, Peter, 183
Beard, William, 168, **170**, 171
Beaufort, Charles Noel Somerset, 4th Duke of, 64, 83
Beckford, Alderman William, 40
Beckford, William, junior, 159-61, 186, **187**
Beckford's Ride, 160
Beechwood, Hampshire, 180
Beere, Richard, Abbot of Glastonbury, 33, **34**
Bennett, Philip II, 102
Bennett, Wayne, 266, **268**
Berkeley, Norborne, 75
Bernard, James and Mary (*née* Carew), 88-9
Berry, Nick, 149-50
Bettiscombe, Devon, 242
Bevan, Miss (of Tintinhull), 234
Biggs, Ken and Ivy, 265, **267**
Billingsley, John, 156
Bishop's Palace *see* Wells
Blackamore, James, 113, **113**, **114**, **colour 16**
Blackdown Wood, 53
Blackdowns, the, 10
Bladud, 75
Blaise Castle, 143-4, **colour 27**
Blanc, Raymond, 265
Blanchard family, 225
Bliss, Sir Arthur and Trudy, Lady, 250
Blomfield, Reginald, 28, 188, 192, 201, 205, 214, 241
The Formal Garden in England, 180, 189, 220, **colour 39**
Blueatt, Richard, 243
boathouses, 124, 126, 147
Bobart, Jacob, **37**, 38-9, 48

294

Bodley, G.F., 189
bone houses, 60, 92, 153, 167-9, **170**, 171
Bonnor, Thomas, 62
Booth, Chris: *Buzzard* (sculpture), 266
Bowden, Samuel, 56
bowling alleys, 226
bowling greens, **13**, 22-3, 27, 29-30, 42-3, 45, 51, 56, 79, 84, 114, 242
Boy Patriots, 97-8, **colour 13**
Boyd-Carpenter, Henry, 231
Brain, Christine, 216-17
Brendons, the, 10
Brentry Hill, 143
Bridgeman, Charles, 50, 139, 256
bridges, 75, 88, **88**, **89**, 93-4, 97-9, 124, 138, 184, 218, **colour 13**
Bridgwater Bay, 11
Bridgwater, Vale of, 77
Britton, John, 160, 162
Brockley Hall, 175-7, **176**
Brockway, Harry: *The Walk*, **4**
Brown, Joy, 23
Brown, Lancelot ('Capability'), 6, 93, 99, 108, **109**, 110, 112-13, 124, 126-8, 141-3, 146, 249, **colour 25**
Brown, Sandy, 269
Brympton D'Evercy, 42-4, **43**, **44**, 180, 229, 232, **colour 38**
Buck, Samuel and Nathaniel, 46-7
Bullough, Susie and Mark, 252
Bunyan, John: *Pilgrim's Progress*, 169
Burne-Jones, Sir Edward, 117, 212
Burrow, Ian, 40
Burrowbridge, 9
Burton, Decimus, 51, **52**
Burton Pynsent, 108-11, **109**, 112, 219, 221
Butcher, Revd Edmund, 13
Byron, Augusta, Lady, 166
Byron, George Gordon, 6th Baron, 178

Caledon, County Tyrone, 57, 60
Camelford, Thomas Pitt, 1st Baron, 98-9, **colour 13**
Camerton Court, 174-5, 265-6, **267**, **colour 59**
Campbell, Colen: *Vitruvius Britannicus*, 55, **55**
canals, 36, 39, 43, **44**, 48, 50-1, 58, 62, 147, 150, **colour 3, 5**
Carew, Sir John, 86, 88
Carew, Thomas, 58, 86-8
Carter, Camilla, 271
Carter, John, 47-8, 126, **colour 6**
Carteret, Sir Charles, 49
Carver, Richard, 153
Cary, river, 9
Casa Bianca (house), Bath, 162

cascades (waterfalls), 82-3, 94, 96, 100, **101**, 102, 105, 118, 137, 141, 158, 185, **colour 10**
Casetta, La (house), Bath, 162
Castle Cary, 9-10
Castle Cary Horticultural Society, 241
Castle Howard, Yorkshire, 50
Cave, Walter, 179, 188, 201-2, **203**
Caveman Restaurant, Cheddar Gorge, 229, 247-50, **248**, **249**
Cecil, William (Baron Burleigh), 24
Chalice Hill, 14
Chalice Well, Glastonbury, 14-16, **15**, **colour 1**
Champneys family, 124-5
Champneys, Caroline Anne, Lady, 121
Champneys, Thomas, 124
Chantmarle, Dorset, 188
Chantry, The, 157-9
Chantry Pond, 157
Charleville, Ireland, 55
Charlotte, Queen, 162
Charmy Down, near Bath, 104, **colour 15**
Chatham, 1st Earl of *see* Pitt, William, the Elder
Chatham, Hester, Countess of (*née* Grenville), 98, 108, 110
Cheddar Gorge *see* Caveman Restaurant
Chedington Court, Dorset, 218
Chelford Manor, Cheshire, 246
Chinese features, 82-4, 100, **101**, 115, 118, 216
Chittenden, Biddy and Jeremy, 206, **colour 42**
Christopher family, 228
Clack, E.J.: *The Expulsion Group* (sculpture), 270, **271**
Clapton Court, 251-2, **252**
Claud Lorraine, 81
Claverton church, 97
Claverton Manor, 173, 177-8
Clevedon Court, 33-6, 179-80, **colour 3**
Clive, Captain Edward, 232
Clive, Violet, 229, 232-3
Clusius, Carolus, 31
Cobham, Richard Temple, Viscount, 98, 109
Coker Court, 13
cold baths, 57, 59-60, 80, 115, 126, **127**, 226, **colour 8**
Coleridge, Samuel Taylor, 11
Coles, John, 182
Collins, John, 78-80
Collinson, John, 18, 20, 38, 52, 62, **63**, 79, 86, 105, 126, 156
columns, 109-10, **109**, 112, 126, 221
Combe Down, 93
Combe, Richard, 112
Conran, Jasper, 48
conservatories, 51, 173, 177-9, 181, 183, **colour 37**
convents, 89, **90**, **colour 12**
Conway, Henry, 107
Conygar Hill, 84

Cook's Folly, 144, **colour 27**
Coombs, James, 120
Cooper, Colonel Reginald, 242, **243**, 244
Corfe, 11
Cork and Orrery, Charles Boyle, 4th Earl of (Baron Boyle of Marston), 54-6, **55**, 58, 92
Cork and Orrery, John Boyle, 5th Earl of, 56, 59, 162
Cork and Orrery, Margaret, Countess of (*née* Hamilton), 56-7, 59-60, **colour 8**
Corsham Court, Wiltshire, 99
Corston Brook, 142, **colour 25**
Cosimo III, Grand Duke of Tuscany, 41
Cote Bank, 143
Cothay Manor, 229-30, 242-4, **243**, **colour 54**
Cothelstone Manor, 29-31, **31**
Cothelstone Park, 89
Country Life, 186-7, 201, 205, 207, 210, 221, 226-8, 232
Cox-Hippisley, Elizabeth Anne, Lady (*née* Horner; then Hippisley-Coxe), 139
Cox-Hippisley, Sir John, 139
Cranmore Hall, 179
Cricket House, 173, **colour 34**
Cricket St Thomas estate, 138
croquet lawns, 158, **159**, 173-4, 227
Crosse, Andrew IV, 147
Crosse, Andrew V, 147-53, **150**, **151**, **colour 28**
Crosse, Cornelia, 149
Crosse, Richard, 148
Crosse, Susanna (*née* Porter), 148
Crossley, Anthony, 222
Crossley, Clement, 222
Crossley, Sarah (*née* Peto), 219, 221
Crowcombe, 86-90, **88**, **89**, **90**, 156, **colour 12**
Crowe Hall, 99, 184-5, **185**
Crowe, Sylvia, 229, 234, 239
Curry Moor, 9
Curtis, William, 121
Curzon, George Nathaniel, Marquess, 27

Darly, Matthew, **106**, 108
Darwin, Charles: *Origin of Species*, 172
Davenport, Shropshire, 99
Davis, Edward, 162, **colour 31**
Davis, Thomas, 121
Deanery Garden, 216
Dee, John, 14
deer parks, 11, 24, 47, 54, 88, 237
Defoe, Daniel: *A Tour through ... Great Britain*, 96
Delany, Mary, 60-1
de Morgan, Augustus, 166
Denzell Gardens, Cheshire, 255
de Salis, Charles and Carolyn, 253
Digny, Henry, 7th Baron, 121

Dillington Hall, 266, **268**, 269
Dodoens, Rembert: *Cruydeboek*, 32
Don, Monty, 265
Donne, Samuel, 26, 29, 115
dovecotes, 45, 205
Dowdeswell Manor, Gloucestershire, 233
Druids, 74-5, 81, 171, 222, **colour 33**
Drury, Thomas, 190
duckeries, 118, **119**, **colour 17**
Duckworth, William, 180
Dudley, Robert, Earl of Leicester, 17-18, 20
Dughet, Gaspar, 81
Dunnant, Nigel, 245
Dunster Castle, 12, 83-4, 86
Dutch style, 48, 214, 216
Dyrham Park, 143

Earnshill, 112-13, **113**, **114**, **colour 16**
East Lambrooke Manor, 229-32, **colour 51**
Eavis, Michael, **colour 2**
Edgar, James, 22
Edwards, Karen, 269
Egmont family, 76
Egmont, John James Percival, 2nd Earl of, 126
Egremont, Charles Wyndham, 2nd Earl of, 40, 54
Egremont, George O'Brien Wyndham, 3rd Earl of, 54
Elizabeth I, Queen, 17-20, **21**, 24, 32
Elton family, 33-4
Elton, Sir Abraham I, 36
Elton, Sir Abraham IV, 35
Elton, Dame Agnes, 180
Emmerson, Thomas, 162, **colour 31**
English Heritage, 40, 47, 120
Enmore Castle, 76, 126
Entwistle, Pam and Roger, 222
Escott, Richard, 62, 75
Esdaile, Edward Jeffries, 29-30
Ethandun, Battle of (878), 9
Evans, Charles, 207
Evans, Sylvia Hope: *Book of Nailsea Court*, 207
Evelyn, John: *Sylva*, 43
Exedras, 190, **191**, **192**, **colour 40**
Eyles, Francis, 112

Facey, Peter, 222
Fairfield, 11, 42, 45-6, **colour 5**
Fane, Lady Georgina, 180
Fane, Richard Ponsonby, 233
Fane, Sir Spencer Ponsonby, 232
Farrand, Beatrix, 215
ferneries, 183
Fielding, Henry: *Tom Jones*, 100
Fiennes, Celia, 39, 41

Fiesole (house), Bath, 162
Fish, James (engraver), 42, 47
Fish, Margery (*née* Townsend), 229-34, 237, **colour 51**
Fish, Walter, 230-1, 233
Flitcroft, Henry, 115
follies, 121-3, **122**, 147, 149-51, **150**, 272, **272**, **colour 27**, **28**
Fonthill Abbey, Wiltshire, 40, 186, **187**
Forbes, J.E., 216
Forbes, Romeo, 121
Ford (of Exeter), 121
Fordbury Water (Whatley Brook), 156-7
Fort, Thomas, 114
Fortescue, Hester, Countess of (*née* Grenville), 165
fountains, 17, 20, **21**, 23, 201, 218-20, 236
Fox, Sir Stephen, 114
freemasonry, 73-5, 97
Frend, William, 166
Freshford, 100
Frome, 10
Frome, river, 41, 124-9
Frost, Terry, 269
Fussell family, 156-7
Fussell, James, 157-8, **colour 30**
Fyne Court, 147-51, **150**, **151**, **colour 28**

Gammack, Helene, 178
garden houses, 12-13, **13**, 27, **53**, 54, 190, 223-4, **224**
Gardeners' Chronicle, 178
Gardeners' Question Time (radio programme), 230
Gardenesque style, 48, **127**, 137, 143-4, 146, 155-6, 158, **colour 34**
Garner, Thomas, 189
Garnerin brothers, 152
gatehouses, 28-31, 34
gateways, 190
Gaudi, Antonio, 157
gazebos, 34, 36, 190, **191**
George, Sir Ernest, 218, 223
George, George, 158-9, **159**
Giant's Cave, Orchard Wyndham, 54
Gibbs family, 189
Gibbs, Antony, 201
Gibbs, Blanche, 178
Gibbs, Emily Ann, 190, **191**, **colour 40**
Gibbs, Henry, 189
Gibbs, James, 40-1
Gibbs, Philip, 272
Gibbs, William, 178, 189
Gilbert, Alfred, 190
Gilpin, William Sawrey, 118
Ginestar, Josep: *Two Pieces* (sculpture), 269
Gingell, William Bruce, 163
Glastonbury, 14-16, **15**

Glastonbury Tor, 14, 16, 25
Glencot House, 218-19
Goffe, Robin, 221
Goldney, 158
Goodfellow, Simon, 246
Goodridge, Henry Edmund, 159-60, 162
Gore Langton, Bridget (*née* Langton), 142
Gore Langton, William, 141-2
Gothic (Gothick), 11, 61, 77, 79, 83-4, 88-9, **88**, **90**, 92, 94, **95**, 98-9, 103-4, 115, 118, **119**, 120, 125, **140**, 141, 144, 149, 155-6, 158, 169, 178, 187, 272, **272**, **colour 12**, **15**
Gough's Cave, Cheddar Gorge, 248
Grange, Richard, 48-50, **49**
Grant, E., 114
Great Elm, 157-8
Greek Revival, 179
Greencombe, 229, 237-9, **238**, **colour 52**
Grenville, George and Richard, 98
Grenville, Hester (*née* Temple), 98
Griffier, Jan I, 54
Griffier, Robert, 53, 54, **colour 7**
grottoes, 57, 74-5, 79-80, **80**, 89-90, **91**, 94, 123-4, 139, 146, 153-6, **154**, 158-9, **159**, **161**, 178, **colour 19**, **29**, **30**
Guest, Lady Theodora, 186-7
Guest, Thomas Merthyr, 185-7

Hackwood, Hampshire, 50
Haddon, Norman, 237
Hadspen House, Pitcombe, 10, 229, 239-42, **240**, **colour 53**
Hagley Hall, Worcestershire, 61, 79, 98
Halsway Manor, 89
Halswell, 61-4, **63**, **64**, 73-8, **73**, 80-1, 83, 97, 126, **colour 9**
Hamilton, Frances (*née* Coles), 182
Hapsford House, 158-9, **159**
Harbin, George, 48
Harford family, 145
Harington, Sir John, 18-25, **21**, 225
  The Metamorphosis of Ajax, 19, **24**
Harland, Peter, 250-1
Harptree Court (*formerly* Richmond Hall), 128, **128**, 137
Hartrow Manor, 237
Harvey, John, 33
Hatch Court, 78-81, **78**, **80**, 271-2, **272**
Hawkins, Sir Caesar, 126
Helyar family, 13
Hepworth, Dame Barbara, 269
hermitages, 59-60, 79, **80**, 83, 103-4, 120, **colour 14**
Herrick, Brian and Denise, 255
Hestercombe, 62, 78, 80-4, **85**, 86, 90, 148, 150, 180, 213-15, **215**, 225, **colour 10**, **11**, **45**
Hestercombe Gardens Trust, 214
Hewitt, Henry, 120

Hewlett, James, 162
Hext, Sir Edward, 24-5, **25**, 35, 37
Heythrop, Oxfordshire, 57
Hidcote, Gloucestershire, 231, 233
Hill, The, Hampstead, 225
Hill family, 12
Hill, Oliver, 251
Hill, Sir Roger, 12
Hill, William, 12
Hinkley Point power station, 11, 46
Hinton House, Hinton St George, 41-3, 206-7, **207**
Hippisley-Coxe, Henry, 139
Hippisley-Coxe, Richard, 138-9
Hoare, Henry, 10, 62, 81, 86, **colour 10**
Hobhouse, Niall, 10, 241
Hobhouse, Penelope, 10, 229, 234, 236, 239, 241-2, **colour 53**
Hogarth, William, 64
Hogg, James, 152
Holy Thorn Tree (*Crateagus monogyna praecox*), 15
Honeywick House, 271
Hooper, George, Bishop of Bath and Wells, 48
Hopper, Thomas, 143, 146
Hopton, Sir Ralph, 40-1
Horder, Percy Morley, 188
Horner family, 32, 117, 211, **213**
Horner, Edward, 117
Horner, Frances
   33, 117, 211, **colour 43**
   Time Remembered, 120, 211
Horner, Sir John, 32
Horner, John, 117
Horner, Thomas, 117
Horner, Thomas, the younger, 32, 117-18, **119**, 120-1
Horner, Colonel Thomas Strangways, 117, 121, 125
Horton, Mark, 48, **colour 6**
Huish Episcopi, 10
Hunt, James Henry Leigh, 162
Hurford, John, 239
Hussey, Christopher, 244
Hyett, Benjamin, 99
Hylton, Alice, Lady (*née* Hervey), 208
Hylton, George, 3rd Baron, 208-9

icehouses, 79
Iford Manor, Wiltshire, 218, 220
Ilchester, Elizabeth, Countess of, 116
Ilchester, Henry Edward Fox-Strangways, 5th Earl of, 114, 211
Ilchester, Stephen Fox-Strangways, 1st Earl of, 114, 116
Iles, Rob, 22
Institute of Landscape Architects, 250
Inwood House, 185-7, **187**, **colour 39**
Ireson, Nathaniel, 49, 87, 117

Iron Age Cadbury Camp, 225
Ironstone Cottage, 157
Isle, river, 112
Italian style, 21-2, 144, 162-3, **164**, 173, 178, 208, **209**, 210, **210**, **colour 31**

James I, King, 18
James, Montague Rhodes, 171
Jamieson, Elaine, 151
Japanese Gardens, 186, 221, 233, 266, **colour 48**
Jardine, Ernest, 252-3
Jarrett family, 174
Jarrett, Anne, 266
Jarrett, John, 174
Jay-Z, 14
Jekyll, Gertrude
   180, 188, 211, 213-17, **215**, 226, 232, 240, **colour 45**
   Colour in the Flower Garden, 217
   Garden Ornament, 232
Jellicoe, Geoffrey, 229, 246, 248, **249**, 250
Jenkins, Alison, 227-8, **colour 50**
Jenner, Sir Walter and Flora, Lady, 31, 205-6
Jerwood Sculpture Park, Warwickshire, 266
Jocelin, Bishop of Wells, 47
John, King, 11, 14
John, William Goscombe, 190
Johnson, David, 245
Johnston, Lawrence, 233, 242
Jolliffe, Colonel John, 125
Jolliffe, Revd Thomas, 125
Jolliffe, Thomas Samuel, 125, 209
Jones, Barbara: *Follies and Grottoes*, 123-4
Jones, Richard, 98-9
Jordans, Ashill, 153-6, **154**
Joseph of Arimathea, 14-16

Keene, Henry: *Ancient Architecture*, 77
Kelston Manor, 18-24, **21**
Kelston Park, 126-7
Kemeys-Tynte, Sir Charles, 61-3, **63**, 73, 76-8, 80-1, 83, 86-7, 148, **colour 9**
Kemp, Edward, 179
Ken, Thomas, Bishop of Bath and Wells, 48
Kenilworth Castle, Warwickshire, 17, 20
Kent, William, 94
Keuper Marl, 9
Kilmersdon Lodges, Ammerdown, 125
Kilver Court, 252-3, **colour 56**
Kingsbury, Noel, 244
Kingston, Francis, 116
Kip, John and Leonard Knyff: *Britannia Illustrata*, 42, **43**, **45**
kitchen gardens, 26, 45, 51, 57, 112-13, 117, 137, **140**, 141, 157,

184, 220, 223, 236-7, 239-40, 244, 256, 265, **colour 16**
Knatchbull, Captain Charles, 265
Knight, Edward, 79, 81, 83
Knight, Richard Payne, 81, 143
knot gardens, 34
Kyle, Thomas, 48, **52**

Lady Farm, Chelwood, 229, 244-6, **244**, **colour 55**
Ladymead House, Wolcot, Bath, 36
Lafontaine, Alfred Cart de, 189
Laird, Mark, 116
Landsford House, Wiltshire, 218
Lane, Mike, 265
Laneham, Robert, 17
Langbourne, Dr, 82
Langley, Batty, 77, **95**, 271
Antient Architecture, 77, 94
Langton, Joseph, 141-2
Langton, William *see* Gore Langton, William
Lansdown, Bath, 103-4, 159-61
Larkins, Simon, 206
Law, George Henry, Bishop of Bath and Wells, 48, 167-9, **170**, 171
Lawrence family, 123
Leadbetter, Stiff, 141-2
Leasowes, Worcestershire, 61, 81-2
Leat, river, 48
LÁger, Fernand, 266
Leicester, Earl of *see* Dudley, Robert
Leigh Court, near Bristol, 143-6, **145**, **colour 26, 27**
Leisure Hour, The (journal), 166
Leland, John, 33
Lilliput Castle, Lansdown, **102**, 103, 105, **colour 14**
Lindsay, Harry, 212
Lindsay, Norah, 211-12, **colour 43**
Line Wood Walk, Hatch Court, 78-80, **78**, **80**, 110
Literary Gazette, 149
Locke, John, 222
Lockett, Henry, 86-7
Loder, Captain Simon, 251-2
lodges, 11, 29, 118, 120, 124-6, 137, 142, 145, 158, **colour 20, 21**
loggias, 51, 79, 94, 137, 145, 201-2, 221-2, 246
London Electrical Society, 148-9
London, George, 48
Longleat, Wiltshire, 48, 99, 248-9, **249**
Loraine, Joan, 229, 237-8, **238**, **colour 52**
Loudon, J.C., 254, **254**
Lovelace, William King, 1st Earl and Ada, Countess (*née* Byron), 163-6
Low Ham, 10, 24-5, **25**, 35, 37-9, **37**, 40, 48
Lucas, Colonel and Mrs Alfred, 233
Lucas, Michael, 236
Lucy, George, 141

Lullington, 124
Luttrell family, 83, 86
Luttrell, Henry Fownes and Margaret, 84
Luttrell, Sir Hugh, 12
Lutyens, Sir Edwin Landseer, 114, 117, 126, 188, 205, 208-9, **209**, **210**, 211, 213-17, **213**, **215**, 225, **colour 45**
Luxborough, Henrietta, Lady, 94
Lydeard House, 181-4, **183**
Lyle, Andrew, 216-17
Lyle, Colonel Arthur, 216
Lyncombe Pleasure Gardens, 102
Lyte, Henry: *Niewe Herball*, 31-2, 206
Lyte, John (1558), 31
Lyte, Thomas, 32
Lytes Cary, 31-2, 205-6, **colour 42**
Lyttelton, George, 1st Baron, 61, 81, 98

McGarvie, Michael, 120-1, **colour 8**
McKenna, Reginald, 217
McVicar, Jekka, 265
Malins, John, 234
Mannerism, 19, 192
Manoir aux Quat' Saisons, Oxfordshire, 265
Maperton House, 179, **colour 37**
Mapletoft, George, 234
Markham, Elizabeth, 19
Marston Bigot, 54-9, **55**, 92, **colour 8**
Martineau, Louis and Guy, 251-2, **252**
Mary II (Stuart), Queen, 48
Mason, William, 116
masons *see* freemasons
Masters, Charles Harcourt, 29, 103, 128, **128**, 137
Mathern Palace, Monmouthshire, 205
mausoleums, 25, **25**, 83-4, **85**, 90
Mawson, Thomas, 188, 205, 223-5, **224**, **colour 49**
Medlycott, James, 48-9, 54
Mellor, James: 'Garden of Correspondence', 169
Mells Manor, 27, 32-3, **34**, 117, 211-13, **213**, 217-18, **colour 43, 44**
Mells Park, 117-18, **119**, 120-1, **colour 17, 18**
Mells Stream, 156-8
Menabrae, Luigi Federico: *Sketch of the Analytical Engine Invented by Charles Babbage Esq.*, 166
menageries, 115
Mendelsohn, Erich, 250
Messiter, George and Lucy, 123
Midford Castle, 126, **colour 22**
Midsomer Norton, 10
Miles, Philip John, 143, 146
Mill Wood, Halswell, 73-7, **colour 9**
Miller, Anna, Lady (*née* Riggs), 104-5, **106**, 107-8
Miller, Captain John, 104-5, 107
Miller, Philip, 50

Miller, Sanderson, 97-8, 272
Milton Lodge, 202-5, **colour 41**
Mimi (sculptor), **244**, 245-6
modernism, 247-50, **248**
Moignes, Les (house), Wrington, 163
Monmouth Rebellion (1685), 9
Montacute, 26-9, **27**, 30, 192, 201, 237
Montagu, Lady Barbara, 105
Montagu, George, 104-6
Montebello (house), Bathwick Hill, Bath, 162
monuments, 30
Moores Cottage, Kelston, 23
More, Hannah, 222-3
Moses, 73-4, 93-4, 96-7, 102
Mother Shipton's Stone, Orchard Wyndham, 54
Mr Nicholas' Farm, Charmy Down, 104
Mrs Busby's Temple, Halswell, 62
Munnings, Sir Alfred, 117

Nailsea Court, 207-8
Nash, John, 142, 175
National Gardens Scheme, 213
National Trust, 26, 94, 206, 216, 234-7, **235**
Naylor, Jonathan, 256
Nesfield, William Andrews, 174, **colour 35**
Nether Stowey, 11
Nether Stowey Manor House, 36-7
Nettlecombe Court, 126-8
Newman, Grace and John, 122-3
Newton Park, near Bath, 141-2, **colour 25**
Newton St Loe Manor, 141
Newton Surmaville, 122
Nicholas, Mr: farm at Charmy Down, **colour 15**
Nicolson, Sir Harold, 242
Ninney Castle, 46-7
North Cadbury Court, 225
Northcliffe, Alfred Harmsworth, Viscount, 230
Norton, John, 153, 178
Nuneham Courtenay, Oxfordshire, 116
Nunney Castle, 46-7
Nynehead Court, 174, **colour 35**

Oakhill, 158
Oakwood (*formerly* Smallcombe Villa), 161-3, **colour 31**, **32**
obelisks, 18, 92, 122-3, 266
Old Court, The, Misterton, 222, **223**
Oldbury Court, 143
Olive, Revd Dan, 238
orangeries, 113, **114**, 117, 153, 174, 201, 208, **209**, 210, 214-15, 227
Orchard Portman, 11, 42, 44-5, **45**
Orchard Wyndham, 42, 53-4, **53**, **colour 7**
Orchardleigh, 124-5, 173, 180-1, **181**, **colour 20**, **21**
orchards, 29, 34, 45, 206, 255

Orrery (earldom) *see* Cork and Orrery
Ossory, Anne, Countess of, 107
Oswald, Arthur, 187, 222
Othery, 9
Oudolf, Piet, 244, 247

Page, Russell, 229, 246, 248-50, **249**
Page, William, 180
Paget, John Moore, 179
Painswick, Gloucestershire, 99
Palace Farm, Wells, 270
Palfreman, Aaron, 51
Palladian style, 10, 51, 79, 93, 95, 97-9, 112, 138, 184, 190, 192, **colour 8**, **13**
Palmer, Thomas, 46, **colour 5**
Palmer, William, 46
Parish's House, Timsbury, 174-5
Parker, Charles: *Villa Rustica*, 163
Parkinson, John: *Complete Herbal*, 207
Parr, Rene, 55
Parrett, river, 9
Parsons, Alfred, 188, 202-4, 218, **colour 41**
parterres, 34, 48, 51, 58, 174, **181**, 183-4, **183**, 210, 211, 218, **colour 35**
Patrick, Judith, 202
pavilions, 41, 100
Payne, Mary, 229, 245
Pearce, Judy, 229, 244-5, **colour 55**
Pearce, Malcolm, 244, 246
Peirce, Jeremiah, 97, **102**, 103-4, **colour 14**
Pelet, Richard, Count de, 186
Pelham, Henry, 98
Pen Pits, 250-1
Penslewood, 246, 250
pergolas, 182-3, 209-10, 214, 224-5, **226**, 227-8, 271
Periam, John, 51
Peto, Harold Ainsworth, 100, 188, 205, 218-22, **219**, **223**, 233, **colour 48**
Peto, Helen, 219
Peto, Sir Henry, 218
Pevsner, Sir Nikolaus: *Buildings of England* series, 10
Phelips family, 40
Phelips, Sir Edward, 26, **27**
Phelps family, 270
Phelps, Richard, 61-2, 83-4, **85**, 87-90, **89**, **90**, **91**
Phillips, Niall, 269
Phillips, Sir Richard, 149
Picturesque, 81, 89, 124, 143, 146, 161, 163, 175, 177, **colour 31**
Pinch, John, 157
Piranesi, Giovanni Battista, 123, **colour 19**
Pitt, Hester *see* Chatham, Countess of
Pitt, William, the Elder (1st Earl of Chatham), 97-9, 108-11, **109**, 112, 221

pleasure gardens, 94, 104, 115, 118, 125, 128, **140**
Pocock, Richard, Bishop of Meath, 40, 57-9, 61, 93-4, 104-5
Pondsmead, 158-9, **161**
Pope, Alexander, 93, 96
Pope, Sandra and Nori, 10, 240
   Colour by Design, 240
   Colour in the Garden, 240
   Planting with Colour, 240
Porteous, Beilby, Bishop of London, 222
Portman, Edward, 214, 216
Portman, Edward Berkeley Portman, 1st Viscount, 180
Portman, Sir William, 44
Poulett family, 41, 86
Poulett, William John Lydston, 7th Earl, 206, **207**
Poundisford Lodge, 12
Poundisford Park, 11-13, **13**
Poynton, Revd Francis: *Memoranda*, 22-3
Pratt, Dallas, 177
Preater, Tom, 238, **238**
Price, Dr S.J.M., 233
Price, Sir Uvedale, 143
Priestley, Joseph: *History of Electricity*, 148
Prior Park, 93-4, **95**, 96-9, **colour 13**
privies, 20, 23-5, **24**
Protheroe, Edward, 144, **145**
Prowse, Thomas, 76, 78, 81, 272
Pryce, Benjamin, 142-3
Pynsent, Sir William, 108-9, **109**, 221

Quantocks, the (hills), 10-11, 29, 54, 86, 126
Quilter, David and Elizabeth Tudway, 204

rabbit warrens, 38
Radstock Lodges, Ammerdown, 126
Radway, Warwickshire, 97-8
Ragley Hall, Warwickshire, 266
Randolph, Dr (Vicar of Banwell), 167
Raven, John, 234
Raven, Sarah, 242
Ravoe, Miss, 104-5
Rawle, George, 88, **88**
Redlynch, 112-17, **115**, 211
Reiss, Phyllis (*née* Lucas), 229, 233-7, **235**
Repton, Lady Elizabeth, 175
Repton, George Stanley, 174-5
Repton, Humphry
   111, 124, 137-9, 141-5, 265, **colour 24, 26, 27**
   Red Books, 112, 137-9, **140**, 141-3, **145**-6, 174
   Fragments, 137
   Observations, 137-8
   Sketches and Hints of Landscape Gardening, 121
Richards, Christine-Anne, 269
Richmond Hall *see* Harptree Court

Rigden, Nick, 269
Riggs family, 105
Robb, Alastair, 242-3
Robb, Mary Ann, 229, 242-4, **243**, **colour 54**
Robin Hood's Hut, Halswell, 77
Robins, Thomas, 62, 94, 99-100, 102-5, 118, **colour 14, 15**
Robinson, Peter, 254
Robinson, William, 203, 208, 214, 231, 241, **colour 51**
Roches, Peter des, Bishop of Winchester, 11
rock gardens, 265
rockwork screens, 62-3, **64**, **73**, 78
Rococo style, 51, 62, 75-6, 84, 93-4, 96, 99, **101**, 103, 114, 117, 150, **colour 14**
Roebuck, Henry Woolhouse Disney, 126
Roos, Alexander, 178
Roper, Lanning, 233-4
rose gardens, 157, 178, 205, 208, 210, 223, 232, 253, 266, **colour 36**
rotundas, 105, **106**, 124
Rousham, Oxfordshire, 256
Royal Commission on the Historical Monuments of England, 37, 40
Royal Fort, 143
Rutter, John: *Delineations of Somerset*, 167-9, **170**, 171, 175

Sackville-West, Vita (Lady Nicolson), 237, 242
St Aubyns, 11
St Audries, 153
St Catherine's Court, 225-7, **226**, **colour 50**
Sales, John, 232
Salisbury, James Cecil, 3rd Earl of, 38
Sandhill Park (*formerly* Hill House), 51-2
Sassoon, Siegfried, 117
Savage, James, 86, 164
Savage, Robert, 155
Scheemakers, Peter, 98
Scott, James, 57
Scott, Mackay Hugh Baillie, 188, **226**, 227-8
Scott, Sarah, 105
Scotts of Merriott (nurserymen), 239
sculpture *see* statues and sculpture
Seaborough Court, 219
Sedding, J.D.: *Garden-Craft Old and New*, 189, 205
Selley, Lee, 269
Selwood, Abbot of Glastonbury, 33, **34**
Sentence of Momus on the Political Amusements of a Villa near Bath, The, 108
Seymour, Jane, 228
Shakespeare, William, 32
   As You Like It, 18
Sham Castle, Bath, 97
Sharpham Park, 253
Sharpshaw, 55
Sheldon, Edward, 19, 22

shell structures, 79 *see also* grottoes
Shelley, Mary
    149, 168
    Frankenstein, 151-3
Shelley, Percy Bysshe, 149, 151-2, 168
Shenston, William, 61, 81-2, 84
Shepton Mallet, 10
Showerings family, 253
shrubberies, 48, 50, 211
Shrubland Park, Suffolk, 178
Simes, William, 49
Sissinghurst, Kent, 232, 242
Skinner, Revd John, 175, 266
Skrine family, 178
Slocombe, Thomas, 90
Smith, Alistair: *Reclining Female Figure* (sculpture), 266
Smyth, Sir Hugh, 138
Smyth-Pigott, Ann, 175
Smyth-Pigott, John Hugh, 175-7, **176**
Soane, Sir John, 121, 125
Society of Antiquaries, 75
Souls, The (group), 117, 189
South Lodge, Enfield Chase, 110
Speke family, **154**
Speke, Georgina Elizabeth (*née* Hanning), 154-5
Speke, William, 154
Speke, William, junior, 154
Spenser, Edmund, 32
Spyers, John, 108
Stainer, Mark, 232
Stancomb, Michael, 239
statues amd sculpture, **21**, 47, 59-60, 76, 89-90, 92, 94, 102-3, 123, 177, 184-7, **187**, 190, **191**, **192**, 206-7, 209-10, **210**, 218, 220, **238**, **244**, 245-7, 266, **267**, **268**, 269, **colour 59, 60**
Stawell, Elizabeth, 37
Stawell, John, 2nd Baron, **37**, 38-40
Stawell, Sir John, 30, **31**
Stawell, Ralph, 1st Baron, 38
Stoberry Park, **268**, 269, **colour 60**
Stogumber, 10
Stogursey, 11
Stoke Park, near Bristol, 75
Ston Easton, 124, 138-9, **140**, 141, **colour 23**, **24**
Stony Lane ironworks, 157
Stourhead, Wiltshire, 62, 81, **colour 10**
Stowe, Buckinghamshire, 94, 98, 108-9
Strode House, 216
Strutt, Charlotte Elizabeth, 226
Strutt, Geoffrey St John, 228
Strutt, Colonel J.H., 226
Strutt, Richard, 226-8
summerhouses, 15, 22, **31**, 35, 52, 54, 62, 79, **80**, 83-4, 92, 100, **101**, 122, 126, 169, 178-9, 205, 211, 236, 256, 266, **colour 36, 41**
sundials, 186, 202-4, 210, 220, 224
Sutton Courtney, Oxfordshire, 212
Swan Circle, 16
Switzer, Stephen, 54-7, **55**
    Hydrostaticks and Hydraulicks, 54, 56
    Ichnographia Rustica, 52
    Practical Fruit Gardener, 56
Sydenham, Sir John Posthumous, 42, **43**

tabernacles, 73, 97
Taunton Deane, 79
Taunton, Vale of, 82-3, **colour 11**
Taylor, Patrick, 239
Taylor, William, 44
Temple, Christian (*later* Lyttelton), 98
Temple, Richard Grenville, Earl, 108-9
temples, 62, 74-7, 79, 81-3, 94, **95**, 110, 115-16, 120, 142, 144, 171, 182, 217, 222, 232, **colour 11**, **18**, **33**
Tennyson, Alfred, 1st Baron: *The Lady of Shalott*, 125
Terhill, 89-90, **91**, 92
terraces, 38-9, 180-1, 190, 203-4, 214, 220-1, 243, **colour 38, 47, 49, 58**
Thomas, Francis Inigo, 188-90, **191**, 192
Thomas, Graham Stuart, 205-6, 234
Thorp, Thomas and John Overton: *Survey of the Manors*, 99-100, 104
Tilden, Philip, 188
Tillemans, Peter, 34-6, **colour 3**
Tintinhull House, 229-30, 233-7, **235**, 239-40
Tipping, Henry Avray, 187, 188, 205, 207, 216
Tomkins, William, 84
Tone, river, 9, 243
topiary, 113, **113**, 177, 222, **223**
Tree, Sir Herbert Beerbohm, 189
Trentham, Staffordshire, 247
Trevelyan family, 127
Trevelyan, John, 127
Trevelyan, Sir John, 127-8
Tudor Pole, Wellesley, 14-16, **colour 1**
Tudway, Charles Clement, 202-4
Tugwell, George, 184
Tugwell, Henry, 184
Turkish (?Chinese) Tent, **colour 39**
Turner, Robert, 150
Twickenham: Pope's garden, 96
Tynte, Sir Halswell, 44
Tyntesfield, 173, 178-9, 189, 201-2, **203**, **colour 36**

Upper Langford Manor, 207
urns, 79-80, **181**, 183, 222
Urquhart, Lulu and Adam Hunt, 265

Vachell, Horace Annesley, 100, 222
vegetable gardens *see* kitchen gardens
Veitch, James, 178
Veitch, Thomas, 127
Ven House, 48-51, **49**, **52**
Verney, Elizabeth (*later* Palmer), 46
viaducts, **140**
Vignola, James Barozzi of, 19
Vincent (Beckford's gardener), 160
Virgil: *Aeneid*, 18
Vivian, George, 163, 177-8
Vivian, John, 177
Vivian-Neal, A., 12

Wadsworth, Edward, 251
Walker, Anthony, 94, **95**
walled gardens, 53-4, **113**, **114**, 147, 177, 179, 184, 201, 207, 224-5, 240, 266, 269, **colour 44**
Walpole, Horace, 104-5, **106**, 107, 116-17
Walton Castle, 35, 176
Wardour Castle, 19
Ware, Miss (of Tintinhull), 234
Warmley, 158
Warwickshire, 17
water features, 57, 76, 96, 112, 138-9, 141, 157-8, 217, **240**
water gardens, 22, 214, 216, 220, 231
Wayford Manor, 219-21, **219**, 225, **colour 47**, **48**
Webb, John, 167
Wells: Bishop's Palace, 41, 47-8, 269-71, **270**, **271**, **colour 6**
Werkmeister, Mike and Gail, 230
West Newton, 9
West Quantoxhead, 153
West Sedge Moor, 108, **109**, 110, 272
Westminster family, 185
Weymouth, Henry Thynne, Viscount (*later* 6th Marquess of Bath), 248-9, **249**
Weymouth, Thomas Thynne, 1st Viscount, 44, 48
Whalley, Robin, 218
Wharf Lane Concrete Company, Ilminster, 209
Whatley Brook *see* Fordbury Water
Whigs, 97
White Gardens, 217, 231, **colour 46**
White, Philip, 83, 214
Whitelegg, George, 253
Whitty, Maureen, 232
Wickham (Horner's agent), 121
Wicksted (Wicksteed), John, 102
Widcombe Manor, 99-100, **101**, 173, 184-5, 222
wildernesses, 39, **49**, 50-4, 73, 94, 97, 266, **colour 3**
Wilkins, Vaun and Colin, 181, 184
Wills, Henry Herbert, 223-4, **224**, **colour 49**
Wilson-North, Robert, 37-8, 40-1
Wilstar, Jacob de, 75

Wilton House, Wiltshire, 97-8
Wimbleball Reservoir, 239
Wincanton, 49
Wise, Henry, 48
Wishart, Maureen Lehane, 157
Witham Charterhouse, 40-1, **colour 4**
Witham, Vale of, 56
Wood, John
   93, 102-4, **102**, 184
   Origin of Building, 97, 103
Woodruff, Charles and Konstantia, 12
Wootton House, Butleigh Wootton, 205
Wordsworth, William, 11
Worthy Farm, 14, 16, **colour 2**
Wotton Underwood, Buckinghamshire, 98
Wray Wood, Yorkshire, 57
Wright, Thomas (of Durham)
   73, 75-6, 78, 81, 83, 116, 124
   Arbours, 63-4, 75, 78
   Grottos, 63-4, 78, 124
Wyatt, James, 125, 208
Wyatt, Thomas Henry, 124, 180
Wyatville, Sir Jeffry, 125, 177-8
Wyndham family, 40-1
Wyndham, William, 40, 53

Yarlington House, 253-4, **254**
yews, 12, 27, 153, 177, 179, 208, **210**, 220, 224, 226, 236, **243**, 254, **colour 16**
Young, Arthur, 74-5, 77, 82-3
Young, Frances, **268**, 269, **colour 60**
Young, Tim, 269